Praise for *The Journey of Crazy Horse*

"The legendary Lakota leader receives due honor in this searching biography. . . . A fine and necessary work."
—*Kirkus Reviews* (starred review)

"Captivating and enlightening . . . poignant . . . This reader was left with the feeling of having just experienced a cultural epiphany."
—Chuck Lewis, *True West* magazine

"Marshall's gloriously poetic and sweeping chronicle ushers in a new genre of American history—indigenous, oral, formerly supressed, a thrilling narrative based upon personal stories and hidden accounts only a trusted Indian scholar could collect and only a true-born writer could dramatize in print. Marshall renders the man and his times passionately alive. A tour de force."
—Peter Nabokov, professor of American Indian Studies and
World Arts and Cultures, UCLA, and author of
Native American Testimony

"Born about one hundred years after Crazy Horse, Joseph Marshall has drawn on oral histories passed down across the generations to find the human being behind the hero who has become a legend for Lakotas and non-Indians alike. The result is a remarkable portrait of a remarkable man."
—Colin G. Calloway, professor of history and Samson Occom
Professor of Native American Studies, Dartmouth College

"This story of treachery and honor has never been told better. Crazy Horse is no longer merely a symbol for the Oglala, or even for the Lakota, but has become an inspiration for all. Marshall's scholarship is meticulous, his passion gripping. This is as composed and crafted as a fine novel."
—Roger Welsch, Ph.D., anthropologist and author of *It's Not
the End of the Earth, but You Can See It from Here*

ABOUT THE AUTHOR

Joseph M. Marshall III, historian, educator, and storyteller, is the author of six previous books, including *The Lakota Way: Stories and Lessons for Living,* which was a finalist for the PEN Center USA West Award in 2002. He was raised on the Rosebud Sioux Indian Reservation and his first language is Lakota. Marshall is a recipient of the Wyoming Humanities Award, and he has been a technical advisor and actor in television movies, including *Return to Lonesome Dove.* He makes his home on the Northern Plains.

The Journey of Crazy Horse

A Lakota History

Joseph M. Marshall III

PENGUIN BOOKS

PENGUIN BOOKS
Published by the Penguin Group
Penguin Group (USA) Inc., 375 Hudson Street, New York, New York 10014, U.S.A.
Penguin Group (Canada), 90 Eglinton Avenue East, Suite 700, Toronto,
Ontario, Canada M4P 2Y3 (a division of Pearson Penguin Canada Inc.)
Penguin Books Ltd, 80 Strand, London WC2R 0RL, England
Penguin Ireland, 25 St Stephen's Green, Dublin 2, Ireland (a division of Penguin Books Ltd)
Penguin Group (Australia), 250 Camberwell Road, Camberwell,
Victoria 3124, Australia (a division of Pearson Australia Group Pty Ltd)
Penguin Books India Pvt Ltd, 11 Community Centre,
Panchsheel Park, New Delhi – 110 017, India
Penguin Group (NZ), 67 Apollo Drive, Rosedale, North Shore 0632, New Zealand
(a division of Pearson New Zealand Ltd)
Penguin Books (South Africa) (Pty) Ltd, 24 Sturdee Avenue,
Rosebank, Johannesburg 2196, South Africa

Penguin Books Ltd, Registered Offices:
80 Strand, London WC2R 0RL, England

First published in the United States of America by Viking Penguin,
a member of Penguin Group (USA) Inc. 2004
Published in Penguin Books 2005

19 21 23 24 22 20 18

Map illustration by Anita Karl and Jim Kemp

THE LIBRARY OF CONGRESS HAS CATALOGED
THE HARDCOVER EDITION AS FOLLOWS:
Marshall, Joseph.
The journey of Crazy Horse / Joseph Marshall.
p. cm.
Includes bibliographical references and index.
ISBN 0-670-03355-3 (hc.)
ISBN 978-0-14-303621-0 (pbk.)
1. Crazy Horse, ca. 1842–1877. 2. Oglala Indians—Kings and rulers—Biography.
3. Oglala Indians—Government relations. 4. Oglala Indians—Wars.
5. Little Bighorn, Battle of the, Mont., 1876. I. Title.
E99.O3C72457 2004
978.004'9752—dc22
[B] 2004049618

Printed in the United States of America

Dedicated to the memory of two warriors

To one who died young

PRIVATE MELVIN C. MARSHALL

Forty-fourth Infantry Division
United States Army

Born—16 October 1926
Wounded in action—8 June 1945
Died of wounds—12 June 1945

Ohitiya Otanin
(His Courage Is Known)

Oglala/Sicangu Lakota

and

To another who made the most of the opportunity the first did not have

JOHN R. WILLIAMS, ED.D.

Husband, father, teacher, Korean veteran, and friend

Born—13 June 1931
Died—4 September 2001

Mato Ihanbla
(Bear Dreamer)

Oglala Lakota

Contents

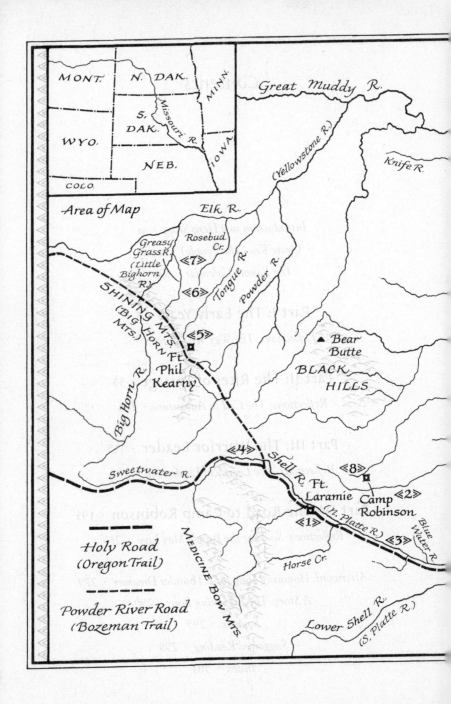

MONT.   N. DAK.   MINN.

S. DAK.

WYO.   IOWA

NEB.

COLO.

Area of Map

Great Muddy R.

Knife R.

(Yellowstone R.)

Elk R.

Greasy
Grass R.
(Little
Bighorn
R.)   Rosebud
           Cr.   ≪7≫

SHINING MTS. (BIG HORN MTS.)   ≪6≫

Tongue R.   Powder R.

≪5≫
Ft.
Phil
Kearny   Bear
              Butte

Big Horn R.   BLACK HILLS

≪4≫   Shell R.   ≪8≫

Sweetwater R.   Ft.
                     Laramie   Camp
                     (N. Platte R.) Robinson ≪2≫

≪1≫   ≪3≫   Blue Water R.

MEDICINE BOW MTS

Horse Cr.

Lower Shell R.   (S. Platte R.)

Holy Road
(Oregon Trail) - - -

Powder River Road
(Bozeman Trail) - -

Events in the Life of CRAZY HORSE

≪1≫ Grattan Massacre, August 19, 1854

≪2≫ Approximate area where Light Hair experienced his vision

≪3≫ Harney's attack on Little Thunder's Sicangu encampment, September 3, 1855

≪4≫ Battle of Platte River Bridge, July 25, 26, 1865

≪5≫ Battle of the Hundred in the Hand, December 21, 1866

≪6≫ The Rosebud Battle, June 17, 1876

≪7≫ Greasy Grass Fight, June 25, 26, 1876

≪8≫ Crazy Horse killed, September 5, 1877

Miles

0 _____ 75

0 _____

Kms.

(Missouri R.)

White Earth R.
(Big White R.)

Great Muddy R.

Running Water R.
(Niobrara R.)

SAND HILLS

(Missouri R.)

Loup R.

S. Loup R.

©2004 A. Karl / J. Kemp

Miles

White Earth R.
(Makizita R.)

Running Water R.
(Niobrara R.)

SAND HILLS

Great Smoky R.

Missouri R.

Loup R.

Grand R.

N

Introduction to a Hero Story

The winter of 1866–67 was bitterly cold and snows were deep along the foothills of the Shining (Big Horn) Mountains in the region the Lakota called the Powder River country, in what is now north-central Wyoming. Buffalo were scarce and hunters had great difficulty finding elk and deer. Crazy Horse, then in his mid-twenties, and his younger brother Little Hawk did their share of hunting, risking their lives in the frigid temperatures as they searched for whatever game they could find. One day a sudden blizzard forced them to seek shelter, but in the midst of it they happened to see several elk that were also hiding out of the wind. After the storm abated somewhat the two hunters brought down several elk with their bows and arrows, not easy to do in extreme subzero weather. They transported the meat home and saved their relatives and friends from starvation. Only weeks before, on another unbelievably cold winter day, Crazy Horse had led nine other fighting men in luring eighty soldiers into an ambush by several hundred Lakota and Cheyenne warriors and into a battle known in the annals of Western history as the Fetterman Battle or Fetterman Massacre. It was a hard-fought battle and a decisive victory for the Lakota and their Cheyenne allies. During the decoy action Crazy Horse stopped well within enemy rifle range and calmly scraped ice from his horse's hooves just to infuriate the pursuing soldiers.

He didn't know, and wouldn't have cared if he did, that he

was laying the foundation for the myths and legends that surround his legacy.

Say the name Crazy Horse and immediately events such as the Fetterman Battle, the Battle of the Rosebud, and, of course, the Battle of the Little Bighorn come to mind for those who have some inkling of Western American history. They think in terms of the *legendary* Crazy Horse. Crazy Horse *was* the Lakota battlefield leader who, in the span of eight days, got the best of two of the United States Army's field commanders: Brigadier General George Crook and Lieutenant Colonel George Custer. His exploits off the battlefield are less well known, however. Deeds such as finding meat in the middle of a blizzard endeared him to those who knew him as an ordinary man. He became a hero to them long before he became a legend in other peoples' minds after Little Bighorn and the defeat of the Seventh United States Cavalry.

Crazy Horse has been my hero since I was a boy. He was arguably the best-known Lakota leader in the latter half of the nineteenth century, a turbulent time on the northern Plains. His name floats in the consciousness of most Americans, along with the names of indigenous leaders and heroes from other tribes, such as Geronimo of the Chiracahua Apache, Chief Joseph of the Nez Perce, Washakie of the Eastern Shoshoni, and Quannah Parker of the Comanche, to name a few. He is certainly no less known than Sitting Bull, the Hunkpapa Lakota medicine man and political leader who was his friend and ally, or Red Cloud, his fellow Oglala, who was not among his friends.

At first I knew Crazy Horse only as a fighting man, the warrior. I didn't know or care what he felt, what he thought; I cared only that he was Lakota and that he was brave and performed deeds that fired my imagination. But as time went on there were more stories. I now know Crazy Horse as a man first and a legend second, a very distant second. In fact, he is much like my father and my uncles and all my grandfathers. He walks straight, he is polite, and he speaks softly. But there is also an aura of mystery about him, as though sometimes I am seeing him in a mist that blends legend and reality. It's that aura that seems to appeal most to people and I'm convinced that many want to connect with the mystery more than they want to identify with the man.

I can consciously remember hearing his name for the first time the summer I was six years old. My grandfather Albert and a man I knew as Grandpa Isaac and I had just crossed the Little White River and stopped to rest. As they both fashioned their roll-your-own cigarettes, one of them compared the slow-moving Little White to the Greasy Grass River. I learned later that the Greasy Grass was in south-central Montana and was also known as the Little Bighorn. In the shade of a thick grove of sandbar willow, the two old men spoke about a battle, and names that I had never heard before—or at least that I couldn't remember hearing before—rolled off their tongues that day along the river. *Pizi, Tatanka Iyotake, Inkpa Duta,* and *Tasunke Witko* and *Pehin Hanska.* Of course, they were talking about Gall, Sitting Bull, Red Butte, and Crazy Horse and Custer. *Pehin Hanska* meant Long Hair, the name many Lakota had for George Custer.

The battle they spoke of was fought seventy-five years prior, ten or so years before either of them was born. They talked, however, as if it had happened only the day before. They could because they had heard of the battle from their fathers and uncles and from a generation who had been alive in 1876, and from some who had been there in the great encampment along the Greasy Grass.

Long Hair and his soldiers had been decisively defeated, as far as I could tell. The *Sahiyela,* the Northern Cheyenne, were there with the Lakota. The soldiers had attacked the south end of the encampment along the Greasy Grass River, then the north end. Those from the south were stopped and routed completely, chased across the river to the top of a hill where they dug shallow pits in the earth to hide. Those who tried to attack from the north were stopped at the river and chased up a long slope. They were forced to fight a running battle, falling and dying as they fled until only a small knot of them were cut off at the end of a long ridge and were killed.

One name was repeated more often than others in the story of that battle: *Tasunke Witko,* or "His Crazy Horse." He was a leader of fighting men and his mere appearance on the battlefield was apparently enough to inspire others to fight. *Tasunke Witko* had led a charge of warriors against the soldiers in the second engagement of that battle. A Sahiyela leader commented on that particular action when recounting the battle years later by saying, "I have never seen anything so brave."

By the age of six I had already listened to many stories from these two grandfathers. I was well aware that being a fighting man was one way of being a man in the Lakota ways of old. I knew that men were often injured or wounded in battle and sometimes killed. And I knew that in battle a man could prove himself. For one man to obviously evoke such reverence and respect from the two grandfathers who told the story of the 1876 Greasy Grass Fight—the Battle of the Little Big Horn—was of some consequence. In my six-year-old world I could think of only two or three other old men in the same category as these two grandfathers, so when *they* respected someone it was no small thing. That day by the Little White River, *Tasunke Witko* became part of my life.

Like any Lakota boy that heard of Crazy Horse's exploits on the battlefield, I was awestruck, and immediately made him larger than life, thus setting him apart from reality. I can't recall the exact moment I realized that the essence of Crazy Horse had something to do with more than his physical appearance and attributes or his accomplishments as a fighting man and a leader of fighting men. But the realization came because the stories from my grandfather and other elders took on a more realistic tone as they added details to correlate with my intellectual and emotional growth. Crazy Horse became more defined and I began to paint him with the brush of reality rather than the distortion of legend.

In that reality every Lakota boy of the time grew up on a horse and Crazy Horse was no exception. As an adult he was described as a skilled horseman. Many who rode with him into battle remembered that he used two horses for a combat, a bay and a sorrel. He favored the bay, a gelding. Later he had a favorite riding horse, a yellow paint. He preferred geldings because they had more endurance than mares and stallions. The bay was not only fast but had unusual endurance. It was the horse he rode in many encounters with both native and white enemies. Crazy Horse liked to rest and refresh his horse by riding him to the top of a hill to catch a breeze or stand in the wind.

Like every Lakota male, he was probably highly skilled with his bow because of the type of instruction and training he was given. In his day it was not unusual for teenage boys to hit grasshoppers on the fly with an arrow. Surprisingly, my boyhood image of him as a warrior was not too far from the truth. As a full-fledged fighting man he did prefer a stone-headed war club for close combat, and it was said he was highly skilled with it, especially mounted and in a running fight. Out of necessity, however, he did a acquire a single-shot muzzle loader and later a repeating rifle.

Crazy Horse was certainly not the tallest or the strongest among the Lakota fighting men of his day. He was probably somewhere between five feet six inches and five feet ten inches tall. But courage and daring are not dependent on size or ability. In another way, however, he was not the prototypical Lakota fighting man in that he didn't participate in a ritual called the *waktoglakapi* or "to tell of one's victories." It was a simple ritual in which fighting men were expected to recount their exploits on the battlefield. As a matter of fact, Crazy Horse barely talked about his exploits to his immediate family.

Sometimes, however, Crazy Horse does seem to tower over

me. He is intense and his eyes flash. These moments happen, I suspect, to remind me that there is a legacy that is larger than life, an aspect to Crazy Horse that sets him apart from others who have gone before us. In a real sense it has to do with something beyond his exploits, something that traditional Lakota know and understand, something often misunderstood by the non-Lakota world.

My grandfather liked to watch the clouds building to the west on late summer afternoons, the kind of clouds that are folded and gray-blue, with quiet thunder rolling in their bowels uttering a promise of lightning and rain. One summer evening as we watched storm clouds approaching and listened to that distant, quiet thunder, he made a soft comment. *Wakinyan ihanble ske.* They say he dreamed of the Thunders. He was speaking of Crazy Horse. So among other things he was a Thunder Dreamer.

Anyone who dreamed of the Thunder Beings, the *Wakinyan,* was called upon to walk the path of the *Heyoka* (heh-yo'-kah), also known as *wakan witkotkoka,* which is roughly translated as "crazy in a sacred way." A Heyoka was a walking contradiction, acting silly or even crazy sometimes, but generally expected to live and act contrary to accepted rules of behavior. In doing so a Thunder Dreamer sacrificed reputation and ego for the sake of the people. Throughout his adult life and with his last breath, this is exactly what Crazy Horse did.

He has left us a legacy that is both a trail to follow and a challenge to follow it.

Much later, when I was an adult, I realized that my research into the life of Crazy Horse had begun that day by the Little White River in the summer of 1951, nearly seventy-four years after his death at Camp Robinson, Nebraska. That research happened in the most natural way possible for me as a Lakota child.

Home for me is the northern Plains because I was born there and shaped by the influence of the land as much as the people who were closest to it. I was privileged to grow up in and around the communities of Horse Creek and Swift Bear on the Rosebud Sioux Indian Reservation, where I had access to the friends and relatives of my maternal grandparents, Albert and Annie (Good Voice Eagle) Two Hawk. I also spent a few years in the Lakota community in and around Kyle, South Dakota, on the Pine Ridge Reservation, where my paternal grandfather, Charles J. Marshall, served as an Episcopal deacon. There, too, were many elderly Lakota who were friends and relatives. All of these elders were born in the 1890–1910 era. Their parents were born in the 1860–1890 era.

All of the Lakota elders I had contact with were unselfish in sharing their knowledge, opinions, and stories. To a child, of course, stories are simply stories. But as I grew older I began to gradually realize that I was hearing essential historical and cultural information. Those elders were the best of authorities regarding the cultural values, traditions, customs, and historical events—well known and not so well known—that existed in the time of Crazy Horse. As a matter of fact, it was intriguing to listen to discussions and debates about what he might have felt and thought at a particular moment. Those elders not only provided my first glimpses into the life of Crazy Horse, but they were an almost never-ending source of information about him and about Lakota life of the past.

I was related to most of them from Horse Creek and Swift Bear (see list on pages 295–98) through both of my maternal grandparents. Those from the Pine Ridge Reservation were acquaintances of my paternal grandparents. They were all great storytellers and never passed up an opportunity to tell stories to an eager youngster. On many occasions it was simply a matter of mood meeting opportunity and someone would launch into a story. On just as many occasions, especially as I grew older, I sought them out with questions to seek clarification or to revisit a story. Of course, the one most accessible to me was my maternal grandfather, Albert Two Hawk. He was a man of many talents. To me he was the best possible example of a hardworking, humble, unselfish, and deeply spiritual person. He exemplified all the things he told about in his stories, as did my grandmother Annie.

A grandfather, Isaac Knife, was cut in the same mold. A big man with a gentle manner, he worked for many years for the railroad. His sister Eunice was a strong woman. She married a man named Black Wolf and was widowed young. One of her sons was killed in a shooting. Another from her second husband, named Running Horse, was killed in an accident while in the army. She had to be strong to survive that kind of tragedy and hardship. But she was always quick to smile and pat my face with her strong hands.

Wilson Janis from Kyle, South Dakota, was blind with snow-white hair. His wife Alice was a small, slender woman, also with strong hands. It seemed somehow a contradiction that many of my aunts and grandmothers with gentle souls and eyes to match had such strong hands.

The last of them to finish their earthly journey was one of my paternal grandmothers, Katie Roubideaux Blue Thunder, my father's aunt. She, too, was small. She was born in June of 1890 (thirteen years after the death of Crazy Horse) and died in 1991, a month short of her one hundred and first birthday. She liked to watch the dances and tell stories of them and of how midwives were considered special people in the old days.

The list goes on and so do the memories. All of them, each of them, gave me information and insight I likely would never have gained on my own without them. This is more their work than mine.

None of the elders who told me stories of Crazy Horse had ever claimed to have seen him, of course, because they had been born too late. But they were the children and grandchildren of people who lived in the time of Crazy Horse, some who had managed to at least catch glimpses of him or hear firsthand accounts from those who had actually seen him. So their stories and descriptions were always preceded by the Lakota word *ske,* meaning "it was said." So it was said that Crazy Horse was slender and had wavy, dark brown hair, and his complexion was not as dark as that of most Lakota. His eyes were dark, however, and he had a narrow face with a typically long, straight Lakota nose, and a wide mouth. This manner of passing on information was, of course, part of the process and mechanism of the Lakota oral tradition that had existed for hundreds of generations.

We Lakota did not invent the oral tradition, however. It has been an integral part of human societies for longer than anyone can remember or document. Simply defined, it is the passing down of information from one generation to the next solely or primarily with the spoken word. Within the parameters of "information" is family, community, tribal, and national history, as well as practical knowledge that insures physical survival, provides for philosophical development, teaches societal roles, social behavior, norms, and values, and insures preservation of spiritual beliefs. Though the written word has supplanted the spoken word as the primary conveyance of information, every human culture and society has used oral tradition at some point in their societal evolution. We Lakota today are a culture that still uses the oral tradition and our sole use of it is only three generations past. It is still a viable mechanism for us.

Although the non-Lakota world has created myths and legends around and about Crazy Horse, he is a genuine hero to Lakota people who have a sense of what he was really about. Documentation does exist on the non-Indian side of history regarding Crazy Horse, but the thought that such documentation is the only credible source limits our access and view of that history. There are many sides to any story, history especially, and all sides can provide depth and substance when we incorporate them all as part of the story. A wealth of cultural information and historical knowledge has not been made available to non-Indians because of a basic suspicion on the part of many Lakota (and other indigenous peoples). The suspicion exists because too many non-Indian noses are turned up at the thought that oral tradition should be considered credible. I suspect that this is a political and ethnocentric debate that will continue indefinitely, and as long as it is not resolved we all lose. At least for the parameters of this work, I have chosen to listen to both sides.

In my opinion, history is something owned collectively by all of us, although there has been a monopoly on the reporting and interpretation of it on the part of those who perceive themselves to be the "winners" or "conquerors of the West" or "tamers of the land." In spite of the self-serving labels and posturing, we are entitled to hear all viewpoints on our history and all the voices that have something to tell. Indeed, we must insist on it.

It is highly likely that another Lakota writer would approach the topic of Crazy Horse differently than I have. Nonetheless, a Lakota viewpoint about Crazy Horse needs to be put in front of those who have only a narrow view. Crazy Horse is much too important to the Lakota for us to be indifferent to the misconceptions about him. My Crazy Horse long ago ceased to be a one-dimensional hero impervious to the foibles of being human. I have done my best to make him real. I accept him for what he was as a man—as a Lakota person shaped by his environment, the times he lived in, and the culture that nurtured him. I am inspired by his legacy as an ordinary man, as much as by his legacy as an extraordinary leader. I feel connected to him when I speak my native language, when I handcraft an ash-wood bow or willow arrows, and when I do what I can to address the issues and challenges facing my tribe in these times. The customs he practiced, the traditions he followed, the values he lived by are still viable today because he did what he could to preserve them. He defended them by living them and fighting for them. For all those reasons he will always be my hero. For all those reasons he will always be as real to me as my mother and father are, as real as my grandmothers and grandfathers are.

To me, Crazy Horse will always be the irrepressible warrior and leader of warriors. He wasn't fearless, but he did act in spite of fear. He was a man who looked realistically at this environment and the circumstances within it. He understood the awesome responsibility and high honor of leading men into combat, as well as the daunting responsibility of living his life as a positive example for everyone to see. I think of him as *wica* or "complete man" (not to be confused with *wicasa* or "man," which is primarily the gender designation). *Wica* is what every Lakota man strove to be. A *wica* was the kind of a man who demonstrated the highest Lakota virtues of generosity, courage, fortitude, and wisdom.

Crazy Horse wasn't perfect but he was generous with his material goods and his efforts on behalf of others. He demonstrated courage time and again on and off the battlefield. His fortitude enabled him to hang on to his values, beliefs, and principles during a time of traumatic change for the Lakota, and he worked to acquire wisdom, realizing that it comes from failure as well as success.

He was much the same as other Lakota men of his day, indeed the same as most Lakota men of the nineteenth century. Like them, Crazy Horse was many things and fulfilled many roles. He was a son, husband, brother, father, and teacher. He was a crafter of weapons and tools, a hunter and tracker, horseman, scout, and fighting man, to list a few. He was also a deep thinker, a shy loner, a fierce defender of all that he held dear, a keen observer, a rejected suitor, a moral person, a family man, and a patriot. In short he lived his life, he made decisions, he took action, he reacted, he made mistakes, and he enjoyed or suffered the consequences of who and what he was and what he did or didn't do. That is his legacy.

A word about names. In English, Crazy Horse is how the world knows him. In Lakota, as I mentioned earlier, his name is *Tasunke Witko* or "His Crazy Horse" or "His Horse Is Crazy."

According to many of the elders who told stories of him, his childhood name was *Jiji,* or "Light Hair," and that is the name I chose to use in reference to him as a boy.

The format for this book was the cause of long inner turmoil and a certain amount of discussion with my editor because I was torn between writing an in-depth discussion of the life and times of Crazy Horse and a straight biography. The result is both, but it is also something more, though not new.

The biographic narrative is an attempt to unfold the life of Crazy Horse as a storyteller would. In the old days there were hero stories, stories that were told to boys and young men to make them aware of the long-standing tradition of the *wica,* the "complete man." Part of that was to be a warrior, of course, and many of the stories were about warriors. But these were not made-up stories; they were about real men and their actual exploits and accomplishments. There was no better way to inspire the young.

One of the old people would say, *Hiyu wo, takoja, wica wawoptetusni wan tawoecun ociciyakin ktelo.* Literally, it meant "Come, grandson, I want to tell you of the deeds of a hero." Colloquially, it meant "Come, grandson, I want to tell you a hero story." The word *wawoptetusni* has several meanings. It could mean "beyond reproach," "accomplished," or even "bigger than life." That was the kind of men the hero stories were about.

The narrative is augmented with essays—entitled Reflections—that add some dimension from the contemporary viewpoint on the life and times of Crazy Horse and his Lakota world.

Any shortcomings here are mine and certainly not due to the subject of this work or the elderly storytellers who gave their words and their hearts, and thus gave us a meaningful glimpse of the past.

So here is a hero story, the way I know it to be.

—Joseph Marshall III

Oyate Kin
(The People)

xxiv   Oyate Kin (The People)

across the Missouri River. Ihanktun was anglicized into Yankton and their subgroups are:

Ihanktunwan—people
Ihanktunwanna—little people of the end (meaning a smaller group).

Lakota

"Seven Fires," popularly referred to as the

Ogdalo—to scatter
Niwape—burnt leg or thigh;

The nation is comprised of three groups, two eastern and one western. The names of the groups mean "an alliance of friends" and represent a dialectical as well as a geographic distinction. All three groups understand one another's dialects. Each has subgroups or divisions.

Dakota

The Dakota are also known as the *Isanti.* The name comes from the Dakota words *isan* or *knife* and *ti,* meaning "to live or dwell." Long ago the Isanti encamped in areas where they gathered stone for making knives, primarily across the Missouri River to the northeast. Isanti eventually became Santee, and their subgroups are:

Mdewakantunwan—people of Spirit Lake;
Wahpekute—leaf shooters (or to shoot among the leaves);
Wahpetunwan—people living among the leaves, or people of Lake Traverse; and
Sissetunwan—people of the marsh.

Nakota

The Nakota are also known as *Ihanktun,* loosely meaning "village at the end" because their villages were far to the southeast across the Missouri River. Ihanktun was anglicized into Yankton, and their subgroups are:

Ihanktunwan—people of the end; and
Ihanktunwanna—little people of the end (meaning a smaller group).

Lakota

The Lakota were also known as *Titunwan,* meaning "to live where they can see" and also "people of the prairie." *Titunwan* was anglicized into *Teton.* The Lakota lived west of the Missouri River, and their subgroups are also known as *Oceti Sakowin* or "Seven Fires," popularly referred to as the Seven Council Fires:

Oglala—to scatter;
Sicangu—burnt leg or thigh;
Hunkpapa—those who camp at the end;
Mniconju—to plant by the water;
Oohenunpa—two boilings or two kettles;
Itazipacola—without bows; and
Sihasapa (sometimes *Siksika*)—black soles or black feet.

The Lakota Calendar

The annual calendar used by the Lakota was based on the thirteen lunar cycles, so there were thirteen months. Names for months were based on natural events, though different Lakota groups often used different names for the same months. The Middle Moon was so named because it had six months preceding it and six months following it. Because of the twenty-seven- and twenty-eight-day lunar cycle, the Lakota months did not coincide exactly with the modern calendar; in fact, they overlapped, so comparisons are approximate.

Tioheyunka Wi—Frost in the Lodge	January
Cannanpopa Wi—Popping Trees	February
Istawicanyazanpi Wi—Snowblindness	March
Magaglihunnipi Wi—When the Geese Return	April
Ptehincala Sapi Wi—Red Calves (are born) *Pehingnunnipi Wi*—When Horses Lose Their Hair	May
Wipazuke Waste Wi—Ripening Berries	June
Wicokannanji Wi—Sun Stands in the Middle	July
Wasutun Wi—When All Things Ripen *Ptehincala Sapapi Wi*—When Calves Turn Dark	August
Canapegi Wi—Leaves Turning Brown	September
Canape Hinhpayapi Wi—When Leaves Fall	October
Waniyetu Wi—Winter	November
Waniyetu Cokan Wi—Midwinter	December
Wiotehika—Hard Times	January

Part I

The Early Years

✧

One

His mother brought him forth in the place that symbolized the Lakota world, the place called *the heart of all things,* the Black Hills. Not new to the pain of giving birth, she silently endured it with the gentle help of She Who Takes the Babies, the midwife, an old woman whose hands were the first guidance, the first welcome felt by many newborns. Other women were in attendance in the tipi pitched slightly apart from the small encampment, a circle of knowledge and support watching the tiny head with coal black hair emerge into a Lakota world. Later they clucked and cooed and exchanged smiles of satisfaction as he opened his eyes, so deep brown they appeared black.

The circle of women worked quietly, laying the mother down and cleaning off the new life. One of them poked her head out the tipi door to announce to waiting girls that it was a boy, a future provider and protector of his people. So the word was carried to his father waiting nervously in his family's home, as all expectant fathers do.

As he heard the news he loaded the bowl of his pipe with tobacco and offered it to Mother Earth, Father Sky, to the Powers of the West, North, East, and South, and finally to the Grandfather, and then quietly smoked his thanksgiving for this new life, this new Lakota come into the world.

The new life suckled his mother's breasts eagerly, anxious to begin his journey. The women in attendance were pleased. One of them sang a soft lullaby, a soft rhythmic chant like a slow heartbeat. Soon his mother helped with the chant, her soft voice joining in, her eyes filled with love as she held her new son close, feeling his moist skin against her bare breasts even as one of the women wrapped a large warm robe around them both, binding mother and son together.

By 1840 much of the northern Plains of North America was unmistakably a Lakota world. From the Muddy River (Missouri) on the east, the Running Water (Niobrara) and the Shell (North Platte) rivers on the south, the Shining Mountains (Big Horns) to the west, and the northern border stretching from the Elk River (Yellowstone) east to the Knife flowing into the Muddy, the size of this far-flung world was in keeping with the population of the nation and the determination to protect it. Within this world the people lived by hunting. The people moved camp several times each year to flow with the change of seasons and the movement of the animals they depended on for food and clothing. The *tatanka,* the bison, was the main source of livelihood. The horse had arrived several generations before and was by then a very important part of Lakota life. It was the other reason the territory was so large.

In this Lakota world the life path for sons flowed in two directions that were closely tied to each other, like twin trunks of the same tree. Every boy grew up to be a hunter and a warrior, a provider and a protector. Every boy born was a promise that the nation would remain strong. Families prayed that each boy would grow up strong of body and mind, that he would heed the lessons of his fathers and grandfathers and honor the path already laid out for him. This was the way. So this new life come into the Lakota world, into the small community encamped in the place known as *the heart of all things,* was welcomed as new hope, and the people prayed that he would grow straight and strong.

The next morning the circle of women who had attended the birth escorted the mother and her new son from the woman's tipi into the main encampment, to the door of her own lodge, singing songs as they went. People watched and some joined the procession and gifts of welcome were laid next to the door. Among the gifts was a tiny bow with its own tiny arrow, an unmistakable sign of the journey that lay ahead for the new life.

Bison robes covered the floor of the lodge and painted rawhide containers—some square and some rectangular—were neatly arranged against the interior wall. A small girl, no more than three, waited anxiously, as did the man of the lodge. The woman entered and walked around the center fire pit and then lowered herself and her bundle carefully into a willow chair set next to the stone altar at the back of the room. Rattling Blanket Woman opened the bundle to show her daughter the thatch of wavy black hair atop her new brother's head, and then lifted the baby into his father's arms.

He was a modest man, a healer. Crazy Horse was his name, the same as his father's and which was passed down to him. They were a humble family, part of the Hunkpatila band[1] of the Oglala Lakota. She was Mniconju Lakota. Their children thus carried the blood of the Oglala and Mniconju Lakota people. The little one, this new life, this new hope for the people, squirmed in his arms and Crazy Horse felt the promise of goodness and strength within the tiny bundle he held.

So the father sang a welcoming song for his new son.

Thus the journey began.

---

1. A sub-band of the Oglala Lakota.

Two

The father of an infant boy would sometimes say to his wife and to all the women in his family, "He is yours for the first years of his life." Even if it were not spoken, it was the way things were done. And so for those first important years when a child plants the roots of his being that will support him throughout life, he is left entirely to his mother and grandmothers, not to mention all the mothers and grandmothers in the *tiyospaye,* the community, who might take a liking to him.

For most of the first year of his life the son of Crazy Horse and Rattling Blanket Woman stayed quite contentedly within the protective folds of his cradleboard, which, if not strapped to his mother, was propped within easy reach. Sleep was mostly what he did, bound snugly inside the portable cradle. And even after the boy began to venture beyond the cradleboard and his mother's immediate reach, his older sister hovered closely by watching over him like a hawk. Beyond her were the women and girls of the community, the second line of mothers and grandmothers for all the children. So the boy, like all Lakota children, grew with the reassuring knowledge that someone would always be there to see to his needs, even if it was only to take him by the hand and guide him back to his mother's lodge. Just as important, because his mother and all the women in his immediate environment nurtured him with gentleness, it was one of the first virtues he learned.

The boy also learned patience. Most of his whims and impulses were indulged as he explored the limits of his environment more and more, driven by his childish curiosity and inquisitiveness. Except to keep him from harming himself, the others did not dissuade him from any path he chose. Consequently he learned small but important lessons: the prairie cactus grew sharp thorns and therefore must be avoided; it was impossible to climb the side of a tipi; all grandmothers were good for at least one handful of freshly washed chokecherries; and so on.

The longer and stronger his legs grew, the wider he roamed in the village, and his world broadened. He played among the meat-drying racks and watched the women scraping hides stretched out on the ground, or he helped a grandmother carry firewood to her lodge. Curiosity drew him toward the horse herd often grazing just beyond the outskirts of the village, and he was more than a few times warned away by an older boy posted to watch the herd. Or he played the Keep-the-Hoop game where he joined a noisy gaggle of boys rolling a large willow hoop with long sticks, trying to keep it away from everyone else as long as possible. Fun was the obvious reward, but of course the game also developed quickness and coordination as well as determination. It also taught each participant to depend on himself. Thus the son of Crazy Horse and Rattling Blanket Woman was no different than any Lakota child, except in one way.

Every Lakota baby was born with thick, shiny black hair that stayed black for most of adulthood. But the hair of the son of Crazy Horse seemed to grow lighter even as he lost his baby fat, which happened to him quicker than in most children. To his mother and the other women in his life it was an endearing characteristic, although they worried that it would prove to be troublesome for him later in life. Outside the reach of his sharp ears he was referred to as *Jiji Kin,* or "The Light-Haired One."

"*Jiji Kin wanlaka he?*" someone would ask. "Have you seen the Light-Haired One?"

To his face he was simply called *Jiji,* or Light Hair.

"Huyu we, Jiji, wanna inunkin kte," his mother or sister would say. "Come, Light Hair, you will go to bed now."

Brown hair was not unknown among the Lakota, though it was much more common for girls. But when a boy had brown hair *and* the color of his skin was also lighter than usual, it did mean trouble. By giving him a name that called attention to an obvious physical characteristic, Light Hair's mother wisely made it less of an issue for him to face as an older child.

Four winters came and went in those first and formative years—a time as carefree as the adults in Light Hair's world could make it. In spring the people moved from sheltered winter camps to find good grazing to fatten the horses after a winter of thin, snow-covered grass. Summers brought several villages together. So the Hunkpatila winter camp of twenty families, about a hundred people, grew to nearly a hundred families and about four hundred people in summer. For Light Hair those factors were not important, only that the number of his playmates increased as well as the number of doting mothers, aunts, and grandmothers. More playmates meant more interesting adventures.

Light Hair was fed when he was hungry, his scrapes and bumps treated and healed, and his disappointments and losses softened by the indulgent attention of the females in his extended family. His father, Crazy Horse, and the other males of the family were always there on the periphery of his world, but they were busy working to provide and protect. As yet Light Hair was not fully aware that their path would be his, only that as he grew older he felt more inclined to seek his father's approval and was becoming more and more curious about him. It was a subtle change that the women allowed, albeit a little sadly, because the carefree boy was beginning to leave their world. He was taking the first hesitant steps onto the path he would follow for the rest of his life. His mother and all the grandmothers had done their part by teaching him the strength he would need to travel that path. Since before anyone could remember it had been said "a boy will learn the way of the warrior from his fathers and grandfathers after he learns courage from his mothers and grandmothers."

So the women, in their way, gave the boy to his father and grandfathers. There was no definable moment in which the next phase of the journey came, as much as a traveler doesn't know that it is a certain place at which he must go from a walk to a trot—only that it is time to do so. The men in the family simply began to give the boy more and more attention.

There came a day when someone handed Light Hair a bow and a quiver of arrows suited to his size and strength. It was the first tangible sign of the life that lay ahead, and his mother smiled because she was proud her son would follow the path of the hunter and warrior.

After the gift of the bow came the gift of knowledge. Light Hair instinctively knew what to do with the bow. Every child, for that matter, understood the bow was a weapon, significant enough that every man, young or old, carried one or always kept one within easy reach in every household. Light Hair was not left solely to his boyish whims to form his relationship with the weapon, however. It was that significant to the life of the Lakota. So, beginning with his father, various adult males taught him the proper way to carry it, care for it, and shoot it effectively. Careful and patient instruction from the knowledge and experience of seasoned hunters and warriors turned the gift of the bow into the gift of change. Light Hair couldn't look at the process in those real and figurative perspectives, of course. For him the immediate impact was in ownership of the bow and the connection it had with the adult males in his family and in the community. Something important was happening and he felt good, he felt different.

The words "He is yours for the first few years of his life" must have seemed to his mother to have been spoken only days earlier. Those first few years passed much too quickly for her. Her son, her only son as it would turn out, was no longer exclusively hers. Perhaps she sensed that she would not be there to see him fulfill his life's path.

Change came into Light Hair's life in yet another way. She who gave him life lost her own. In the perception of a child time can often be irrelevant, especially in a culture that was not given to measuring it. He was too young to understand that death is a part of life. Later he would realize that his mother's time on Earth had been much too short.

Perhaps Light Hair could not comprehend what had happened to his mother, but he could certainly perceive that all of the constant realities that were his mother—her voice, her reassuring touch, her busy hands at work, her physical presence—were suddenly no longer part of his daily routine. Perhaps he wondered at the sudden attention directed at him and his sister and their father and about the inordinate amount of weeping among adults. Something had happened that caused unusual behavior. Older women relatives took him and his sister into their homes and acted in an uncharacteristically somber manner, all the while treating them with utmost love and respect.

Such behavior was not totally unfamiliar to children. Death was part of their environment. Adult men were killed in battle or during a hunt. The elderly died of old age and people died from illness or women in childbirth. Although children were not excluded from the rituals and ceremonies surrounding mourning and burial, they were not directly involved unless, of course, someone from their immediate family or a close relative had died.

Few children would know exactly what to do or how to behave. Light Hair and his sister could do no more than react to the mood of the adults and grieve in the same way everyone was. One day they were taken to a secluded area and to a long bundle atop a platform on four poles, a bundle of buffalo hide. There they left tiny bundles of prairie sage tied to the poles and an old man sang an honoring song. From the platform hung some small personal possessions they recognized as belonging to their mother. Perhaps it was at that moment they might have realized somehow their mother would never come home from wherever she had gone.

So she left Light Hair when he was at that turn in his new journey that would take him beyond those first formative years. She gave him life, thus filling what Wakantanka had created her to do, and she gave him a foundation on which to build the balance of his life, thus fulfilling the expectation held for all Lakota mothers. Her work on Earth was wholly fulfilled, it seemed, because she gave her son all that he would need: life and a foundation.

Losing one's birth mother was not unknown among the Lakota, but in reality there were no orphans. Other mothers and grandmothers filled in because they had always been there.

The seasons did not stop, however. Sun rose and traveled its daily journey. Moon graced the night without missing its more than ancient cycle. In the Hunkpatila encampment life went on. There came a day when Crazy Horse and his woman relatives made a feast and invited everyone to eat, and they talked of the woman who had been a shadowy guest in all their grieving hearts and in so doing let her rise from their grief into the light of the next life. And so, finally, she was on her next journey.

More seasons turned. Leaves colored and fell, the autumn winds grew colder until they became the gusty breath of winter blowing the snow as it fell across the land. Spring came once again with its ancient promise of renewal, then summer with the fulfillment of that promise. And one day Light Hair and his sister were given their new mothers.

They were sisters, quiet and polite as they walked into the circle of their new life as the wives of Crazy Horse and the mothers of his daughter and son. They were the younger sisters of a man renowned among his own Sicangu people, one whose name was spoken often in reference to courage and leadership: Spotted Tail. Even Light Hair had heard the name, though unaware as yet that his new uncle, a tall, stalwart man, would influence his journey on this Earth.

A man having more than one wife at a time was not unusual among the Lakota. Such an arrangement had to be worth the added responsibility, however. Now and then a man would take his wife's widowed sister into the family circle, for example. Crazy Horse, though of modest means, was much in demand as a healer and he had as much of an obligation to the community as he did toward his children. Thus a new wife was a necessity, and two—in his case—would turn out to be a blessing for his children.

Crazy Horse had told Light Hair and his sister that they would have new mothers. It was a tentative declaration though, not in the sense that it might not happen, but stemming from a feeling of trepidation. There was the real fear that Light Hair and his sister would not accept their father's new wives as their new mothers. But although there was uncertainty on both sides of the new family, day by day they grew to tolerate one another. Tolerance, in the end, was the mother of acceptance and in time the sisters of Spotted Tail became, in practice and in the heart, mothers to the children of their husband.

Crazy Horse was relieved, for he did have the welfare of his children in mind when he offered gifts to the family of Spotted Tail. His duties as a medicine man kept him busy and away from the home and he knew that his new wives were thought of as good young women well taught in the art of keeping a home. And like all Lakota women, they knew their eventual calling was to be mothers whether the children they cared for and raised were only born to them in the heart. As for Light Hair and his sister, the emptiness that had been in their lodge began to slowly fill in with soft voices and laughter and the sense of purpose and comforting presence only a mother could provide.

The lodge of Crazy Horse became whole again, not because the two new wives and mothers replaced her who had been the first mother, but they came with their own presence and their own ways. There was still a sense that someone should be there in the hearts of the children she had left behind. Yet there was the growing sense that beside the empty space was the reality of mother embodied in two. The specific memories of she who had given them life began to fade and take much of the pain with them. They would always have memories of her, but over time they would grow more into feelings than images.

Three

Light Hair knew his father was different from other men because he spent many days and nights away from his family. He knew he was curing fevers or treating broken legs or rattlesnake bites, and he also helped families prepare for burials when there was a death.

The boy didn't completely understand all about his father. But he did know that Crazy Horse didn't hunt like the other men or go to war. A father who was a medicine man and didn't do the things all men did caused the boy to feel all the more different. He wondered most of all why he looked different than other boys. Each summer gathering when several encampments came together, he always looked for other boys with light hair like his. To his dismay, the only other children with light hair were girls. Older boys also noticed and teased him by pulling on his breechclout—their way of suggesting that he should be wearing dresses instead.

Light Hair was about to begin a journey that, in the end, would make him even more different than the boys who teased him mercilessly. But first, he would become a hunter.

Hunting was the Lakota lifeblood. Like the wolf, fox, eagle, mountain lion, and hawk, the Lakota were hunters. At age seven, Light Hair realized more and more that hunting was the way to have fresh meat, and deer and elk hides for clothing, and buffalo hides for lodge coverings. He also sensed that he would be part of the process somehow.

Like all boys, Light Hair was becoming skilled with his bow. He had progressed to a stouter bow, stronger than the first he was given—one made in proportion to his size and strength. His favorite game had changed as well. Shooting arrows through a rolling willow hoop had become too easy and boring, so his uncle Little Hawk and a few other men introduced him to a new game—shooting at grasshoppers. The rules were simple: Walk along the prairie with an arrow on the bowstring, and shoot at a grasshopper when it flew. A rolling hoop was a much easier target. A grasshopper was about the size of his little finger and flew erratically, and fast. The men would suppress smiles when, at first, the boy was unable to get off a shot. Before he could pull back the string the insect was back in the grass. But as he learned to hold his bow ready, he could send an arrow in the general direction of the flitting grasshopper. Shooting at grasshoppers was not boring. It was, he learned, a very humbling experience.

As the summer wore on, his reaction became faster and more and more his arrows only narrowly missed. Grasshoppers, an old man told him, have much to teach. Many Lakota hunters bring down rabbits or deer because grasshoppers taught them how to shoot with unerring marksmanship. If you want to sharpen your shooting eye, they said, or if you ever think you are as good as you'll ever be, chase grasshoppers.

But fortunately for Light Hair there was more to his training than humiliation by grasshoppers. Across the prairies, through brushy creek bottoms and up mountain slopes, he followed his mentors, and each kind of terrain offered ample opportunities to learn. Whitetail deer, he noticed, left a nearly perfect, matted circle in the grass where they had been resting the day away. They lay in hiding most of the day and grazed at night. A wolf's paw print was almost as large as a grown man's hand. After sundown, warm air flowed up from the floor of a valley; therefore, the best place for a night camp was high on the slope.

Lying beneath the branches of a pine tree, Light Hair watched a young coyote approach. "Stare at him," whispered the teacher. "Stare at his eyes." Light Hair did as he was told. The coyote was about to pass when he stopped and turned to stare back directly at the boy hidden among the branches, and then fled.

"No matter how far, the eyes have the power to draw the eyes," said the teacher. "A good thing to know when scouting in Crow lands. Do not stare at the enemy's eyes too long. He will feel your stare. He will know you are looking. Just as the coyote did."

Light Hair's teachers were not loud, vociferous men. They made no speeches espousing grandiose philosophy. Their approach involved action more than words. They took him away from the comfortable confines of his boyhood environment and into the realm of their knowledge and experience. They introduced him to the various dimensions of his world. Day by day he learned its rhythms, its moods, its colors and textures, and he began to form his own experiences, build his own knowledge, and develop his own intimacy with it. What he thought was merely endless space had its own life, its own spirit. He began to appreciate that the grasshopper had something to teach him. More importantly he began to understand that, like the grasshopper, he had a place in the world around him.

As a child, Light Hair saw men ride into the encampment with deer, elk, and antelope either hanging across the back of a packhorse or on drag poles behind the horse. It was a mystery to him how exactly the hunters were able to find such game. Buffalo hunting was not so much a mystery. He'd watched a few chases from hilltops, horses and riders on the edges of an undulating black river, dust billowing, a low rumble coming across the prairie. It was the most exciting thing he had ever seen. He knew it was dangerous, but he couldn't wait to chase buffalo. Now, under the tutelage of men like his uncle Little Hawk, he began to understand the practical aspects of hunting.

Much of it was repetition and practice, which was not exciting at all. Sitting along a game trail waiting for a mountain black tail was almost as boring as shooting arrows through a rolling willow hoop. He would have preferred to watch the clouds billowing above the horizon, or the eagles circling overhead. But if he didn't have the patience to wait for the deer to come, or the patience to wait for it to come into range of his bow, and if he missed when he had the right shot, his family would go hungry.

"The family of a good hunter looks well fed," he was told. "They wear fine clothes because he takes deer and elk so the women can tan the hides and sew them into shirts and dresses and make moccasins. The family of a poor hunter is thin, with worn clothes because there are no new hides to sew. What do you want everyone to say about how you provide for your family?"

So Light Hair took his lessons seriously.

Some lessons had nothing to do with improving his physical endurance or distinguishing between elk and deer hoofprints. They were nonetheless just as important.

One afternoon Light Hair spotted a hare resting beneath a clump of sagebrush well within range of his bow. The teacher took the bow away. "Run," he said, "chase it and catch it with your hands."

Light Hair put down his weapon and did as he was told, or tried. The hare was off and running in a heartbeat and out of sight before the boy had run ten strides. He returned complaining that he couldn't catch the animal.

"But it's only a hare," replied the teacher, "and you are a human being. You are the hunter."

Like all boys caught in such a predicament, Light Hair humbly reasoned that he couldn't bring down the hare without his bow and arrows.

"True," said the teacher. "Remember that we all have weaknesses and strengths. Sometimes the hare will win, sometimes you. Even the wolf fails more often than he wins, but he doesn't stop. He has great fangs, he can smell a trail two days old, and he can hear you over the next hill. But his real strength is endurance. He never quits."

As he was learning the skills necessary to hunt, Light Hair was also learning that the hunter had much in common with the hunted. We all live to sustain the life of others, he was told. The grass feeds off the earth; the rabbits, buffalo, elk, deer, and antelope feed off the grass, and wolves, foxes, and men feed on them. In the end, the hunters feed the earth when the life of even the mightiest hunter comes to an end. To acknowledge this practical and spiritual connection, Lakota hunters performed a simple ceremony. Light Hair was taught to offer a bundle of prairie sage to acknowledge the gift of life the animal had given, whether it was a squirrel or an elk.

As the days passed he unknowingly attracted the interest and curiosity of a man called High Back Bone. He was a Mniconju with an Oglala wife, and he liked what he saw in the shy Light Hair. Perhaps it was the boy's quiet determination or his innate humility.

High Back Bone himself was a quiet man, not given to pursuing the path of glory, but he was deeply committed to achieving the status of *wica*, the complete man. The complete man embodied the best qualities of the hunter and the fighting man. Though all men necessarily filled roles of both provider and protector— the hunter/warrior—not everyone could achieve the highest ideals for both callings. High Back Bone was one of the few.

High Back Bone was a leader of fighting men, muscular and broad shouldered, exuding the confidence of a man who not only had physical strength but also a lifetime of experience and accomplishment. He knew that Little Hawk and the Light Hair's other teachers had taught him a variety of physical skills, but had also laid the foundation for an important quality that would stand him in good stead throughout his life: self-confidence. Most important, he also saw in the boy the proverbial stillness of deep water. The day he visited the lodge of Crazy Horse and asked to take the light-haired boy under his wing was the beginning of a lifelong friendship. From the first time High Back Bone rode out of the camp with Light Hair at his side, the future of the Oglala Lakota rode with them.

The Oglala had been slowly pushing westward from the Black Hills before Light Hair was born. By the time he was seven, there was a consistent Lakota presence as far west as Elk Mountain at the northern tip of the Medicine Bow Mountains, and north into the Powder River country east of the Shining Mountains. Buffalo and pronghorn antelope were plentiful on the prairies, as were the elk and deer in the mountains. All were essential to survival and comfort. The Snakes, also known as the Eastern Shoshoni, had prior claim to the lands near Elk Mountain. Likewise, the Crow, who called themselves Absaroka, long roamed the Powder River region. Those ancient Lakota enemies grudgingly gave way but only because they were outnumbered. Numerical advantage was the basis for strength. A willingness to fight added to it, and when the Lakota did fight and win, their victories stayed in the minds of those they defeated. They were not better than their enemies, simply stronger. And Light Hair would learn where that strength came from.

High Back Bone reminded the boy that he was born in the Year a Hundred Horses Were Taken. In a daring raid on a Snake encampment, a handful of Lakota warriors swooped in and drove off a hundred horses without losing a single man or horse. Perhaps it was a sign that he was born in a year designated by warrior accomplishments. Every man was a hunter and every man was a warrior. A few warriors set themselves apart with their exploits on the battlefield. Such men seemed to be born to the calling, more than others. High Back Bone sensed that in his slender, light-haired charge. The stillness of deep water.

High Back Bone's choice did not go unnoticed. A man with his reputation might have been expected to pick the son of an influential family, the kind of association that would enhance High

Back Bone's standing in the community and in the warrior societies. More than a few men were puzzled over his selection of the light-haired son of a humble medicine man. On the other hand, Crazy Horse's wives were the sisters of Spotted Tail, an important man among the Sicangu. Perhaps, some said, High Back Bone selected the nephew of Spotted Tail, rather than the son of Crazy Horse. But the Mniconju paid no heed to such opinions. If anyone would have asked him, he would have told them, but no one did.

A broad-shouldered man with serious, chiseled features and a shy slender boy with wavy brown hair were an unlikely pair, but they became a familiar sight in the Hunkpatila camp. Light Hair emulated his teacher from the way he rode his horse to how he wore a quiver of arrows across the small of his back. The boy was a willing student and never failed to attempt to do anything High Back Bone asked him to do. He was slowly being shaped into a warrior in much the same way the fire-cured bow is made.

The preferred process for curing a wood stave for a bow was to cut it in winter when the sap was down, hang it high in the lodge beneath the smoke hole, and simply allow it to cure for five years. But the Lakota had made their living and protected themselves with the bow for countless generations and had learned effective shortcuts out of necessity. Using fire, it was possible to cure a green stave in a matter of days.

The summer of his eighth year, when the Hunkpatila were encamped near the southern fork of the Powder River, Light Hair and High Back Bone found a stand of young ash trees guarding a spring in a gully. A straight tree a little taller than the boy was selected. Before he instructed the boy to chop it down, High Back Bone smudged it with sage and offered tobacco bundles to the tree to acknowledge its life and the sacrifice it was about to make. With a hand axe the boy cut the tree down, marking the bottom. They hauled it to their camp where a fire with a deep bed of coals was already burning.

The slender stave, no wider than a man's wrist, was stripped of its bark and hung over the fire. At appropriate intervals it was turned so that it dried uniformly.

"The fire is like life when it strengthens a man through hard times," a bow maker would point out.

Over a bed of hot coals the fresh stave, mostly white in color, slowly turned a deep yellow as it became harder and harder. After the fire-cure came the tools: a hand axe, several knives, a flat piece of sandstone, and elk antler tines. An outline was carefully drawn on the stave to mark the bottom end, and to show the excess wood to be removed with the axe. That done, a knife was used for the next phase of shaving off excess wood.

The bow maker watched his pupil closely, with a patient word here and there, making sure the bow was taking shape as it should. Then he took the bow and refined it, explaining his methods as he worked. Finally, the bow had the desired shape and design. In the exact middle it was two fingers wide from side to side and tapered away to each end, which was about the size of a man's little finger. From the top to bottom profile it gradually tapered away to each end.

On the top near the tip a single notch was carved in one side for the bowstring. On the bottom two notches were carved, one on each side. Just as it is important to mark the bottom of the tree so that as a finished bow it remains in line with the flow of life, upward from the Earth, when the bow is kept in its natural direction, it is less likely to break. Strength comes from balance, as all bow makers know. The bow stands on its feet, bow makers are quick to point out, like humans do.

With the antler tine the bow maker rubbed the wood, giving it a smooth sheen as well as closing the grains to give it more strength. With the addition of a sinew string the weapon became a force to be reckoned with. Shaping a stave into a bow was the story of any boy's journey on the path to becoming a warrior.

High Back Bone watched the slender boy and wondered what

fires of adversity lay ahead on his journey. Of one thing he was certain: the boy would become strong as a result, in the same way the ash stave became harder as it dried over the coals. The fires of adversity, as High Back Bone knew, were already smoldering along a wide, flat river far to the south known as the Shell.

The Shell River flowed north out of the Medicine Bow Mountains, turned east on the sagebrush plains, then southeasterly as it entered the short grass prairies until it emptied itself into the Great Muddy River after a slight turn to the northeast. People traveled west along this river, though they were calling it the Platte and then the North Platte. The corridor along the river was called the Oregon Trail. The travelers were a trickle the two summers past, but now the trickle grew to a thin but steady stream. These were a people strange to the Lakota, though not unknown. Their kind had been encroaching on Lakota lands for several generations, perhaps for nearly a hundred years, though only a little at a time.

These travelers along the Shell were from the nation of whites to the east beyond the Great Muddy River. They had already established outposts mostly on the fringes of Lakota lands, and traveled up and down the Great Muddy in large smoke-belching houseboats. A trading settlement northeast of the Medicine Bow Mountains along the Shell became an outpost called Fort Laramie. Soldiers in blue coats came to the fort, carrying knives as long as a man's arm. Thus they became known as the Long Knives. And they and the travelers heading west along the Oregon Trail were the first wisps of smoke from the smoldering embers that would grow into flames of adversity for all the Lakota, and for Light Hair.

In the summer of his ninth year Light Hair's Hunkpatila encampment moved southeast to the area northwest of Fort Laramie. They were curious about the stories coming from the southern encampments that seemed difficult to believe—stories of lines of wagons pulled by teams of cattle, mules, and horses

moving west along the Shell, not unlike the migration of large
buffalo herds. Men, women, and children rode in the covered
wagons and many walked as well.

The corridor on either side of the Shell River had been a trail
for elk and buffalo for thousands of years. Human beings used it
as well. The first whites in the area were trappers and mountain
men, who learned of the trail from the Ponca people to the east
and the Kiowa and Blue Clouds, called the Arapaho by many, to
the south as well. When one ant sets off on a trail, others follow.

Light Hair accompanied High Back Bone to the Shell. There
they joined over a hundred other curious men and boys sitting
on the hills and ridges north of the river to watch a line of wagons plodding westward. The stories were true.

Amusement was the predominant state of mind. Men and
boys stood, sat, or reclined in the grass and among the rocks on
the hills. There were many questions and much speculation.
Where were these people going? And why did they obviously
leave behind their homes? Some of the older men told alarming
stories connected with whites. The whites, they said, likely carried illnesses that were very dangerous. The Kiowa far south of
the Shell had lost half of their people in less than two months to
disease brought among them by whites, it was said. Perhaps as
many as four thousand Kiowa had died, it was said, and this only
the past summer.

The Lakota themselves had suffered. The Sicangu living near
the Great Muddy had lost over a thousand to the running-face
sickness, called smallpox, just over ten years earlier. One of the
large houseboats came up the Great Muddy, stopping at various
landings to trade or take on wood. People and goods from the
boat had come among the few Sicangu who met the boat to
trade. Very soon after the boat departed upriver smallpox swept
through several encampments. People became ill, their faces and
chests marked with pustules. Death came in a matter of days.
Though medicine men worked day and night, they were power-

less against the illness that moved like a wind-driven fire. The only possible cause of the sudden and terrifying outbreak was contact with the people and goods from the houseboat. In the autumn, word came down from the upper reaches of the Great Muddy that the People of the Earth Lodges, the Mandan, had been all but wiped out by the same running-face sickness. They had also traded with the houseboat.

The men and boys who heard the stories for the first time stared somberly from the hills and ridges at the line of wagons and people. For some, curiosity turned into a sense of foreboding. Perhaps something should be done, a few suggested. Perhaps they should be prevented from coming into Lakota lands. In spite of their concerns, the Lakota men did nothing more than watch. Most, if not all, of them had never seen a white man up close.

Light Hair watched as well, but he didn't know what to think. The distant wagons and people yielded no specific features. Though some of the Lakota described white men as having beards, it meant nothing to those on the hill because the people in the wide valley below were small, shadowy outlines. On either side of Light Hair were men and boys with brown skin, long hair flowing in the breeze or worn in tight braids, most of them dressed in leggings, breechclouts, and moccasins due to the warm weather. Dozens of pairs of curious or intense dark eyes fixed on the spectacle below. He knew them, who they were and what they were. The people below, although he was aware there were men, women, and children, were nothing more than distant shapes moving slowly to some unknown destination for unknown reasons.

Light Hair had never seen a wagon. *Canpagmiyanpi*—"Wood that is rolled," they were called. No doubt difficult to move since four horned cattle in line two by two were needed to pull them. He returned to the Hunkpatila encampment with High Back Bone, saying little and nothing at all about the wagons and the shadowy travelers.

Four

One fact of life for the Lakota was movement. Clouds, wind, the buffalo—all were in constant motion. Winter, spring, summer, and autumn also lived a never-ending cycle. Life itself moved from infancy, to childhood, to adulthood, and to old age, and all the various layers of life also had a beginning, and an ending.

Like most Lakota boys approaching the age of twelve, Light Hair was a proficient hunter. The game trails and seasonal migration habits of white tail and black tail deer and elk in every region in which the Hunkpatila people pitched their lodges—from the Black Hills to the Powder River country—were common knowledge. Like all hunters, Light Hair learned to sit motionless in a driftwood blind along a creek for the better part of an afternoon waiting for a white tail to move within the effective killing range of his bow, which was as far as he could throw a stone with all his might. He knew to cut the jugular in the animal's neck and the femoral arteries on either side of the back legs so that the warm carcass would bleed out profusely and so that the fresh meat wouldn't spoil.

His skill with the bow was approaching the expert level. More than a few grasshoppers on the fly fell to the deadly flick of his arrows. Though he was not much larger than he was at the age of ten, there was the confidence of a man in the way he handled a weapon and in the manner in which his eyes appraised everything around him. More and more there was the stillness of a deep pool. If the taunts of other boys about his light hair touched a nerve, he didn't give them the satisfaction of a reaction. Perhaps it was this characteristic that drew a thin, gangly boy to him, a boy with dark, inquisitive eyes.

Lone Bear and Light Hair became close friends and shared the usual activities of boyhood. They ranged far beyond the encampment in pursuit of adventures small and large as they yearned for the excitement they knew was waiting for them as young men. On their horses they patrolled the perimeters of the camp or hid among rocks on a hilltop to watch for enemies, wishing, almost hoping, that one would appear so they could be the first to spread the alarm, or charge forward to meet the threat.

When no enemies came, they resorted to games like the one called Knocking-Them-Off-the-Horses. Armed with thin willow or driftwood rods and sitting astride their horses, they faced one another, looking for the right opening to poke the opponent hard enough to force him off the horse. More often than not it was Lone Bear who fell to the ground. When they tired of that they would practice the wounded-man-drag. They fell from their horses pretending to be wounded, a long rope attached loosely around their chests and the other end around the horses' necks. The horse was expected to drag the "wounded man" to safety. Sometimes the horses cooperated and other times they were more interested in grazing in a particularly lush patch of grass.

But their favorite game was imitating a buffalo chase. First one, then the other, would be the "buffalo" and gallop away on his horse from the "hunter" who approached from the right side at a full gallop, a blunt arrow held to the bow string and aimed at the running buffalo. Even in the absence of a real herd thundering across the prairie, the game did present some of the real dangers of a buffalo chase. Uneven ground, unexpected obstacles, or a horse swerving unexpectedly could cause both riders to lose balance and fall. Of course, one tumble from a galloping horse was often enough to motivate the rider to keep his seat the next time, no matter what. Skinned elbows, knees, and faces, not to mention a roll through a cactus patch, were the wounds that turned playful boys into earnest men one game and one small adventure at a time.

There were, of course, other amusements that were not as dangerous. Light Hair and Lone Bear often passed most of a quiet summer afternoon reclining on a grassy slope observing the land and the sky. Such episodes of seeming inactivity had purpose, however, because they provided intimate contact with everything around them that could be detected by any of their senses. It was this kind of connection that enabled a being like the wolf to become part of the land, not simply live on it. While boys didn't have the wolf's unimaginably keen sense of sight, smell, and hearing, they nevertheless like the wolf learned to connect with the land. That connection would make them skillful hunters and dangerous warriors. While the dangerous games were the substance of the preparation for the trials that lay ahead of them as the hunters and warriors they would be, moments of quiet introspection and observation would help them to understand why.

Other groups of boys were learning by playing as well, but Light Hair and Lone Bear seemed to be a particularly odd pairing. Lone Bear, with his glistening black hair and dark brown complexion, was the total opposite of Light Hair, with his light brown hair and fair complexion. The others didn't understand that the remarks and the teasing they hurled at the pair were helping to solidify a friendship that would be ended only by death.

One of those who tried to be especially hurtful with his words was a soft-handed, always ceremoniously dressed boy who was given the name Pretty One by an uncle unhappy with the boy's bent for fancy clothes. Pretty One was of an influential family with a father skilled in oratory and accomplished as a leader. The boy was certainly aware of his family's status in the community and it was from that lofty perch, which he somehow perceived as based on his own merits, that he hurled verbal barbs at Light Hair and Lone Bear. Little did the two friends know that the immaculately dressed boy would always be like a bothersome pebble beneath their moccasin soles.

But if Pretty One would be a growing problem, so would a place they had yet to see, a place called Fort Laramie. Lone Bear listened intently as Light Hair described the day he rode with High Back Bone to see for themselves the wagons traveling west along the Shell River. Many of those wagons stopped at Fort Laramie, it was said, and many Lakota were curious about them. There was talk among the old men, many of them suggesting that a closer look at what was happening at Fort Laramie might be wise, and to learn why the Long Knife peace talkers had sent out a call to meet with the Lakota, and others.

So the encampment moved further south.[1] For anyone who had never seen a white man, there was a strange anticipation, much like wanting a closer look at a rattlesnake but knowing there could be some danger involved. What were they like, many thought, these people living in wagons?

Fort Laramie was several large buildings and a trading post near the Shell River. Soldiers in blue clothing were everywhere, some carrying the long knives. It was clear that the Long Knives were fond of the strange shape of the square—the wagons were of a similar shape—but the more astonishing fact was the number of whites.

Lone Bear and Light Hair rode to a slight rise north of the fort, warned by Crazy Horse and High Back Bone not to go nearer. But it was a good enough vantage point to see the buildings and the surrounding area. A wide trail led to the fort from the southeast and away to the west. On either side of the main area of activity, which was among the light-colored buildings,

---

1. Summer of 1851.

and along the trail were what they could only assume were abandoned wagons. They resembled skeletons, most of them stripped down to the frames.

Whites were everywhere, along with their horses, mules, oxen, and cattle. The occasional barking of dogs reached the boys' ears. South of the buildings they could see the tops of several Lakota lodges. A few Lakota stayed near the fort from the days before the soldiers had taken over, in the days when it was only a trading town. Now, the rumors were, the soldiers had come to protect the travelers along the Shell River trail. They were afraid of the Lakota and the Blue Clouds to the south and the Snakes further to the west. Perhaps that was the reason the Long Knives wanted to meet and talk. The call had gone out as well, it was said, to some who were enemies of the Lakota, such as the Crow and the Blackfeet. Light Hair and Lone Bear sat on their horses and watched the town of white men busy with whatever was part of their everyday lives. The old men were hoping that the whites would keep going west. There was nothing wrong with trading, they said. They had tobacco and coffee and other good items, like butcher knives. Some old Lakota said the good things made by the white men were one thing, but the white men themselves were questionable.

Light Hair and Lone Bear stayed on the hill until the sun sank low and sent shadows from the rolling hills across the gullies and meadows. As the days passed, they grew tired of watching the whites, and there was more talk of the Long Knives' call for a great "peace" meeting. Peace talks when there was really no war seemed more than a little suspicious to many of the old Lakota who were children when the whites were only occasionally passing through, sometimes lost. Since then their numbers had grown steadily and a man needed only to spend a summer afternoon watching the Shell River trail to feel a cold fear in his belly from the sheer numbers of people traveling west. What if, some asked, they decided to stay?

Lone Bear and Light Hair liked to lie next to the rolled-up sides of the council lodge to listen to the old men talk the evenings away, sometimes far into the night. If there was to be talk with the whites, the Lakota had to make certain their concerns about the wagons on the Shell River trail were heard, some said. Others were more insistent. The whites had to leave, give up Fort Laramie, and stay off the Shell River trail.

The trail had quickly become marked by deep side-by-side ruts from the iron-rimmed wheels of the wagons. Strange-looking, strange-shaped items of wood and some of iron had been discarded along the way, according to some eyewitnesses—not to mention the rotting animal carcasses, and some human graves, too. Something had to be done before the land was killed for good.

When the wagons first began to appear on the trail, they, and the whites in them, were regarded as little more than a curious occurrence. At first, there had been trading of small items such as knives, plugs of tobacco, and cloth. Both sides were understandably nervous and cautious, but there had been no outright conflicts. But when a few Lakota demanded payment to let the wagons pass, the whites' nervousness turned into fear. And fear always clouded good sense. An old man reminded everyone about the incident when a few outriders from the wagons had opened fire on a few Lakota boys who had wandered closer to have a better look. One of the boys had been killed. Now the Long Knives at Fort Laramie were saying the wagons had to be protected. The Lakota had to allow safe passage or the soldiers would punish any who harmed any person or animal traveling with the wagons. They started the trouble, some of the old men complained, and they threaten us because of it.

But there was another consequence just as troublesome. Because of the yearly human travel along the trail, the seasonal movement of buffalo herds was changing. Buffalo scouts reported that many of the herds no longer grazed in the Shell River floodplain because the grass was trampled or cropped down by the oxen, mules, and horses of the wagon trains. And for two or three springs, though the rains had been good, the grasses didn't grow as thick along the wagon trails.

Movement was nothing new to the Lakota; it was a constant part of life. Such a thing was normal and reassuring. But not all movement was understandable, or welcome. The buffalo moving away from the Shell River trail was disturbing. These things the old men talked about in the council lodges in the Lakota encampments, and many people, young and old, stayed near to listen. There were no ready answers. Perhaps, one or two would suggest, the buffalo had the answer. Perhaps it was wise to move away from the trail until the wagons stopped coming altogether. The trouble with that, some replied, was that when one thing moved away from a place, something else often moved in.

The consensus that rose like acrid smoke from the council lodges was to listen to what the Long Knife "peace" talkers would have to say.

Five

The Lakota called it the Council at Horse Creek. The white peace talkers called it the Fort Laramie Treaty Council of 1851. One of them, known as Broken Hand[1] to some of the Lakota, had sent word beyond Lakota lands and gifts had been promised. Many of the Oglala camps were the first to arrive, since this was their territory. The Sicangu were not far behind. From the middle days of summer the prairies around Fort Laramie began blossoming with lodges. In the Moon of Dark Calves, others began arriving. Ancient Lakota enemies, the Blackfeet, came from the mountains to the northwest of the Elk River, and the Crow from the north. From the west beyond the Wind River came the Snakes. The Mandan, Hidatsa, and Arikara came from the Knife River country in the upper reaches of the Great Muddy. The Sahiyela and Blue Clouds, good friends of the Lakota, came from south of the Shell. And, of course, their close relatives the Dakota and the Nakota came from east of the Great Muddy, at least those who could make the crossing.

Nearly eight thousand men, women, and children of all the nations gathered around the Long Knives. And there were fewer than three hundred of their soldiers.

Old enemies put aside ancient animosity to pitch their lodges deep in Lakota lands—mostly because the curiosity about the manner of people who could audaciously talk to them as if they

---

1. Thomas Fitzpatrick.

were children had to be satisfied. A bit of grumbling arose because the promised gifts were late, and some began to talk about breaking camp and heading back to more familiar territories. But the Long Knives assured them the wagons loaded with gifts were on the way.

The horse herds quickly grazed down the prairies all around the fort, and the camps and the heavy smell of horse droppings soon became a constant annoyance. A few of the headmen met with the commander of the Long Knives and it was agreed to move the camps a day's ride southeast to Horse Creek where there was fresh grass.

The Long Knives pitched a long tent and invited the various headmen to parley. In between the horse racing and trading among the various camps, the leaders from each went to sit under the tent and listen to the white peace talkers harangue. The white peace talkers were surrounded by rows of warriors from the different tribes but it was the headmen who attracted the most attention. All of them were garbed in their finest feather bonnets and their keenly decorated shirts made from elk, deer, mountain goat, and big horn sheep hides. Such a colorful or powerful assortment of leaders had never before gathered together.

It was mainly the forbearance of the old men leaders that kept the large gathering in order, for such a thing was not without its problems. The promised gifts were late in arriving, but the chief complaint was the lack of interpreters available to translate the peace talkers' words into nine other languages. Delegations from the different tribes could not all clearly understand and agree on the intentions of the whites, but they could all agree that the white peace talkers seemed to be confused.

Yet as the various people talked among themselves and sent messengers from one camp to another, they arrived at the consensus that the whites wanted three things. First, they wanted no more fighting among the people gathered. The Blackfeet and the Crow were called upon to live in peace with the Lakota and the

Lakota were in turn to live in peace with the Snakes, and so on. (Tell the wind to stop blowing, some reacted, or the rivers to stop flowing.) Second, the whites seemed to want to say where the land ended and where it began by drawing a picture on a parched hide. Beyond a certain line was Crow land and behind it was Blackfeet, but who could find that line on the earth? some wondered. Third, the travelers on the Shell River trail must not be molested, they said, for they were traveling under the protection of the "great father" who lived in some city far to the east of the Grandfather River. The "great father" would know if his people on the trail were harmed. The trail must be holy in some fashion, suggested an old Lakota man wryly. Thereafter, the Shell River trail became known as the "Holy Road."

For agreeing to these three things, the peace talkers said, the "great father" was empowering them to pay annuities[2] that amounted to many, many thousands of their money in dollars. The annuities would be in the form of food (beef cattle, flour, and beans, for starters), and various other goods, such as plows, hoes, and other farm implements. There were many raised eyebrows and helpless shrugs at the listing of the "other goods," but in the end they were accepted. Those who had seen such goods before described how they had melted down metal implements for lance points, arrowheads, and knives.

The feasting and dancing and talking went on for days. Through it all, the solemn-faced, bearded white peace talkers acted like stern fathers while their Long Knife soldiers paraded around in lines and strange squares. To show their power, they fired one of their big guns mounted on a short wagon, the shell tearing up the ground and shattering trees. It was an impressive weapon, powerful and loud. But in between the loading of it,

---

2. The promised annuities totaled $50,000 a year for fifty years. When the Senate ratified the treaty, the duration was reduced to ten years, with the possibility of a five-year extension.

some fighting men observed, several good men on fast horses could charge a small contingent of soldiers and wipe them out.

Wagons filled with the promised gifts finally arrived: glass beads, small hand mirrors, butcher knives, blankets, and rolls of cloth, among other things—trinkets intended to soften the hearts of opposition. The old men leaders watched as their names were made in ink at the bottom of a paper with a feather marker. The paper held the words the peace talkers said were forever binding, once all the headmen from the various tribes touched the marker making their names.

At first the camps began to leave in scattered groups as lodges were struck and columns of people with their horses pulling drag poles disappeared over the horizons around Horse Creek. But soon enough, hundreds of drag poles raised dust. And once more, only Lakota lodges dotted the plains around the island of whites at Fort Laramie and the lines of wagons.

In time, the Blackfeet again raided the Crow, who, of course, had to retaliate. The Lakota raided Snake territory, and thus, the first condition of the binding paper of the Horse Creek Council was obliterated by the powerful winds of long-standing tradition. Try as they might, no one, not the Blackfeet nor the Lakota nor the Mandans nor anyone else, could ever find a line on the earth that showed where their lands ended and someone else's began. It was always a mystery.

As for the Holy Road, young Lakota men stood back and watched as the wagons pulled by oxen or mules slowly creaked into Fort Laramie, took on more supplies, and creaked off to the west to some unknown place close to the setting sun. The peace talkers had said the wagons needed no more space than the width of their wheels, but the trail—the Holy Road—had more than one line of ruts because the wagons made new ruts each summer. The wagon ruts began to spread to several wagons wide. They lined the hills still, some of the young men watching with a growing anger at this strange intrusion into their lands and their lives, an uneasy feeling growing in the small of their backs. Some grumbled that it would not be difficult to gather enough warriors to turn back the wagons at the edge of Lakota lands to the east near where the Blue Water River flowed into the Shell. Then there would be no worry about how wide the wagons or ruts were then, and the land could begin to heal itself, and the buffalo would return to water in the Shell and graze along its banks. But, the old warriors counseled, remember the Kiowa and our Sicangu relatives and the sickness that killed thousands of them. How close does one have to be to the wagon people to catch one of their sicknesses? So beneath dark, angry scowls dozens and dozens of warriors watched the line of plodding wagons, keeping their hands on their weapons. The white men and their bullets they could confront, but the sicknesses that caused strong men to take to their deathbeds in a matter of days was another matter. So, for the most part, the wagons and their occupants plodded along unmolested, not because of words on a paper or the power of a "great father" but because of the fear of sickness.

Fort Laramie and the Holy Road were part of Lakota life— bothersome realities that left wise old people scratching their heads and wondering how that had come to be. Perhaps when the people in the wagons had all arrived someplace in the west there would be no more Holy Road. No more Holy Road and no more need for Fort Laramie. It was a fool's hope, some said. The whites won't go away of their own accord. It was a fearful thought Lone Bear and Light Hair heard many old men utter, as if they had tasted spoiled annuity meat. In time they would see firsthand how prophetic those fears were.

Three years after the Council at Horse Creek, during Light Hair's fourteenth year, Fort Laramie remained, and more wagons crept along the Holy Road each year from late spring until summer. The fort was busier than ever as more whites bustled about. Many Lakota couldn't ignore the annuities distributed by the whites and so they came to wait, though they were still fearful of the whites' sicknesses. The more cautious kept their encampments half a day's ride from the fort, the Hunkpatila among them. Some Lakota, however, pitched their lodges within bow shot of the fort, their sense of caution pushed by curiosity and a desire for white-man things. In time those careless ones would come to be known as Loaf About the Forts, or Loafers.

Red Cloud and Smoke were said to be somewhere, a sure sign that the Long Knives would be pressed over some significant concerns. Smoke was the head of an influential family, the source of many Lakota leaders in time of war and peace. Red Cloud, in spite of being part of a feud that had resulted in the death of a young Lakota, was building a reputation as a fine orator, one who was not afraid to speak his mind about the whites. And there were several concerns for Smoke and Red Cloud to drop at the feet of the whites. More dead animal carcasses were left to rot each summer along the Holy Road, more graves were left as well, and discarded possessions were scattered along the trail. The biggest worry of all was that the buffalo stayed further and further from the trail, both to the north and south.

But there was a new problem. The annuities were late and some of the Lakota who had grown to depend on the annuity cattle for meat instead of hunting were becoming nervous. Others scoffed at the foolishness of depending on the white man to feed their families, but, sadly, the white man and his annuities were like the thorn buried deep in the foot. It couldn't be removed without some blood flowing.

Each summer's lines and lines of wagons were not the same as those that had come the summer before. They carried a different group of whites who had never seen a Lakota or a Kiowa or a Blue Cloud, but who had been filled with stories about the dangers from brown-skinned marauders. So, wide-eyed and fearful were the whites who arrived at the fort—not comforted by the sight of scores of scowling Lakota men.

But the Lakota were likewise troubled at the sight of so many white men. Some of the old ones would shake their gray heads and speak a warning. In any land among any kind of people, three human weaknesses are at the root of trouble—fear, anger, and arrogance.

Those weaknesses were about to be mixed.

Six

Life has a way of creating strange circumstances that often lead to a bad end, or an unexpected turn. Several Lakota camps were in the vicinity of the fort in the Moon of Dark Calves, idling away the hot months waiting for the annuities, especially the longhorn cattle. Though the meat wasn't nearly as tasty as buffalo, it was meat nonetheless and many were becoming impatient.

Sometime during the summer, the Long Knife commander at Fort Laramie decided to designate an old Sicangu man named Conquering Bear as a spokesman for the Lakota, ignoring the fact that the Lakota already had their spokesman. But it just so happened that Conquering Bear was respected and thought of as a wise man by many among his own people because he cared for their welfare, a fact unknown to the white officer who made the "appointment" for his own convenience. And it was into Conquering Bear's camp that an old footsore cow wandered on an especially hot afternoon.

The Lakota didn't own any cattle, of course, so it was correctly assumed that she had been lost or abandoned by some white man. Trying to escape barking dogs, she was running between lodges knocking over meat racks. After the laughter stopped someone realized that, although old and thin, she was fresh meat.

A young Mniconju visiting relatives in the Sicangu camp dispatched the old cow, butchered it, and divided the meat among the old ones. Word came soon after from the fort that a white man called a Mormon was complaining to the soldiers that his cow had been stolen. Trouble might be brewing at the fort, the messenger warned old Conquering Bear.

The story of the "stolen" cow was relayed to Conquering Bear. The Mormon had tried to turn her away from the Sicangu camp, but when he couldn't, he immediately ran for the fort. He was undoubtedly too afraid to go near the encampment to recover his animal, so instead he told the commander of the soldiers, a young man named Fleming, that it had been stolen.

The next morning Conquering Bear rode to the fort to settle the matter by offering payment for the cow, explaining that it had been butchered because it appeared to belong to no one. But his offer was ignored, and Fleming demanded that the man who had killed the cow be turned over for punishment.

The old Sicangu politely tried to explain. The cow was dead, and the offer of a good horse, better than the cow was in her good days, was fair, the old man insisted. There was no need to punish anyone over a cow. But Fleming was insistent because the Mormon was demanding to have his cow returned. The old man returned to camp, angry and frustrated with Fleming. In the evening, he went to sit in the Oglala council lodge to talk with Man Whose Enemies Are Afraid of His Horses, and Smoke, and Bad Wound. He informed them that Fleming wanted the killer of the cow turned over, or he would come with a few soldiers to take him away. If the Mniconju refused to go with the soldiers, what was to be done? And what Lakota in his right mind would willingly go with the soldiers for any reason?

Word of the predicament spread quickly through the camps. The next afternoon the soldiers started from the fort in two wagons, and with two wagon guns. But the man leading them was not Fleming. It was one called Grattan, a new officer lately come from the east. With him was a man married to a Lakota woman, a "speaks-white" brought along to translate.

Grattan, it was later learned, had been loud about his disdain for the Lakota. As they passed other camps along the way he shouted for everyone to stay in their lodges. At the Conquering Bear camp, men had been gathering since early morning, positioning themselves to watch for trouble. And trouble was coming.

When the soldiers reached his camp, Conquering Bear left his lodge to meet them. Even as they jumped from the wagons and formed into two lines facing the camp, the old man was still trying to stop the trouble. But his efforts were ignored. Meanwhile, the speaks-white rode up and down the line of soldiers shouting threats at the Lakota.

South of the camp, hidden in low shrubbery, Light Hair and Lone Bear watched the old man and strained to hear him, but couldn't. Grattan stepped down from his horse and helped load one of the wagon guns aimed into the camp. The officer shouted, the wagon gun blasted, and all movement seemed to come to a stop, if but for a heartbeat.

The tops of a lodge's poles splintered into many pieces, then the soldiers aimed their rifles and fired before the echo from the wagon gun had faded. Astonished and unable to immediately perceive the reality unfolding before their eyes, the two boys watched Conquering Bear fall back, struck in the chest and stomach. The second wagon gun boomed and then the Lakota men reacted. Before the soldiers could reload their rifles to fire again, a few Lakota guns boomed, arrows flew, and then angry men ran toward the scattering soldiers. Grattan was one of the first to fall. The speaks-white fled from the camp at a gallop.

A hundred or more Lakota warriors swarmed the soldiers as a few women ran to carry the grievously wounded Conquering Bear away. But the incident was quickly over. Many of the soldiers died within a few steps from where they had stood and fired their rifles. Several managed to flee a little way before being cut down. The speaks-white tried to hide in the death lodge of an old man who had died days before, but several angry Lakota dragged him out screaming and begging to be spared, to no avail.

Soldiers lay dead, scattered at the edge of the camp. Angry warriors swarmed about although the fight was over. Light Hair and Lone Bear cautiously left their hiding place and crept up on the dead soldiers. They had never seen a dead white man. Already the bodies were stripped or being stripped, their guns and powder cases taken.

For the moment, any possible consequences to what had just happened were on no one's mind. The two boys felt the heavy excitement in the air. People were already gathering around the lodge of Conquering Bear. Women wept. Several warriors dragged away the bodies of the soldiers while others took up defensive positions to protect the Conquering Bear family. In a moment the boys found their horses and started for their own camp, an unexpected sense of elation mixing with a sense of dread as they galloped.

Angry warriors rode to the trading post near the fort run by a Frenchman named Jim Bordeaux, who was married to a Lakota woman. They talked of attacking the fort itself and wiping out all the soldiers and shutting down the Holy Road once and for all. Their anger continued to rise like flames, fanned by the thought of an old Lakota man mortally wounded because he tried to seek a peaceful solution to a dangerous situation. Groups of armed warriors rode through the hills and the breaks wanting to fight, wanting to attack someone. When they gathered together and began to harangue one another into even more frenzied anger, a veteran warrior and a man of high repute rode among them and spoke. His name was Swift Bear, a Sicangu.

He warned them that attacking the fort or any white people in sight would only bring tragic consequences. If there is one thing that is certain, white men would not hesitate to kill Lakotas, he told them. If all the whites hiding in the fort—soldiers or wagon people—were to be killed, it would not close the Holy Road or the fort. The whites, he said, would only send more Long Knives and more wagon guns and would start killing. Still, he reminded them, attacking and killing the soldiers that opened fire on the Conquering Bear camp was undoubtedly the right thing to do— the only thing to do because men are bound to defend the helpless ones. Perhaps there were thinking men among the whites who also have good hearts and will understand why it all happened. And perhaps they would think clearly enough to influence others.

Swift Bear's calm insistence cooled the men's anger and they left to see to their families. Already the camp of the wounded Conquering Bear had been moved, except for one lodge. The old man's family stayed with him, afraid to move him because of his wounds. In fact, all the camps relocated further from the fort. In a few days, even Conquering Bear's lodge was taken down and he was moved to a place of safety where the Sicangu and Oglala had encamped together, carried on a wooden litter by six strong men walking so that he wouldn't have to endure a jarring ride on a pony drag.

Light Hair and Lone Bear stayed near and watched men like Spotted Tail, Red Leaf, and High Back Bone come and go from the home of Conquering Bear—Crazy Horse, too—helping to make the old man comfortable.

The anger among the younger warriors had not completely faded, however, especially after they had learned that some of the annuities had indeed arrived but that the soldiers were holding them in storage houses. Intent on collecting the annuities, perhaps two hundred armed men rode into the fort early one morning. High Back Bone took Light Hair with him.

If there were Long Knives about, they could not be seen. The fort stood as if deserted. Before long, the storage houses were found, doors were broken down, and bags of food were loaded onto horses. Unchallenged, the men rode away. The old men decided soon after that it would be best to move further from the fort and the Holy Road.

The Oglalas headed north back toward the Powder River country while the Sicangu traveled east toward the Running Water River. Conquering Bear was growing weaker by the day. The farther from the fort and the Holy Road they moved, however, the fresher the air seemed. Trouble seemed far away under the shadow of the western horizon. Crazy Horse and his family stayed among his wives' Sicangu relatives. High Back Bone also decided to stay with the Sicangu camp to be near the dying Conquering Bear. Lone Bear was with his family in the Hunkpatila camp by now somewhere near the Powder River. Light Hair spent most of his time alone or helping his mothers.

The Sicangu camp finally reached an area near Snake Creek and decided to let the wounded Conquering Bear rest. It was difficult for the people not to think about the incident that was taking the old man's life. The old men talked of it in the council lodge and the younger warriors talked around their fires under the night sky. But now the flush of anger was wearing away and the men relived the incident as something to be examined from all sides rather than a source of anger and pain.

Light Hair followed High Back Bone to the door of the Conquering Bear lodge on a warm evening. Through the opening, his gaze found the sunken eyes of the dying man—an overall picture so different from that of a man so vital until the shell from the wagon gun knocked him to the ground. There was no light in the old man's eyes, only a shadow caused by fading life. An immense confusion and sadness washed over the boy. Walking aimlessly back to his own lodge he caught his horse and rode for some far hills.

He rode north from the camp. The horse picked his way over the uneven ground until he reached the top of a long ridge. There was thunder in the west. Light Hair dismounted on the ridge and let the horse graze. Night fell with deeper darkness as he sat on the ridge. Behind him to the east, perhaps three or four days' travel, was the sand hill country known to him only through the eyes and memories of others. To the north was the country where his mothers had known their childhood. They talked softly about the White Earth and Smoking Earth Rivers, the second a tributary of the first.

Light Hair lay down, keeping his feet to the west in the direction of the thunder and lightning. The Thunders were the source of power. He stared up at the stars.

Morning came, bringing hunger with it. Thirst came as the day grew hot and passed slowly into the afternoon. Once again the clouds rose up behind the western horizon and the Thunders spoke again. Another evening slid into darkness and the Thunders spoke louder and louder, and the lightning turned the land blue-white for a heartbeat each time it flashed. He saw to his horse then curled up against the hunger and growing thirst. Sleep came again sometime in the night.

Hands pulled at him and Light Hair jumped to wakefulness, instinctively moving away from the faces looking down at him.

High Back Bone and Crazy Horse were kneeling over him. The sun was in the morning half of the sky, the land bright. They pulled him to his feet, their faces scowling as they scolded him for his carelessness. The Kiowa and the Pawnee and the Omaha were known to be around at times, they told him.

Light Hair rode silently behind his father and High Back Bone as they returned to the camp.

Reflections:
The Way We Came

On my wall hangs a color copy of a photograph of a petroglyph.

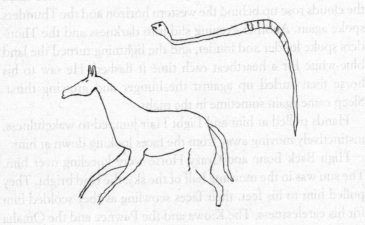

after Sweem

If the story associated with the petroglyph is true, then the man who carved it was Crazy Horse. A Northern Cheyenne friend of his is believed to have been with him and witnessed the carving of it into a sandstone wall along Ash Creek a few miles southeast of the Little Bighorn River and the Little Bighorn battlefield. The photograph was taken by the late Glenn Sweem of Sheridan, Wyoming—a history buff and a fine, fine gentleman.

The carving is said to have been done a few days before the Battle of the Little Bighorn. I have no reason to doubt the authenticity of the petroglyph and that Crazy Horse was its creator, but then I may feel that way because I *want* it to be real. I have not seen it with my own eyes and never will if the last report I heard is true. The sandstone bluff, I was told, was washed away. Plaster replicas of the wall with the images on it have been made, however.

Some who have seen the actual petroglyph or the photograph or the plaster replicas believe it to be Crazy Horse's signature. It is, of course, open to interpretation. I think it was more of a statement than a signature.

The snake, to some Lakota, symbolizes *toka,* or "enemy." If the carver of this petroglyph was using the snake in this manner, then the horse—and whomever and whatever it represented— was being pursued or followed by an enemy or enemies.

At that point in his life, in 1876, Crazy Horse was certainly well aware that he had detractors, men who were envious of his status among the Lakota. When I see the photograph on my wall, I feel as though Crazy Horse was saying *Lehan wahihunni yelo,* or "This is where I am in my life."

Or perhaps he was simply saying *I was here.*

Whatever the message, it does reach across from then to now, at least for me.

Crazy Horse came into the world at least four generations ahead of mine. He was born in the early 1840s, perhaps as late as 1845. I was born in 1945. As Lakota males, he and I have much in common. Enough of Lakota culture has survived through the changes during those four generations, fortunately, to allow my generation to identify strongly with his.

My childhood was similar to his in several ways. I grew up in a household where Lakota was the primary language, as did he. I heard stories told by my grandparents and other elders who were part of an extended family, as did he. My maternal grandparents, who functioned as my parents, were very indulgent, as Light Hair's parents and the adults in his extended family were. I recall vividly the solicitous attention from my grandmother and from all the mothers and grandmothers who were part of the extended family circle, not to mention the women in the community of families in the Horse Creek and Swift Bear communities in the northern part of the reservation. Given these experiences, I know how it was for him as a boy growing up. The society and community and the sense of family—all of which were operative factors in his upbringing—were much the same for me. My 1950s lifestyle was certainly different than his 1850s lifestyle as a consequence of interaction with Euro-Americans, but traditional Lakota values and practices of rearing and teaching children have remained basically intact in the more traditional families and communities of today.

In my early days, as in Crazy Horse's, every adult in the family's extended circle and those in the community (village) were teachers, nurturers, and caregivers. The concept of "babysitting" was alive and well because everyone watched over all the children all of the time. In a sense there were no designated or hired "babysitters" because everyone was. Though the biological mother and the immediate family were the primary caregivers, the entire community or village had a role in raising the child. But in traditional Lakota families today these values and practices are still upheld and applied. Furthermore, among us there were and are no orphans. Though one or both biological parents may be lost to the child, someone in the immediate or extended family circle is ready to step in and function as a parent. A friend of mine on the Pine Ridge reservation had a particularly close relationship with his mother. I was surprised to learn later that the woman was, in our contemporary terminology, his stepmother because—as he explained it—his "first" mother had died.

The village itself, however, has changed. In the early days of the reservations in South Dakota, the old *tiyospaye* or family community groups attempted to remain together as much as the system of land ownership would allow. Actually owning the land, as opposed to controlling a given territory, was a new concept. As a consequence of the Fort Laramie treaties, the Lakota (and other tribes of the northern Plains) were "given" collective ownership of enormous tracts of land. Collective ownership—everyone together owning all of the land—was not too far removed from the entire group or nation maintaining territorial control.

While the Lakota were still conceptually adapting to owning the land, the Dawes or Allotment Act of 1887 changed the rules; it changed collective ownership to individual ownership. Though the implementation of the act took several years because reservations had to be surveyed in sections, quarter-sections, and so on, and the population of adult males (eighteen years and older) counted, the culmination was the allotting of 160-acre tracts to family men and 80 acres to single men. Women were not eligible for initial allotment. Essentially the new system forced Lakota families to take up "homesteading," and the encampments of old—several families living together—gave way to single families living on their tracts of land. Though the nearest friend or relative might be as close as just over the boundary line, the close physical proximity of living in a village was no more.

Even so, the ancient social more of functioning as a village still persisted. Mere distances could not destroy the sense of belonging to a group or a community. Friends and families came together at every opportunity and to meet every necessity. Dances, weddings, give-away feasts—and until the 1940s, going to the various government issue stations—were some of the reasons to gather together. Traveling by foot, horseback, or in horse-drawn buggies and wagons, the communities clung to as many of the old ways as possible.

Clinging to the old ways was not easy, however. In Light

Hair's boyhood the whites were unwelcome interlopers. At the other end of the hundred-year spectrum, in the 1940s and 1950s, we Lakota were still living under the firm control of the interlopers in the guise of the Bureau of Indian Affairs. Government and parochial boarding schools took children from their families, and the process of learning became a group activity motivated by the prospect of punishment for failure rather than the one-on-one mentoring where lessons and achievement were more important than the rules.

Light Hair's father was free to pursue his calling as a medicine man, but in my boyhood Christianity was telling us that our spiritual beliefs and practices were passé. As late as the 1940s, Indian agents (now called superintendents), frequently at the behest of white priests and pastors, sent Indian police to roust out Lakota medicine men. Their sacred medicine objects such as pipes, gourd rattles, and medicine bundles were confiscated and sometimes destroyed on the spot. It is likely that many of those objects later became museum displays as cultural artifacts. The medicine men were ordered to cease conducting and practicing their spiritual and healing ceremonies. But fortunately for us Lakota of today, our grandparents' generation by and large employed the "smile and nod" tactic. When raided by Indian police, medicine men would smile and nod to avoid further persecution or even jail time. When the Indian police left they would haul out another pipe or make another one, and they would make sure their ceremonies went further underground.

There was no choice but to go along with the new ways to save what was left of the culture. It was necessary and acceptable to learn English so long as the Lakota language wasn't forgotten, for example. Even today, many Lakota practice both Christianity and traditional religion, and there are enough bilingual Lakota people to insure that the core of our culture is still intact. Smiling and nodding has its rewards.

For me there are positive links between Lakota boyhood in

the 1950s to Lakota boyhood in the 1850s. For example, I learned to hunt and make bows and arrows from my maternal grandfather. His other male relatives or contemporaries were mentors for me as well. I learned the meaning of patience and gentleness (among other things) from my grandmother and every other "grandma" I came into contact with. I was nurtured and taught and indulged much the same way Light Hair was. Childhood for me was wonderful and I'm certain Crazy Horse felt the same about his. Yet it is at times necessary to examine the differences between my boyhood and his.

The state of the Lakota nation as Light Hair entered his teen years was much different than it was during that same period in my life a hundred years later. In the late 1850s the Lakota nation was still strong and maintained a vast territory and the lifestyle of nomadic hunters living in buffalo-hide dwellings. The Fort Laramie Treaty of 1851 was the first treaty to establish static borders not of our choosing. The 1868 Fort Laramie Treaty redefined those borders and identified what is now the western half of South Dakota as the Great Sioux Reservations for "as long as the grasses grow." In the 1950s, we were scattered across the state of South Dakota on eight reservations, the consequence of a series of "agreements" that whittled our traditional territory—then our "treaty lands." The discovery of gold prompted the first "agreement" in 1875, and several others followed that resulted in the eight reservations.

By the time Light Hair was ten or eleven, Euro-Americans were a consistent presence and an increasing annoyance. The Oregon Trail cut across the southern part of the territory, and beginning in the late 1840s it became a steady stream of white emigrants moving east to west from late spring to midsummer. Tens of thousands of people, thousands of oxen, mules, and horses, and hundreds of wagons passed through every summer for twenty years. Those people carried with them many things new to the Lakota, some beneficial such as iron knives and cooking pots, and some destructive such as liquor and disease. Most of all, however, they brought change.

The concerns of the old Lakota leaders of the time are the realities that we contemporary Lakota live with today. Throughout the 1850s the growing Euro-American presence certainly impacted Light Hair and the Lakota who lived near the emigrant trail, derisively dubbed the "Holy Road." Many of the older Lakota leaders of the time worried that the assurances of the white peace commissioners that all the emigrants wanted was safe passage through Lakota territory and space wide enough for wagon wheels were empty promises and a portent of the future.

They were right. In 1868, the Lakota, Dakota, and Nakota returned to Fort Laramie for more negotiations. The Powder River, or Bozeman Trail, War had just ended. The federal government allowed the Lakota to think the soldiers were abandoning the forts along the Bozeman Trail—from south-central Wyoming north to the gold fields of Montana—because they had "lost" the conflict. In truth, they could afford to abandon the Bozeman Trail because they were developing an east-west rail line across Montana, a more direct route to the gold fields. Negotiating from the position of "loser," the government's peace commissioners successfully convinced the Lakota that, as "victors," they had won what is now the western half of South Dakota. Furthermore, portions of the current states of North Dakota, Montana, Wyoming, and Nebraska were designated as "ceded territory" where the Lakota could hunt. In reality, the 1868 Fort Laramie Treaty was the beginning of the end of the free-roaming, nomadic hunting life.

The late 1950s found us living in square houses in scattered communities across the reservations. Our lifestyle was largely indefinable and on the dole of the United States government. The buffalo-hide *tipestola* or pointed dwellings (more commonly referred to as *tipi*) were only memories. We were virtually powerless politically. But those circumstances were irrelevant to me as a child. My grandparents and I lived in a log house on a plateau above the Little White River, which my grandfather referred to as *Maka Izita Wakpa,* the Smoking Earth River. He never ever referred to the river by its new name. Perhaps it was his way of staying connected to the past.

That past came alive in the stories both he and my grandmother told. I can't recall precisely at what point I realized that those stories were much more than just entertainment. There were, of course, the more whimsical stories of *Iktomi,* the Trickster, but even those always had a lesson to offer. Other stories were about people and events, many of which did not find their way into the history books of the interlopers nor coincide with their versions of the same people and events. The information in those stories were our history—family, community, and national history. The impact and the value of those stories, for me, are summed up in something my grandfather said one late summer afternoon when I was five or six. We had been walking along the Smoking Earth River a few miles from our house and came to the top of a hill. We stopped to rest and he grabbed me by the shoulders and turned me so that I could look back along the trail we had walked.

"Look back at the way we came," he said. "Remember the trail we have walked. Someday I might send you down that trail by yourself. If you don't remember it, you will be lost."

That sentiment is why the medicine men smiled and nodded when the Indian police ransacked their homes and confiscated their pipes and medicine bundles. You can take away the things but you cannot take away the knowledge, the awareness. That sentiment is why, in spite of everything, the first generation of Lakota to live on the reservations clung to their ways. That sentiment is why, in spite of the intensive and extensive efforts of the government and parochial boarding schools, there is still a

Lakota language, still a Lakota identity. We haven't forgotten the trail we have walked. Hopefully enough of us have heeded Crazy Horse's message and we will never forget that he was here.

My grandparents and their generation were not too different from Light Hair's parents and grandparents. The elderly Lakota of the 1850s, in the face of the white incursion and the changes brought by them, were telling stories and reminding their children and grandchildren to remember the trails they had walked.

Handcrafting a bow out of ash is almost a lost art for the Lakota. My grandfather taught me because his father, White Tail Feather, and second father (stepfather), Henry Two Hawk, taught him to make bows and arrows. They learned it from their fathers and grandfathers. And the methods and process are the same as those that were taught to Light Hair—exactly the same. Each time I've had the opportunity to make a bow, a thought invariably passes through my mind: *This is the way it has been done for hundreds of generations.*

I make my bows the same way Crazy Horse did.

That is only one of many connections he and I have as Lakota boys.

Part II

The Rites of Passage

Seven

Memory is like riding a trail at night with a lighted torch, some of the old ones liked to say. The torch casts its light only so far, and beyond that is the darkness.

There were, among the Lakota, young people who couldn't remember a time without white men. For some young men, making arrows meant looking for the white man's barrel hoop iron to be chiseled into points, rather than finding the right kind of chert or flint—the stones that had been chipped and flaked into arrow heads for generations untold. Now, most of the young men did not have the skill to make stone arrow points. Likewise, after Grattan and his soldiers were so soundly defeated, the Lakota who lived near the fort—the Loafers—were already complaining that the Long Knives would take away their annuities permanently. Surely there was darkness of a kind, some of the old ones said sadly at hearing about the complaining. How is it that a people whose life path for countless generations has been hunting have forgotten how to hunt and make meat? Living in the shadow of the fort waiting for the annuity cattle was easier than finding and chasing buffalo. But that was not life in the opinion of those who shunned the easy influences of the whites and stayed away from the fort.

At the southern edges of Lakota territory near the rolling hills close to the Blue Water River, which flowed into the Shell, was a new death scaffold. Four poles supported a platform holding a hide-wrapped body. From the platform hung the accoutrements of a warrior's life, a painted shield and eagle feathers. This was the final earthly abode of Conquering Bear.

The passing of the old man left a hole in his family and uneasiness for the Sicangu Lakota—uneasiness born of the new hard times that came with the white man. Someone among the Long Knives at the fort, perhaps the one called Fleming or perhaps on the orders of the "great father" far to the east, had labeled Conquering Bear as the spokesman for the Sicangu. Respected as he was in his own camp and by many Sicangu, other leaders had bristled that the old man seemed to accept the white man's authority in this matter. Others said the old man was simply doing what he would have done in a sensitive situation. Nonetheless, there was disagreement and uneasiness because some blamed him for the Grattan incident.

After the days of mourning, the Crazy Horse lodge and a few other Oglala lodges visiting among the Sicangu departed for the Powder River country. There, they rejoined the Hunkpatila encampment. Light Hair was happy to see Lone Bear and his new friend He Dog.

The playfulness of boyhood was gone now. The concerns of the three boys were now more and more tied to the issues facing their people. They stayed near the council lodge in the evenings hoping to catch as much as they could of the earnest conversations of the old men as they talked of recent events at Fort Laramie. News about the fort was never lacking. According to the latest messenger, the Long Knives were still staying near the fort. They had been so afraid that Grattan and the other dead had been left unburied for days, until the French trader Bordeaux was paid to gather them up for burial. Many of the old men laughed, amazed that the bluster and loudness exhibited by most whites seemed to be nothing more than fog before the persistent sun.

But that didn't mean they were any less of a problem; if anything they would be much more so because they would simply wait until other soldiers came. There was something very strange about a group of people who paid men to do their killing, an old man said. And by all accounts, and especially if the wagons on the Holy Road were any indication, there seemed to be an endless supply of whites. Which meant they had plenty of soldiers. The "great father" needed only to say how many should be sent to avenge Grattan.

Many men came to talk with Crazy Horse as well. Light Hair's father was not only a thinking man, but, as a holy man, he cared deeply about the spiritual balance that every person should carry. Much had happened in the past few years that affected the essence of being Lakota. Most who came to seek his insight were worried most about the effect the white intruders were having on the Lakota way of living. Some thought the best way to react was to stay away from the whites in order not to catch their illnesses or subject themselves to their ways. Others were in favor of taking direct action to drive them away and prevent them from entering Lakota territory. But all were concerned with how quickly many Lakota became attached to the material goods so easily offered by the whites. Trading for a wool blanket was easier than days of hard work to scrape and soften an elk hide.

Change was a part of life, Crazy Horse advised. Yet it is wise to hang on to the things that make us all happy and worthwhile as Lakota. In the days of the far past the lance gave way to the bow and arrow as a hunting weapon, yet the essence of being a hunter didn't change. Trading for a blanket or a length of blue cloth didn't have to change the person trading for or using the blanket or the cloth, Crazy Horse was certain. Anything in the hand didn't have to be given the power to change what was in the mind and the heart. And that, he understood, was at the root of many fears, that the essence of being Lakota could be so easily changed by new and different *things*. It made no sense.

Light Hair, like anyone who listened, heard the worries expressed by the old men in the council lodge and the men who came to sit with his father. Many of them likened the situation to a man staring into the fire until he remembered that his vision would be momentarily spoiled if he had to look into the darkness to find an enemy. One had to look away to clear his eyes so he could see into the dark. Perhaps this was happening to the Lakota, they feared. Many were so blinded by the white man's things that they could no longer see the goodness and strength of the Lakota way.

The days slid into the Moon of Leaves Turning Brown. Buffalo scouts returned with news of good herds to the north. Hunters and their families went joyfully to hunt and make meat, not to enjoy the killing but to honor the pursuit of life. They returned riding on laughter and happiness with their drag poles piled high with meat and hides, their stomachs full and their hearts bursting with a sense of connection. Cool breezes turned sharp as came the Moon When Leaves Fall and the land divested itself of the flamboyance of autumn to humbly await the season of cleansing—winter. Summer camps split, although there were no sad good-bys since no one was farther than half a day's travel away.

Lone Bear, He Dog, and Light Hair—approaching his fifteenth year—put the things and games of boyhood aside in favor of more manly activities, such as helping with the horse herd when the Hunkpatilas moved to a favorite winter spot past the middle fork of the Powder. Light Hair was less talkative than usual and though he divided his time between his friends and his mentor, High Back Bone, he also began to go off by himself. No one knew exactly where he went and he rarely divulged what he had done, but everyone had habits and ways that set them apart. His parents and his friends accepted the fact that Light Hair liked to be alone now and then. They surmised that there was something on his mind.

Winter held the Powder River country in its usual cold embrace, but it was a good winter. The autumn hunts had yielded plenty of meat. Even so, the hunters came home often with fresh elk. Children played even in the cold. Light Hair taught his younger brother Little Cloud, now nearly ten, the snow-snake game since the ice on the Powder was thick and solid. In the game, long, peeled willow rods were slid far across the ice toward a painted stone. The rod, the snow-snake, closest to the stone earned the shooter a pebble. The shooter with the most pebbles after twelve shots won.

Stories were told by the grandmothers and grandfathers at night, or during the days when the wind threw the snow about in confusing swirls. Deep beds of glowing embers kept the lodges warm. During the Moon of Snow Blindness, restlessness crept into the lodges and people were anxious to shed the snow and cold. Toward the last days of the Moon When the Geese Return the days became warmer, although the old ones kept an eye out for sudden storms, knowing full well that spring blizzards were ferocious. The months slid by; summer came and with it a new journey for Light Hair. One of his mothers suggested he spend time with their Sicangu relatives and get to know his uncle Spotted Tail. It was a reasonable thought, easily spoken, but the journey it would bring was the kind that gave strength from adversity.

Spotted Tail's Sicangu were between the Shell and the Running Water, west of the sand hills country. They were on the southern fringes of Lakota territory. Light Hair had been in their camp but a few days when a raiding party prepared to go against the Pawnee and Omaha, who had become too daring of late, coming north well past the Running Water. He accepted the invitation to go along.

The raiders went east toward the Loup River, an area of rolling hills and tall grass and many deer. There they separated into two groups. One turned south to probe into Pawnee country and the other, with Spotted Tail and Iron Shell leading, had spotted an Omaha camp in the breaks east of the Loup. A small number from the group crept close to the camp while the rest hid and waited. Light Hair was one, staying close to his uncle. They crawled in among the horse herd and slowly cut the hobbles from the horses' legs and chased them out of camp. Though the Omaha didn't immediately respond, a large contingent soon started out to recover their horses. Spotted Tail's group waited a little longer, then attacked the camp.

The few Omaha men left in camp fought hard, but so did the Lakota. Spotted Tail charged several times on horseback alone, and Light Hair claimed his first victory as a fighting man. An Omaha tried to attack through some tall grass, but Light Hair stopped him with a well-placed arrow. The confusion and chaos delayed his reaction to what he had just done, though he was vaguely aware of the man's death throes. Seized by a sudden bravado, he crawled through the grass to take the scalp of his first kill. A wave of sickness swept through him. The dead Omaha was a young woman. He turned away. The fighting was over.

The raid had been successful, though the Omaha had recovered some of their horses. Spotted Tail's daring and courage was the talk around the fire. Light Hair sat quietly wrestling with the reality of taking human life. Like all newcomers to it he had learned something about the unfettered violence of combat. Ordinary perception did not exist and senses became confused. The Omaha who attacked him seemed to move so swiftly, too swiftly for a deliberate reaction. On the other hand, when he had let go of her head because he didn't want her scalp, everything around him seemed to move very, very slowly. Her hair was soft, thick, and very long. Light Hair said nothing although he knew the overall outcome of the raid had been good. They had new horses and no one had been hurt. But the face of the dead girl stayed in his mind.

Another raid was carried out, against the Pawnees this time. More horses were taken, and a young Lakota was wounded in a fight. Finally, the raiders decided to go back to their own country.

A man from the fort came looking for Iron Shell with a message from the French trader Bordeaux. The Long Knives had received word that the "great father" was very angry over the killing of Grattan and his soldiers. More soldiers were being sent and their purpose was to punish those who had done the killing. It was an ominous message, but one not totally unexpected. Had the "great father" been told that the soldier Grattan had opened fire first? Had the "great father" been told that more than adequate payment had been offered several times for the worthless cow of the Mormon white man? Why should the "great father" care about such facts, someone asked. That was the problem, everyone agreed; the whites had one truth and the Lakota another.

Summer passed. Light Hair grew taller, his voice deepened, and he walked with a surer step. When there was dancing, he stayed in the shadows, satisfied only to watch. But he liked the feeling of belonging that always came with such doings. Perhaps it was the rhythmic pounding of the drums that represented the heartbeat of the Earth Mother herself, or perhaps it was the outright celebration of life.

The Spotted Tail people joined the camp of Little Thunder nearer to the Blue Water River, which flowed into the Shell. These groups of Light Hair's Sicangu relatives often pitched their camps on the edges of Lakota lands, as if daring the enemies to the south, such as the Pawnee, to cross the Shell. But another enemy crossed the Shell instead.

After days of hunting, Light Hair was returning to the Little Thunder camp early one evening. Over the hills to the east rose a large plume of dark smoke. At first he thought someone had set the prairie grass on fire, but burning grass gave off a thick, whitish smoke. The smoke he saw was black and not moving. A sense of caution gripped him, prompting him to ride down into the gullies and stay off the skyline. Thus he rode a meandering trail toward the encampment.

He stopped below a familiar hill, hobbled his horse, grabbed his bow and arrows, and climbed to the crest to have a look. Thick and dark the smoke billowed. Something was wrong. To the north was movement just beyond some low hills, but it was too far to distinguish what was moving. Light Hair remounted and put his horse into a gallop.

From another and higher vantage point he could see that the smoke was rising from the encampment. A few horses were scattered about, watching to the north, but there was nothing else. No children playing, no dogs running about. Leaving his horse hobbled he ran toward the camp. Light was fading, a dog barked tentatively, and a stench hung in the air. Among the smoking lodges and collapsed poles were objects scattered over the ground.

Whatever had happened was over. An eerie silence hung over the camp—nothing was moving. The horses he had spotted earlier had not moved; they were still gazing intently at something toward the north. Light Hair entered the camp. The objects seen from a distance now took distinct shapes. They were rawhide meat containers, willow chairs, clothing containers, robes, and cradleboards, scattered indiscriminately as if by a sudden, angry wind. But it hadn't been a wind. Someone had attacked the encampment.

The horses had been telling him something, looking north as they had. He walked over to a hobbled mare. She appeared unharmed, so he fashioned a jaw rope, untied the hobbles, swung onto her back, and urged her into a lope toward the north where there had been movement earlier. If the people in the camp were running away, they would be moving as fast as possible. In a bare patch of ground, he saw the grooves left by a pair of drag poles. Pausing to look he saw other signs of drag poles. Then he saw something else. Even in the fading light, the distinctive prints of the metal shoes worn by Long Knife horses were not difficult to distinguish. Unless soldiers had taken to pulling drag poles, something wasn't right.

Throwing caution aside, Light Hair galloped in the direction of the signs. And at the second or third hill, he saw them. People were walking and leading a few horses pulling loaded drag poles, though it was difficult to count how many they were. But on either side was a column of mounted soldiers. They were heading northwest.

Most of the men from Little Thunder's camp had been away hunting. Some of them were bound to return sooner or later, but for the time being, Light Hair was alone. He returned for his own horse so he could take two along to follow his relatives who were captives of the Long Knives.

Back at the burned-out camp he retrieved his gelding and gathered stones from several cooking fires and built a marker, pointing it to the northwest. Anyone would know to go in that direction, especially given the condition of the camp.

He had been only in the south end of the camp, so he led his horses through it to the north end. The mare snorted in apprehension and shied away from a long, dark object on the ground. Light Hair bent to it and felt a leg. It was a woman! She was dead. He discerned other shapes in the growing darkness and went to them. They were all dead. He retched after he bent low over a woman and realized that both her breasts had been cut off. Searching in the growing darkness, he found one dead body after another, all of them scalped or mutilated in some fashion. He retched again and sat for a time before he pulled a robe back from the next body, a child this time, perhaps ten.

Gathering his horses he walked out of the camp. He had covered every body he found—covering the shame of the insults they had suffered after the pain of death. With the shock and the grief came another feeling, starting like a small cloud growing over the horizon. Anger.

He kept going northwest and stopped briefly to rest in a deep gully. A soft noise startled him. In the darkness, he saw a bundle and scrambled toward it. The body he touched was warm. Light

Hair heard the sob, the kind of sob that ends a long weeping when there are no more tears and no more strength to weep. A frightened whisper reached his ear.

He leaned close and recognized her; he knew her to be a young Sahiyela woman. She and her husband had been visiting relatives in the camp. Her name was Yellow Woman. In her arms she held a new baby, whose journey had been like the shooting star, a flash of new light over much too quickly. Yet she clung to him, refusing to part with the tiny lifeless body. Her husband's body, she told Light Hair, was at the end of the gully. He had tried to fight off the soldiers that had trapped them there. A bullet had torn through the body of their new son. Some of the people had gotten away toward the east, trying to reach the sand hill country. She and her husband had planned to follow them, but the soldiers had found them first. As far as she knew, everyone who wasn't killed had been taken captives by the soldiers.

Light Hair coaxed the woman out of her hiding place. They would head for the sand hills, he told her. He would take her there so she could be safe. Weeping, she left the body of her baby with the body of her husband.

Light Hair rode back to the camp and found a set of drag poles; he put them on the mare to give Yellow Woman a place to ride. And so they left the place of killing and death and headed east toward the sand hill country.

Through the long night they went. Light Hair was too angry and still too shocked to let weariness and the need for sleep take hold. He kept the horses at a steady pace, listening to the soft scrape of the drag poles over the ground mingle with the sobs of the grief-bound woman. At dawn he found a water hole and stopped to let the horses drink. Yellow Woman refused water and would not be comforted.

Light Hair decided to rest the horses. He dozed off sitting against the front legs of his gelding; when he woke he noticed a man standing before him. He was a scout from the Spotted Tail camp.

Hidden among the sheltering hills of the sand country, Spotted Tail's camp was well guarded so that the many wounded and injured could have a few days to recover. Spotted Tail, Light Hair was told, lay grievously wounded. Yellow Woman told how Light Hair had found her and brought her through the night. After Light Hair told of finding Little Thunder's camp, he was told about the soldiers.

Early in the morning soldiers had been seen moving up the Blue Water. Spotted Tail and Iron Shell and a few of the warrior leaders rode out under a white banner of truce to talk. The leader of the soldiers was a white-haired and bearded older man who said his name was General Harney. He smoked the pipe with Spotted Tail and told the purpose of his journey. He had come to take the men who had caused the killing of Grattan and those who actually killed the helpless soldiers. Spotted Tail assured him that it was Grattan who started the fight by firing first and wounding an old man. Harney would not hear the truth spoken by Spotted Tail and continued to insist that there would be no trouble if the guilty killers were given up to him for punishment.

On a pretense of agreement, Spotted Tail sent Little Thunder back to the camp to warn the people and tell the warriors to prepare for a fight. At the first sight of the soldiers, some of the women had become frightened and took down their lodges to flee to the hills. But it was too late. While Spotted Tail and Harney had been talking, another large column of soldiers had moved into position around the camp. They attacked before Little Thunder could deliver his warning.

Spotted Tail, Iron Shell, and the other leaders were trapped with Harney's soldiers, but they tried, nonetheless, to defend the camp. They had ridden to the meeting unarmed. Spotted Tail, a tall and powerful man, wrenched a long knife from a soldier and fought on a captured horse. With only the long knife, he killed over ten soldiers, but in the end he fell, weakened from two bullet wounds. Iron Shell fought valiantly as well.

There were too many soldiers. They overran the camp with a mounted charge, killing anything in their path and then setting fire to the lodges. Many of them paused to mutilate the dead, especially the women. They quickly gathered over a hundred captives and headed up the Shell, and the few people who had managed to hide when the soldiers were first seen gathered the wounded. They had to leave the dead behind, unable to perform even the last acts of respect because they were so afraid the soldiers would come back. Among the dead was one of Spotted Tail's daughters and one of the captives was Iron Shell's beautiful young wife.

Light Hair remained with his uncle's people to help guard the camp and hunt while the wounded ones recovered. Eventually they moved northwest, closer to the fort, knowing that messengers would come looking for them once news of the killing had reached the Oglala and Mniconju camps to the north. Word did come. Harney had stopped at Fort Laramie. Since he was the leader of the soldiers, he declared an end to trading with the Lakota, still demanding the surrender of the killers of Grattan. When the story of the attack on Little Thunder's camp on the Blue Water was carried north to other Lakota camps, General Harney was given a new name. To the Lakota he would always be Woman Killer.

In the middle of autumn, Light Hair returned to the Hunkpatila camp. His mothers and his father saw a deeper quietness in him. His shoulders seemed broader, his voice deeper. He didn't talk of his rescue of the Sahiyela woman, though they had heard what he had done from others. But he did tell of his uncle Spotted Tail, how he had fought without weapons until he took a long knife from a soldier, then killed him with it. Only grievous wounds had stopped him.

Light Hair went out to hunt alone and took his turn guarding the horse herd with Lone Bear and He Dog. But even to them he told little of the attack on Little Thunder's camp. They noticed that his eyes hardened at the mention of whites or the fort or the Holy Road.

One evening he returned from a long outing with High Back Bone and waited for his father in their lodge. When Crazy Horse returned, the boy held out a bundle of tobacco. It was a gift, an offering to a holy man when one needed to speak from one's heart. Light Hair needed to tell of a dream—a dream that had come to him the second night he had spent alone on a sandstone bluff. It had been with him every day and night for these many months, he told his father.

Dreams were important, Crazy Horse said, as he took the offering of tobacco from his oldest son.

Eight

Waves of heat would roll through the small, enclosed space each time Crazy Horse poured water over the glowing hot stones in the center pit. There was only the darkness and the heat. Crazy Horse sat to the right of the door inside the low, dome-shaped structure of red willow frames covered with hides. Light Hair sat across from his father.

"All my relations," said Crazy Horse in a low and respectful voice as he pushed aside the door cover. In came the welcome cool air and light. Light Hair sat quietly, the sweat running off his body as though it was water from a pouring rain. Both he and his father were completely naked.

They had ridden away from the great gathering at Bear Butte, only the two of them and a packhorse. After a few days, they finally made camp below the crest of a grassy butte above a narrow little valley with a little stream, though its flow was only a trickle in this early autumn. The father watched his son and knew that the words and the ways and the lessons of High Back Bone had taken root in the boy. He was still slender but his arms and legs were thicker, his voice deeper, and his movements were those of a man rather than an impulsive boy. His younger brother did not resemble him at all in appearance or in action. Where Light Hair was calm and deliberate and given to long moments of quiet introspection, young Little Cloud was always darting about and busy. He was still far from adolescence, while Light Hair was on the verge of manhood.

Everything happens for a reason, many of the old ones liked to say. The ash stave used to make a bow could be cured and seasoned over five years as it hung below the smoke hole of the lodge—or it could be tempered quickly over a bed of hot coals. In either case, the bow made from it would perform well. Crazy Horse knew that his light-haired son had a purpose beyond fulfilling his roles as a hunter and a warrior. His light hair and skin had made him the object of taunts and teasing, but not once had he seen the boy's lips tremble in response, nor did he resort to anger. He had taken the teasing in stride as though sensing he was being held over the fire, being tempered by the difficult moments.

Crazy Horse had been expecting something to happen. Then came the offering of tobacco from Light Hair. There was a change in the boy, the kind caused by more than passing time. Reflected in the boy's eyes was something that the medicine man's experience and insight told him was prompted by a memory rising out of a dream.

Along the banks of the little stream, they built the low, dome-shaped lodge, working together to cut the red willow poles. Together they dug the outside fire pit and the inside pit for the hot stones. They spent most of day on the crest of the butte, sometimes talking but mostly sitting in silence and watching the land and the sky. Hawks, eagles, butterflies, grasshoppers, ants, antelope, elk, and even a lone buffalo in the distance passed by them in one direction or another. A coyote peered over the edge at them and scurried away. As the sun slid lower toward the western horizon, the boy finally told of his dream.

The dream was not difficult to remember, only to tell. It had been a part of the boy since that late summer night near the sand hill country when old Conquering Bear lay dying in the Sicangu camp after the incident with the soldier Grattan and his men. He was almost embarrassed to describe it.

The dream began at a lake, a small still lake. Bursting upward from the blue calmness, a horse and its rider broke through the surface and rode out across the land. The rider was a man, a slender man who wore his hair loose. A stone was tied behind his left ear, a reddish brown stone. A lightning mark was painted across one side of his face. On his bare chest were blue hailstones. Behind them to the west as they galloped was a dark, rolling cloud rising higher and higher. From it came the deep rumble of thunder and flashes of lightning. The horse was strong and swift and it changed colors: red, yellow, black, white, and blue. Bullets and arrows suddenly filled the air, flying at the horse and rider, but they all passed without touching them. Close above them flew a red-tailed hawk, sending out its shrill cry. People, his own kind, suddenly rose up all around and grabbed the rider, pulling him down from behind. And the dream ended.

There seemed to be a warning in the dream. The glorious warrior in the dream was grown, but still young. The faces of the enemies that had sent bullets and arrows at him were not visible, but the people who had pulled him down were like the rider himself. They were easily seen, as was the horse, the hawk, and the Thunders.

The Thunders. They were the powerful beings that lived in the West, perhaps the most powerful of all beings anywhere.

Rarely did anyone dream of the Thunders, and anyone who did had a special calling to be a "sacred clown," the one who did the opposite of what was expected. Light Hair had described the lightning mark on the dream rider's face, as well as blue hailstones painted on his chest. Lightning and hail were both strongly associated with the Thunders.

Crazy Horse closed the door and began singing again, another gathering song to call in the spirits. He poured water on the stones, sending steam and new waves of heat rolling inside the tiny enclosure. Light Hair endured the heat even as he held the dream in his mind's eye, as his father had instructed him to do.

Dying gloriously, making the ultimate sacrifice in defense of the people, was the secret dream of every Lakota fighting man. It was the warrior code, repeated in all the honoring songs. The dream seemed to suggest that the dreamer would gain honor and immortality by living and dying as a warrior. But perhaps there was more to the dream—perhaps there was a warning of a path that could not be avoided.

After a final prayer and a song of thanksgiving, Crazy Horse threw open the door flap for the final time and ended their ceremony. The cool evening air rushed in, bringing instant relief from the heat. They sat unmoving, both reluctant to leave the comforting confines of the sweat lodge. The man motioned to his son and they emerged and walked into the stream. It was only ankle deep so they sat, splashing themselves with its icy water without feeling the bite of its deep coldness. And when they finally did they stood and stepped to the graveled bank and back to the stone altar in front of the lodge door. Crazy Horse offered his pipe to the Sky, the Earth, to the West, North, East, and South, and finally to Grandfather. He lit it and they smoked.

They passed the evening talking and eating in the orange glow of a low fire. The next day they would find the reddish brown stone that Light Hair must wear, and the father would show his son the plants he would need to prepare to make the colors for the blue hailstones and the yellow lightning mark. They would trap a hawk while the weather was still warm and dry out its body. And in the days and seasons to come they would talk about the dream and all its meanings. But for now, for this evening, they would enjoy the solitude.

High Back Bone was one of the first visitors to the lodge of Crazy Horse after the father and son returned. He brought a seasoned ash stave as a gift. The final worth of the gift was in the hands of the boy, he was gently reminded. It would be the first bow he would make entirely on his own.

The time spent with High Back Bone was now even more important. Light Hair had all the requisite skills to be more than an adequate hunter, and experience would mold him even more. Likewise, he had all the skills to ride into battle, because they were the same used by the hunter. But combat was different. Going into battle was not the pursuit of life by taking life; rather, it was the defense of the life of the people by putting one's own life on the line. Those who saw only the glory of being a warrior without seeing the reality of the commitment it required rode behind those who did. High Back Bone, like Crazy Horse, sensed that there was something about Light Hair that would set him apart, something that had to do with the quiet nature and the shyness. Still waters were almost always deep. So the influence of the older warrior went from the hand more to the heart and the mind—for, as every good warrior knows, the deadliest weapons a man carries into battle are not in his hands. Rather, the boldness in the heart and the willingness of the mind are always the difference between winning and losing.

High Back Bone saw something else in the boy. Crossing the threshold from boy to man came with its burdens. Now and then there was hardness in the boy's eyes that hid something behind it. Every warrior remembered that part of his own life, the last vestiges of boyhood burdened with doubts and so many questions. But then, he had not dreamed of the Thunders. In truth, all of the various parts of the boy's dream were a sobering burden. The hidden implications in it would cause any mature man much concern and turn anyone's eyes into a hard façade. Given the boy's already established habit of spending time alone, High Back Bone guessed that he would think about the dream almost constantly now. He expected that the boy would be even more introspective.

Even in the company of He Dog and Lone Bear, Light Hair laughed and smiled less often and didn't participate in their banter as much as he usually did. His friends knew that Crazy Horse had taken Light Hair off somewhere for several days, and that since returning, their light-haired friend was less communicative. But they also knew that he always tried harder to win the games the boys played to emulate warriors. In fact, he rarely lost. He was not always the fastest or the quickest or the best shot, but he simply kept trying. And though he didn't tell them what to do, they still followed him because he didn't hesitate to take the lead. He seemed to know instinctively the best trail to follow or the best way to do something.

Strangely enough, however, He Dog was the first to taste the experience of going on a raid against their ancient enemies. He joined a group that attacked a small Crow camp and took a horse or two and a gun that was left behind. But there were no stories to tell from this little raid, only that it happened and no scalps were taken. In any case, Light Hair's rescue of the Sahiyela Yellow Woman was something any full-fledged warrior would not have found easy to do. So he smiled as He Dog excitedly told of his part in the raid. But He Dog and Lone Bear got the better of him again.

Word of Light Hair's dream had quietly spread among the fighting men. Sooner or later, some said, the boy would have to put his medicine to the test. There was only one way to see if the enemy's bullets and arrows would not strike him, so preparations were made for a raid north into Crow lands. Crazy Horse and Little Hawk had found a reddish-brown stone for Light Hair to wear behind his left ear, and taught him how to paint the lightning and hailstone marks from his dream. Then, a bullet gone astray while someone was practicing grazed Light Hair's knee. Though Crazy Horse carefully treated the wound, to him it was a sign—a worrisome sign directly related to the people in the dream pulling the rider down. For the dreamer there would be danger, or harm, from his own kind.

To Light Hair, it was more than a wound. It was like the teasing he endured as a younger boy. The raiding party went without him, and although they neither failed nor succeeded, he still had to stay behind. But he still envied them their little adventure and listened eagerly as He Dog and Lone Bear described it to him.

The wound healed well and the months passed into winter. Hunting was good in the Powder River country and the Hunkpatilas laid in plenty of meat. But word came from the Hunkpapa and Mniconju to the north and from the Sicangu camps near the sand hill country to the east that the buffalo were hard to find. Such news was received with somber nods because everyone knew the reason the buffalo were finding new trails. The whites. How can anyone so thoroughly contaminate a strip of land just by passing through? many wondered. The Holy Road was still filled with wagons from spring to late summer and newcomers didn't have to be guided along it. All they had to do was follow the grave markers and the decaying carcasses of mules and oxen and the discarded household goods. The buffalo were wise to avoid such a trail and the Lakota couldn't blame them. But when word came that some Lakota camps had to resort to eating horses to make it through the winter, anger rose like a flame pushed by a wind.

Light Hair, Lone Bear, and He Dog listened to the older men talk and heard them say that though the whites were not honorable enemies like the Crow or the Snakes, they were still a threat that had to be faced. Some Lakota were encouraged that one of the new agents at the Horse Creek fort was a man who had married a Lakota woman and who was, therefore, more inclined to understand his wife's people. Others said that *Iktomi,* the Trickster, was twisting the minds of those who thought that an agent with a Lakota wife was a good thing, because the best thing would be that the whites were not around at all.

Winter passed for the Hunkpatilas and spring came as it always did, with its promise of renewal. The ash stave given to Light Hair by High Back Bone was now a new, stout bow. Under his uncle Little Hawk's careful tutelage, he had glued strips of antelope leg sinew onto the back of it, giving it a strength that

unbacked bows didn't have. It sent its arrows with a low, reso-
nant twang and drove them deep into a sand bank or the decaying wood of an old stump. A sinew-backed bow was more
powerful than ordinary bows, in the same way some men had
abilities that set them apart from others.

Crazy Horse gave his son the gift of a weapon, an old muzzle-
loading rifle that had been given to him years before. It was a
good shooter but a heavy thing to carry, not to mention its round
lead bullets. There was also the added need to keep the black
powder dry and in good supply. Powder and shot were hard to
come by, but the rifle was a necessary weapon. More and more
Lakota warriors had one. To add to Light Hair's arsenal, Little
Hawk gave him a cap and ball six-shot pistol he had found on
the body of a dead white man during the previous winter. Overall, it was a spring unlike any other in Light Hair's life.

Spring gave way to summer and the people moved to find
good grazing for the horses. Light Hair rode on a long scout with
High Back Bone toward the southwest near the eastern reaches
of Snake territories. Through the days spent watching the distant
smoke from several camps, the older man was not inclined to do
any more than watch the normal comings and goings of their ancient enemies.

They returned to find that the encampment had grown considerably. News was buzzing about a prominent family planning
a coming-out ceremony for a favored daughter. There would be
much feasting and dancing.

Red Cloud was an impressive figure of a man and had a reputation as an orator. He was the head of a large family and some
said he would be an important man for years to come. So it was
only natural that the people were excited that his niece, Black
Buffalo Woman, was to be honored. As a tiny doe-eyed girl, she
had crossed Light Hair's path now and then. Now she was a
beautiful, willowy girl with long, glistening black hair.

The day of the ceremony came, and Light Hair joined his

friends as they stayed on the outside of the large crowd gathered at the front of the girl's family's lodge. An old man spoke to the gathering, reminding them that all women were meant to be mothers, like the mother of them all, the Earth—that all Lakota women must follow the Earth Mother, to be like her in all ways, to feed, clothe and shelter her children, and to give them a place to rest.

Black Buffalo Woman sat in her mother's lodge keeping her eyes appropriately down as the old man spoke. Beside her were piled fine things to be given away and outside the lodge were a string of horses also to be given away. When the old man finished talking, the girl's father presented him with one of the horses and the feasting began. Light Hair hung back as the crowd moved away and managed to catch a glimpse of her dressed in a finely beaded dress, her hair in two long braids hanging down over her breasts signifying that she was now a woman.

That evening, Light Hair stayed in the back of the crowd during the dancing. Black Buffalo Woman's brothers, her father, and her uncles stayed close to her as a reminder that any would-be suitor could count on having to prove his worth in order to become part of that family. (In the Lakota way, a new husband became part of the woman's family.)

Light Hair made his way back to his own lodge and was given a message from High Back Bone. On the next dawn the man was leading a raid to the southwest. The message instructed him to gather his weapons and his medicine things.

Light Hair made his preparations before he turned in for the night. As any man does on the eve of battle, he saw to his weapons. Outside were the sounds of the drums and laughter as the people celebrated the coming out of a new woman among them, a new woman who would be the mother of warriors.

The drums were still pounding as he drifted off to sleep.

Nine

The enemy was positioned behind large rocks on the point of a hill near the Wind River. High Back Bone had led the Lakota raiding party deep into Snake country, but the men up on the ridge were not Snakes. Nonetheless, they showed a willingness to fight.

High Back Bone called the party together to plan an assault up the slope. The advantage clearly was with the unknown hidden enemy. The only cover on the slopes of the enemy hill was sparse sagebrush and small rocks, so a ground assault would be very risky. High Back Bone decided the best tactic would be to circle the hill on horseback and draw the enemy's fire, causing him to use up his powder and bullets.

Though the Lakota managed to waste a few of their own precious bullets, the enemy on the hill did not fall for the trick. There was no choice but to dismount and use what little cover there was to advance up the hill. Two of the younger boys in the group were dispatched into a gully to hold the horses while everyone else spread out along the base of the hill. At a signal from High Back Bone, they began crawling. Halfway up, the enemy unloosed deadly fire, with the deep crack of gunfire echoing across the broad valley and bullets ricocheting off the rocky soil. Though no Lakota were hit, it was senseless to stay in the open. Someone managed to hit one of the enemy fighters as he moved from behind a rock, but otherwise the enemy was still entrenched. The Lakota moved back down the slope and regrouped.

There were two choices: call it a day and go home or make a mounted charge directly up the slope. The latter alternative was met with an exchange of intense, excited glances. High Back Bone decided they would position themselves all around the base of the hill and charge up from several directions at once.

Light Hair left his heavy muzzle-loader with the young horse holders. The new bow would be his weapon of choice since High Back Bone said there would be close fighting when they reached the top. A good bowman could send off more arrows in a short space of time and the rifle would be good for one shot at best. But he slid the six-shot pistol into his belt.

Waiting for his first taste of battle, Light Hair watched for the signal from High Back Bone, a stone's throw to his right. He had stripped to his breechclout and moccasins, his hair loose in the manner of his dream and the lightning mark and hailstones painted on his chest. At the back of his head he wore the tail feathers from a red-tailed hawk, pointing down as when the hawk was about to strike his prey. Behind his left ear was the reddish-brown stone. In his right hand he held the bow, two arrows against his palm and a third clamped in his teeth. His quiver, bristling with arrows, was tied to the front of his waist to be in easy reach.

A shout came from High Back Bone as he urged his mount into a quick gallop to take him up the slope. Light Hair and the others did the same. Strangely, each rider had only a vague awareness of the others, though they could clearly hear dozens of hooves clattering on the rocky slope. Low, angry-sounding humming noises buzzed past their ears. The experienced fighting men knew it was the sound of passing balls from the enemy muzzle-loaders. The gunshots could be heard less than a heartbeat later.

Light Hair saw the large rocks getting closer with each jump of the horse. A man with a gun stepped out from behind a rock. Light Hair's shot was pure instinct and he didn't see if the arrow had hit its target. His horse pitched forward. The enemy who had stepped from behind the rock had managed to shoot the animal in the chest.

Light Hair rolled across the rocky slope. His horse was dead. His bow was gone. He quickly sliced the drag rope from his horse and ran down the slope, first in one direction, then another. A loose horse came out of nowhere and he managed to grab a handful of mane and swing on. There was gunfire from below and answering fire from the rocks at the top of the hill. The horse was rushing up the slope in blind panic and took his new rider in among the rocks.

With the pistol he snapped off a shot at a man who doubled over from the impact of the bullet. Gaining control of the horse, he raced down the slope, stopping to recover his bow. His quiver was still tied to his waist.

High Back Bone joined him, his horse winded. Together they charged up the slope again and in among the rocks. This time Light Hair used his bow and put an arrow through an enemy's chest. Gunshots rang out from among the rocks and up from the slope. Bullets splattered against boulders or shattered small rocks on the ground. Unable to load another arrow, Light Hair used his pistol again, and another of the enemy went down.

Light Hair jumped from his horse to grab the hair of the dead enemy. A quick swipe with his knife separated a patch of scalp. As he ran toward a second body and grabbed another handful of hair, a sharp, smashing blow to his leg knocked him over. He went down in a heap but hurriedly regained his feet. Shouts and gunfire continued, bouncing off the huge boulders all around. Light Hair went from boulder to boulder as the gunfire waned, and then he hobbled down the slope.

The fight was over. Every one of the enemies had been killed. The Lakota rode among the rocks on the hill to make certain, and then they came down to gather around Light Hair. Most of them had seen him in the fight. Bullets and arrows had not touched him, except when he had tried to take the second scalp. His dream was true, they decided.

High Back Bone took the scalps from him and cleaned the wound in his lower leg. Someone rounded up Light Hair's new horse, and they all rode away from the hill, a few new scalps dangling from lances or belts. Horses and guns were the prize, as well as the emergence of a new warrior among them.

That night around the fire, the full impact of the battle settled in like an uninvited and unwelcome visitor. Men had been killed. Light Hair had killed two men, the second and third human beings he had ever killed. The first was the Omaha girl in the country far to the east three years past.

Ghosts, the old warriors said, were the price a fighting man paid to follow the path of the warrior; somewhere behind the noble and espoused traditions, somewhere behind the achievements and the glory the ghosts waited. And they would always be there. Their dying would forever be part of the path of the man who took their lives, whether the act was honorable or justified or not. Their faces, and often their dying moments, could not be forgotten, unless the heart of the warrior was made of stone. And few could boast of that, though many might have secretly wished it to be so. Somewhere people they didn't know— wives and daughters, mothers and granddaughters—would mourn. They would wail and gash themselves, their hearts torn in anguish. The path of the warrior was indeed strewn with broken hearts like so many stones on a long and winding trail.

The victory dances honored the warrior and the victory stories reaffirmed the tradition of the warrior, but very little, if anything, could chase away the dark memories that always lurked. The ghosts would always dull the edge of arrogance and bring a cold feeling at the most unexpected moments. Such was the price of being a warrior.

High Back Bone sent two of the young men ahead to announce their victory in the Snake country against an unknown people. The encampment was waiting with smiles and laughter and songs. The victory was a good one because only two men had been wounded, no one had been killed, and young Light Hair had passed his first test.

His mothers fussed over him after his father treated the wound in his leg, although High Back Bone already had taken good care of it. His father quietly reminded him that though his victories would be many, he was never to take a scalp or boast of his deeds. That was why he was wounded, his father believed. A Thunder Dreamer must always do the opposite of what people expected. Though the people would expect him, as the warrior he now was, to claim the scalp of his enemy, one who was a Thunder Dreamer had to take a different path. Light Hair must walk the path of humility rather than the path of glory.

That night there was a victory dance. High Back Bone and the others described the battle and their parts in it. Four enemy warriors had been killed. Guns and horses had been captured. Everyone waited for the son of Crazy Horse to tell of his deeds, since according to the other men, he had turned the flow of the battle. But the boy hung back, reluctant to talk. Some thought it a little strange.

The celebration went far into the night, but Light Hair retreated to his parents' lodge to rest his injured leg. Long days of riding had not helped ease the pain, so he welcomed the opportunity to be still, and to think.

The events of the past days had happened so quickly, beginning with the woman's ceremony for Black Buffalo Woman. The family of Red Cloud was well known in many Oglala camps, and as his niece she would be courted by many young men who wanted the influence of such a family to help them in their ambitions. Light Hair knew that was how things worked for such families. It was the way influence was increased. No suitor would be allowed to stand outside her lodge unless he was from an important family.

Morning came with a gray light. The injury was more painful and had kept him awake through the night. The camp was into its usual routine. Horses were being moved from one end of the encampment to a meadow close by where the grass was still high. Dogs barked, children ran about and threw their laughter around. Light Hair's mothers were busy outside, cooking, it seemed. His sister came once to bend over him closely, so he pretended to sleep. Little Cloud came to look as well, and left.

The sun was high when he finally roused himself. The pain in his leg had diminished somewhat and he had managed to doze a little. He sipped tea from the horn cup someone had left by the fire pit and finally dressed. He stepped out from the lodge and was surprised to see a crowd gathered in the camp circle; at the edge of it stood his father, wearing his best medicine robe decorated with long strands of horsehair.

A trilling arose among the women. His mothers stood behind his father, gentle smiles on their faces, and unmasked pride as well. Crazy Horse lifted his voice in a warrior's honoring song, joined by his wives and Light Hair's sister. After the song came more shouts and war whoops and trilling. Crazy Horse lifted his hand and walked forward and faced the crowd.

"I give my first son a new name this day," he said, raising his voice. "I have heard the story of the brave things he did. I am proud, his mothers are proud, all of his family and friends are proud of our young man. So this day I give him a new name. I give him the name of his father and of his fathers before him. From this day forward I call him Crazy Horse!"

From somewhere in the crowd a drum pounded and another honoring song was raised and the crowd surged forward. High Back Bone, Little Hawk, He Dog, and Lone Bear were among the many who came forward smiling.

Crazy Horse.

The name flowed like water over rocks.

Ten

"A good name is like deep roots," many old ones liked to say, "that help the tree stand strong against hard winds."

For a lifetime, the father had walked in humility, honoring the calling that had chosen him and endeavoring not to dishonor the good name given to him by his father. Defining something that cannot be carried in the hand or seen with the eye is not easy, yet a good name can be the most important possession of all. Things born of the Earth eventually return to dust and even the stones will turn to sand, but a good name can rise above the weaknesses of things held in the hand and outlive even the stones. Thus, the father unselfishly passed on part of his own strength—part of his own being—in the gift of an old name to his son. The name will be his roots, he hoped—and yet he knew it would be so. It was an old name earned and established long ago with courage and strong action. So the father also passed on part of his father, and his father before him. He had earned the name not with the same deed that established it, but by not dishonoring it. And he knew in his heart the new bearer of it would not dishonor it and he would lift it higher. So the father passed on the name and took for himself another: Worm, a name of utmost humility. In time, even that name would have meaning, for he would be known as Worm, the father of Crazy Horse.

Boyhood had been left behind on the rocky slopes of a hill west of the Wind River in the land of the Snakes, the place of Light Hair's second taste of combat. The wound from that hard-fought battle healed and the pain of it was fast becoming a waning memory, but the fight itself was still in his mind as if it were only yesterday. Crazy Horse would look back on that day and those blurred moments often in the days and years ahead. That day was a sharp bend in the road that was his journey. All that had happened that day had taken him to a new place in his own mind, to a new way of thinking of himself. In one day, in a few fast and furious moments, he had become a man. He had become Crazy Horse.

Every boy on the verge of manhood comes face to face with a moment that comes only once. The stories of the deeds of men who had lived before push him toward that heartbeat in time when he must answer the question: Will I run or will I face the moment? It is at once an almost overwhelming fear and the ever-present question that will define the road ahead. Some cannot face the moment. Most live through it dragged along by the events and circumstances and the actions of others. A few grab it by the horns.

Since the day of that battle, Crazy Horse had already relived those moments several times each day. He had answered the question, he had faced the moment—greatly relieved that he had not shamed himself or his family. Just as important, he had acquitted himself well in the eyes of High Back Bone. His first reward had been the satisfaction in the eyes of that warrior. He also knew his family would be pleased, but the gift of a new name had been unexpected. Some of the family had been thinking that another old and honored name should be his: His Horse Stands in Sight. But his father had followed an old, old custom and passed on the name that had been passed to him. Crazy Horse knew the story of the name and was humbled by it and truly mystified that it was given to him. Unexpected though it was, the new name gave him also a new sense of purpose. As many men do, he suddenly understood an old saying: We must pray that courage is always the last arrow in the warrior's quiver.

All the Lakota encampments scattered from the Great Muddy in the east to the Shining Mountains to the west did not know the news that another young man had joined the ranks of fighting men. But every year in every season, another young man somewhere made the passage from boy to young man. And every year in every season, Lakota fighting men gave their lives on the path they had chosen. One such young man, killed by the Crows, had been the beloved son of a man named Black Shield. Black Shield was a man with a strong reputation and so his revenge raid against the Crow did not lack for fighting men. Nearly a hundred men followed him to help his family heal their hearts and honor the good name of a good man. Young Crazy Horse was one of those men.

The raiders went far into Crow country, attacking more than one camp. They returned with many horses and guns and victory stories to be told in the warrior society lodges and around the evening fires. Crazy Horse left it to others to tell their stories and showed no inclination to talk about his own actions, though it was known he had fought with such daring that others were compelled to stop and watch him. He gave away the horses he had captured to widows who had to borrow horses to haul their household belongings each time the people moved camp.

His medicine was strong, agreed all who had watched him in action. His father and mothers were proud, but they were happier that their young man was concerned for those less fortunate, especially in light of the fact that his younger brother, Little Cloud, was now approaching fourteen and eager to follow his brother onto the warrior's path. They knew there was more to that path than glory and the spoils of victory, and they wanted Little Cloud to learn that as well. Being a warrior was only a part of being a good man, and a truly good man would not let his horse herd grow to far more than he would need for himself and his family while the old and unfortunate had to walk.

Other facets of life for young Crazy Horse suddenly and unexpectedly opened—as when a long embedded stone on the road of life is finally dislodged and what has been hidden beneath it is revealed. The grain of hope Light Hair had dared to hold as he watched the line of suitors at Black Buffalo Woman's lodge grew into a distinct possibility for the young and daring Crazy Horse. Getting into line with the other hopefuls was no less daunting in its own way than facing an armed and dangerous enemy. But when she came to him and stood beneath the robe for a few precious moments, all the trepidation and expectations of rejection and failure were forgotten. Like any young man inexperienced in such matters, he found no endearing words to speak that wouldn't have been forgotten by the time he had walked away, so he asked some senseless question. He walked away elated by those few precious moments and angry over his clumsiness, but he had the memory of the scent of sweet grass in her hair and the trembling of her lips as she smiled.

The tossing and turning beneath his robe that night did not go unnoticed by his mothers, who worried that he was having pain from his leg wound. But his father knew otherwise. The wounds suffered by the heart were the most grievous of all. While he regretted that his own reputation would not make the path of courtship easier for his son, the father was convinced that the accomplishments of the up and coming warrior would prompt the fathers of many eligible young women to let him walk to the front of the line of suitors. He also knew that young men did not always follow the path of reason when it came to matters of the heart, just as he knew that old men who saw their daughters and granddaughters as the means to an end were apt to let the weight of their own narrow thinking trample the swirl of youthful emotions.

Worm was relieved when young Crazy Horse was asked to join a small group of warriors with plans to see what kind of excitement they could stir up in the territory of the Snakes. A few daring Snakes had tried to steal horses from Oglala encampments. The raids had been unsuccessful, but the fact that they were well into Lakota territory could not go uncontested.

The Oglala departed in the Moon of Ripening Berries and were joined by a few Sahiyela and Blue Clouds who had their own differences with the Snakes; all headed to the southwest. Not far past the Sweetwater River their advance scouts located a large encampment with a sizeable herd of horses. That night they moved in close and rested and planned.

Horses would be the main objective. There were simply too many to be ignored, for one thing. And if anyone wanted excitement and a good fight, the Snakes would certainly not stand by and watch a few of their most detested enemies drive off their horses.

They rode out of the dark morning shadows cast by the rising sun, crossed the Sweetwater, and were well into the still sleeping village before the first shouts of alarm were raised. By then, the herd of several hundred horses were running away from the shouting, blanket-waving raiders.

Surprise was on the side of the Lakota, but the reaction from the camp was swift. By the time the large herd was turned northward, a few Snake fighters who had staked their warhorses at the doors of their lodges were mounted and in pursuit. It was a foolhardy though undeniably brave effort by a few. Their pursuit was strung out in the broad floodplain, with no real hope of regaining the stolen herd.

Crazy Horse was with the first group of raiders. Back across the Sweetwater, he and several others stopped to fight as a rear guard. One Snake warrior on a very fast horse broke through their lines. With a pistol, he killed two Lakota before a hail of return fire knocked him from his mount. Others caught up as well, and Crazy Horse and his companions fought hard to drive them off, but by now, the fighting men of the camp had gathered themselves in larger numbers and were galloping across the flats toward the river.

Crazy Horse and the others gathered up the two dead Oglala and galloped to catch up with the herd. The pursuing Snakes were relentless. What had started out as a horse raid for the Lakota, Sahiyela, and Blue Clouds was turning into a fight for survival itself. Crazy Horse and the rearguard warriors took advantage of a thick stand of trees to dismount and then set an ambush. The Snakes came in fast and a few were cut down with the first shots, but the others began to circle the grove.

Crazy Horse found good cover but was soon surrounded, and his horse had been captured. Incoming fire prevented him from reloading his rifle. Without a horse, his odds of survival were greatly reduced. His best chance was to move out of harm's way, but he knew he had to act quickly. The sound of distant gunfire was growing fainter, meaning the herd of new Lakota horses and most of the raiders were now well to the north. He and the few other Lakota in the trees were left on their own, with more Snakes arriving. Moving from tree to tree, he waited for a Snake warrior to pass close and jumped behind him onto the horse, dispatching the man with one swing of his stone-headed war club. Pulling out his pistol, he opened fire to distract the Snakes circling outside the trees and shouted for the Lakota to make their escape. Making the break from the trees, Crazy Horse and his companions gained a good head start before the Snakes could regroup.

The Snakes continued to pursue the herd, and, at one point, managed to recover a few of their horses, but they had lost several more men and soon disengaged. Never in recent memory had the Oglala Lakota taken so many horses in one raid. But they had suffered losses as well, with at least five men killed.

Victory stories abounded and the dances went far into the night. The Lakota learned that one of the Snake casualties was a son of their headman, Washakie. The young man had been one of the first to pursue the Lakota.

Once more, young Crazy Horse did not participate in the

dancing. In fact, he said nothing even to his father about the new
horse he was riding or the new muzzle-loading rifle he had
brought back. Worm could only guess how his son had acquired
them until one of Crazy Horse's companions, who had been in
the trees surrounded by the Snakes, told what he had witnessed:
that the young man had unhorsed a Snake and captured the gun
in one daring moment. His action had saved them all, the man
was certain.

Twelve years of one-on-one instruction provided any Lakota
male the basic physical skills to be a fighting man. By the age of
fifteen or sixteen, any boy was proficient with all of his weapons.
But unseen factors determined how each would-be warrior
would handle live combat. After the first few encounters with
enemies on the battlefield, young Crazy Horse had demonstrated qualities that eluded many men for an entire lifetime.
Older experienced men, while initially impressed, waited to pass
judgment, however. It wasn't unusual for young men to perform
well in the first face-to-face encounters with enemies, if for no
other reason than that their inexperience made them less cautious. Then the daunting realities of combat became part of their
thinking and the same young men who seemed so daring and
reckless in their first few outings hesitated, taking stock before
taking action.

Caution was good. It turned reckless boys into thinking men
and a thinking man was overall more valuable on the battlefield
than one who placed others in danger because he took unneces-
sary risks. So the old men who heard of the first exploits of
young Crazy Horse nodded knowingly, remembering that
"such-and-such" had started the same way and now he was a
man with a family because there was more to life than glory on
the battlefield.

There were many good men among the Lakota. Three years
after Woman Killer's attack on Little Thunder's camp on the Blue
Water, many still talked about how the Sicangu leader, Spotted

Tail, fought that day—jumping into the middle of swarms of soldiers with his bare hands until he took a long knife away from one of them and killed him, and ten more, with it before he finally fell from several grievous wounds. Black Shield, the Oglala, was still a formidable fighting man though he was nearly sixty. Old Smoke still wielded much influence because he was known for a lifetime of good judgment and honesty. And there were others.

The reckless die young, the old men advised, and their only legacy is a brief moment of glory; but over time it is forgotten. It is the steady and the steadfast that prevail, the old ones said. So while it stirred the heart and the imagination to hear of the exploits of a new young warrior—one whose quiet ways in camp contradicted the stories of daring on the battlefield—the old men puffed on their pipes as they sat around the evening fires and nodded knowingly. Over time, young Crazy Horse would give up his reckless ways, they said. Everyone does.

But even in this one encampment, there was more going on than the campfire conversations about the exploits from the latest raid. After a few days, the initial excitement that rose like a hot wind after several hundred horses were brought back had waned. The warrior societies decided that the families of those who had been killed should have first pick from the new herd, followed by the other participants. So the spoils of victory were thus divided and life went on.

The lines of suitors at the lodge of Black Buffalo Woman were as long as ever. One young man was notable by his absence. Young Crazy Horse had taken his place in line a time or two before the raid into Snake country. Some old women whispered to each other that many of the young hopefuls and fops who stood in line would not in their lifetimes achieve the battle honors that young Crazy Horse had earned in only a few raids. Furthermore, Black Buffalo Woman was not the prize for the heart of any man, they said. The family had gone to considerable effort to affirm their high standing by putting on the Woman's Ceremony for her. And, some said, her family had already picked the man she would marry. Perhaps the man didn't know that himself, but his good fortune was that he had been born into an influential family. It would be a marriage of families, the old women said, not of a man and a woman alone. Therefore, young Crazy Horse would be well served to bide his time and court another young woman who didn't have the high ambitions of her father, uncle, and brothers, who were clinging to her like sandburs on her dress fringes.

Many of the old women, who watched with some amusement the parody being played out at the lodge of Black Buffalo Woman every evening after sundown, had seen the boy Light Hair grow into a shy and respectful young man. Perhaps he was overly shy but he had humility—something not often found in someone so young. And, after all, his family was not completely without status, they told one another. His mothers were the sisters of Spotted Tail and the mention of his name always evoked respect. In time, young Crazy Horse would have the pick of any young woman he wanted, so long as it wasn't Black Buffalo Woman.

Life indeed went on for the Hunkpatilas. More raids were conducted and more successes became stories to tell in the months, and perhaps in the years, to come. Word spread throughout the land that the Hunkpatilas were fat and happy. They had put fear into the hearts of their enemies and even the hunting was better than it had been for many years. They had passed up the opportunity to go into Fort Laramie for their annuities, raising the eyebrows of those who had no choice but to live off the promises and uncertain generosity of the whites. What did the Hunkpatilas have that we don't, they wondered. Yet they knew the answer as quickly as it had crossed their minds—the old way of living by hunting.

The old ways were good, and living off all that the land provided had always been the way. The unwanted realities were what were difficult to face. The Holy Road, messengers from the south said, had been as busy as ever. A new agent had come to the Shell River fort to replace the one with the Lakota wife. The agent was new because a new "great father" had come into power among the whites, it was said. Perhaps the old one was not wise, some Lakota thought, so the whites needed to find another. Wise or foolish, came the response, he looked on the Lakota as children, and the words and the ways of the new agent were less trustworthy because he knew nothing about the Lakota.

Crazy Horse listened to the news and sat at the edges of conversations that rose with the smoke from the evening fires outside the lodges. He said little, though he shared the sentiments of those who were puzzled that any Lakota would give up the free-roaming life to live so close to the whites. He liked especially to sit with his uncle Little Hawk, who was very opinionated about such matters and never hesitated to speak his mind.

So the words and the feelings of old men rose with the smoke into the cool night sky. Crazy Horse sought the light and the warmth of the low flames as much as he sought the wisdom of those who encircled the fire. As Light Hair, he had dared only to stay at the edge of the light. Now he could walk into the light, and at his approach, one or another of the old men would make room and invite him to take a place.

Since the fight on the rocky hill west of the Wind River in Snake country, he had a new sense of himself. Like a man trapped beneath thin ice, he had suddenly broken through to breathe fresh, life-giving air. High Back Bone and other established fighting men of strong experience looked at him differently and invited him into the lodges of the warrior societies. A few small boys had called out his name, "Crazy Horse! Crazy Horse!" But the circle of old men around a small fire offered a kind of acknowledgment he yearned after. Perhaps that was why he always stood at the edge of the firelight as a boy. There was something in the air any time a group of old ones gathered together, whether it was grandmothers talking as they dyed porcupine quills or as now, old men around a fire. He couldn't explain it or understand it yet—except to wonder if the old ones had reached a place that everyone yearned to be.

So the young man with the new name breathed the fresh air of life.

Eleven

Worm, like all old ones, knew there were many un-avoidable realities in life—some good and some bad. The sun rises and sets; warm spring weather follows quickly when the geese fly low. And broken hearts are as certain as snow in winter.

The silence hanging over the lodge of Worm was almost too much to bear. Elsewhere in the encampment were noisy victory celebrations for Red Cloud and his warriors. For nearly a month he had roamed at will in Crow territory with a large and power-ful contingent, claiming victory after victory against the ancient enemy of the Lakota. But now a few old women shook their gray heads knowingly. Red Cloud was celebrating more than victories against the Crow.

Red Cloud had taken to the warpath with all the young men in the camp answering his call to arms. He needed to strengthen his influence as a military leader with a successful campaign, and to solidify his political alliances as well. To accomplish his first objective, he needed warriors to gather to him. For his second objective, a marriage of convenience would serve his purpose.

Just when many people thought that young Crazy Horse had wisely turned his attention away from Black Buffalo Woman, he raised a few eyebrows by taking his place in the line of hopefuls. Her family was encamped with Red Cloud a short ride from the Hunkpatilas, so the quiet young man would slip away now and then in the early evenings and take his hopes and his heart with him. Given his rapidly growing reputation, many weren't at all surprised when the young woman seemed to favor him, much to the disappointment of his rivals. As time went by, even the staunchest skeptics agreed that Black Buffalo Woman and the stalwart young Crazy Horse were a good match and that she would do well to bring such a man into her family. But there were still many whispers behind the hand that her family had plans that didn't take the girl's own feelings into consideration. One of the other suitors was No Water, who of his own accord was no comparison to Crazy Horse. But No Water's older brother Black Twin was a skilled orator and a man of growing influence, and he held many opinions solidly in line with those of Red Cloud. So No Water was suddenly a valuable man. There was nothing for anyone to do but wait and watch with great interest—and great amusement.

Yet there were other things to concern the Hunkpatila. To the north, the Crow were crossing the Elk River and were seen scouting as far south as the head of the Tongue and the Rosebud Rivers. The Oglalas responded swiftly, but the Crow, owing mostly to their good horses, always managed to slip back to the protection of their own lands. Scouts to the southwest reported small contingents of Snakes and perhaps Utes probing into Lakota territory as well. So in the summer of the year that would come to be known as the Winter of Many Buffalo, the enemies of the Lakota provided many opportunities for Lakota fighting men to prove themselves.

Among the new crop of eager young fire breathers was Little Cloud, only recently given the new name of Little Hawk from his uncle, following the example of Worm. The boy was slender like his older brother, though his hair was darker brown. In him burned the same fire of commitment to a dream he had yearned to fulfill since he had picked up his first bow.

Crazy Horse and Little Hawk were a source of pride for their mothers and father. Where the older son was quiet, soft-spoken, and often serious, the younger was always laughing and playful.

But wherever Crazy Horse went, Little Hawk followed, whether it was down a treacherously rocky slope in pursuit of an enemy or into a state of mind that lifted them to a level of daring and recklessness unknown to others. It was hard to comprehend that one was just past twenty and the other barely seventeen. Many who watched the pair in action speculated that the younger brother would eventually win more battle honors—if he could outlive his recklessness, others were quick to add.

Red Cloud had sent out the call for warriors the old way: each of his messengers carried one of the man's individually marked arrows to the headman of a warrior society. High Back Bone took it upon himself to include the sons of Worm, though they had not yet taken membership in any society. He knew no one would refuse them.

After preparations were made, the throng of mounted warriors rode from the encampment to the trilling of wives, daughters, mothers, sisters, and grandmothers. Strongheart songs also rang through the camp to give them courage when they met the enemy. The reputation of Red Cloud was evident in that nearly every able-bodied fighting man in several encampments joined his endeavor.

The tediousness of the long trail to enemy country was overshadowed by the power and spirit carried along by such a large group of fighting men. Rarely did so many warriors carry the banner of war at one time. In the evenings, the older men told stories of past fights and of men whose deeds were still emulated. Hero stories, they were called. Upon hearing them for the first time, most boys didn't realize that the heroes in the stories were real. Some had lived in the time before horses, but the storytellers could make it seem as though it was only yesterday. Young men went to sleep with images of brave men whirling in their minds and awoke to a sense of purpose that drove them to face the long trail ahead.

Every morning a medicine man accompanying them arose

and offered his pipe, asking for good things to ride with them and for courage to face the unknown as well as the enemy with a face. Then the throng would ride strong again.

High Back Bone started out leading a small group consisting of Crazy Horse, Little Hawk, Young Man Whose Enemies Are Afraid of His Horses (Young Man Afraid), Lone Bear, and He Dog. Soon enough, however, other individuals or small groups joined them. The Mniconju leader was known as a courageous warrior, and his reputation was further enhanced by the presence of the daring sons of Worm.

Among those who were invited to ride as part of Red Cloud's immediate circle were Black Twin and his brother No Water. Before the group reached the Elk River, however, No Water began to complain of a toothache. The medicine man was quick to advise that it would be dangerous for No Water to continue since his medicine was from the fang teeth of the grizzly bear. A toothache was a warning, a bad sign not to be ignored. Reluctantly, it seemed, No Water took the trail home alone and no further thought was given to the matter.

They traversed the Elk River at a wide, shallow crossing. Red Cloud decided to keep the entire group together to maintain an advantage. The availability of so many fighting men was as much a tactical advantage as a numerical one. With feints and flanking movements, the Lakota wreaked havoc on each Crow encampment they attacked. Even the largest one they attacked couldn't respond with adequate numbers of fighting men to effectively counterattack. The best they could do was hold the Lakota off long enough for women and children to flee to safety.

From each encampment, the Lakota made off with horses and as many guns as possible. The horse herd became so large that it became a tactical disadvantage. And so the decision was made to head for home.

Crazy Horse had accorded himself well, as had Little Hawk. Together, they had rescued several fallen Lakota, dashing in to snatch them up from under the very hooves of charging Crow warhorses. It astonished those who watched them that neither suffered so much as a scratch. Lone Bear, on the other hand, fell off his horse twice, but would not admit to some type of injury to his knee.

The Lakota crossed back over the Elk with only token harassment from the Crow. They understood that the extent of their success was directly proportional to the amount of shame suffered by their enemy. Therefore, revenge raids should be expected. The Crow were too proud, or too foolish, to let such an insult pass.

Scouts from one of the camps along the Powder River met the returning warriors and were quickly sent back to spread the news of success. But before he left, one of the scouts let slip a bit of news from the Red Cloud camp that was like an arrow into the heart of the young Crazy Horse. No Water, the younger brother of Black Twin, had become the husband of Black Buffalo Woman.

The grain of hope that Light Hair dared to allow himself to hold in his heart had grown into distinct possibility when, as Crazy Horse, he joined the line of hopeful young men waiting outside the girl's lodge. That grain of hope had grown even more each time she stood with him under his courting robe and seemed reluctant to leave his embrace. Or perhaps it was only his imagination; this would not be the first time imagination totally ignored the boundaries and limits of reality.

High Back Bone, He Dog, and the others had been quick to turn their faces away at the news. There was nothing to be done and nothing to be said. Hearts were broken in an instant but they could not be healed in the same manner. Even those who did not feel his anguish were stunned to silence. The usually animated Little Hawk was subdued as his older brother gathered his things and took his leave of the warrior camp.

The land lay unchanged under the evening sky as young Crazy

Horse rode in the general direction of the Hunkpatila camp. He rode on, lost in a new kind of pain, unaware that he had left his warhorse behind at the warrior camp.

The dogs announced his arrival in the Hunkpatila circle of lodges as he dismounted at the edge of the horse herd and turned his sorrel loose. He left his weapons at the door of his parents' lodge and crawled inside.

The silence of the days that followed hung over the home of Worm like a deep, cold fog. Everyone remembered that No Water had returned alone soon after the raiders had left for Crow country. Soon after that, the family of Black Buffalo Woman announced that she had made her choice. Women who had watched the light-haired one grow into a broad-shouldered young man talked among themselves about this interesting turn of events. They remembered that he was so small when he had lost his mother, and that he had steadfastly endured the teasing of other boys because his hair was very light colored and wavy. Not unlike so many, he had already faced much difficulty in his life. So they didn't blame him when he stayed in his parents' lodge for several days. The fickleness of young women was always difficult to understand, they reminded one another. So, too, were the ambitions of grown men.

Days passed and soon enough the celebrations in the Red Cloud camp came to a stop. Little Hawk returned with his brother's warhorse and with questions in his eyes, but his father shook his head and sent the young man on an errand. That evening Crazy Horse emerged from the lodge and announced to his mothers that he was hungry. They took it as a good sign and fed him.

Before the sun rose the next morning he was in the horse herd. The horse guards saw him catch the sorrel he had captured in the raid against the Snakes. But he spoke to no one. When a few old ones awoke to start cooking fires they saw him riding away to the northwest, armed and equipped for whatever he had in mind.

Half a month later he returned, his young face weathered by
the sun and a familiar steadiness in his eyes. He had another new
horse laden with goods that he turned over to his mothers to do
with as they saw fit. They were quick to pass everything on to a
few other families. For his younger brother, he had a fine new
muzzle-loading rifle.

Crazy Horse said nothing of the trail he had traveled for
nearly half a month. Though Little Hawk was full of questions,
Worm understood that the journey was not so much for the
length of the trail or a particular destination. It was more for
what had to be left behind. So the young man took his place in
his family's lodge as if he had never left at all. He teased his
younger brother and carried wood for his mothers and played
the Arrow-in-the-Hoop game with a gaggle of little boys with
dusty toes and bright, excited eyes.

Worm knew that the broken heart was not completely healed
and perhaps it never would be. But he knew as all good fathers
do that sometimes the best medicine for such a wound was life
itself.

Summer passed. As warriors, the sons of Worm rode to the
edges of Lakota lands to watch for enemies. As hunters, they
scouted the buffalo herds or chased the elk into the Shining
Mountains. Sometimes they rode alone but more often in the
company of High Back Bone, He Dog, and Lone Bear. Always
they returned with stories in their eyes or elk tied to their packhorses.

When the first cool breezes of autumn prowled the land,
scouts were sent to select locations for winter camps. Buffalo
scouts returned with news of the herds, and hunters began to
practice in earnest with their best buffalo runners in preparation
for the hunts.

As always there was news carried by visiting relatives or young
men wandering the land in search of adventure. Among the
Hunkpapa Lakota who roamed along the upper reaches of the

Great Muddy to the north arose a leader whose name was Sitting Bull. It was said he achieved many honors on the field of battle as a young man and then turned to a different calling as a holy man, a healer. His keen insight and shrewdness and wise decisions on behalf of the people were invaluable and he was called upon to take on the responsibility of a headman. Further to the northeast from the lands of the Dakota just west of the lake country, the news was not as good. In spite of the marked papers of the white peace commissioners that bound both sides to the agreement, white settlers had overstepped the boundaries that their own kind liked to draw on their pictures of the land. So the Dakota were preparing to defend themselves. Such news brought slow, sad, knowing nods to the gray heads of old men. It would seem all the whites were alike.

On the waters of the Great Muddy, the large fireboats of the whites still paddled their way up and down the river, belching smoke and scaring away the animals and more than a few people as well. The boats stopped to trade now and then, and brought news of a great war between the whites to the east. The white nation had been split in half over the ownership of black-skinned men as slaves, it was said. Each half had raised great armies of soldiers and the war was on. Black-skinned men were not unknown to the Lakota; some had been seen by Sicangu warriors who had raided far to the south along the Grandfather River. What a strange purpose to have in life, some said—to be the property of white men.

So the autumn hunts were planned and done. The buffalo were plentiful in the north. Across the prairies and over the many hills, the thunder of galloping hooves rolled up from the grass like the heartbeat of life itself. Lakota hunters raced into the dark, undulating mass of hundreds and sometimes thousands of animals, each larger than a horse. Crazy Horse and Little Hawk rode among them, astride the fastest sprinters they owned, which were specially trained to overcome their natural fear of buffalo and to maneuver along and inside a herd to position their riders for several lethal arrow shots into the chest cavity of a dark behemoth that could outrun most horses.

A mounted buffalo chase was one of the most exciting things a man could do. There was always the risk of injury and death, but having once hunted buffalo from the back of a horse, no man could resist trying it over and over again. It was one thing to wait in ambush along a trail for black-tailed or white-tailed deer or at a waterhole for the white-bellied pronghorn, but chasing buffalo was the pursuit of life itself, testing one's nerves and skills to the limit as fast as a horse could run.

The meat racks were bent under the weight of meat drying in the sun. Grandmothers were busy chasing hungry dogs and playful little boys away, to keep them from making off with too much. Later, the painted rawhide meat containers in each lodge were filled to bursting. The winter ahead would be the kind the old ones enjoyed the most, plenty of meat and little worry. Let the snow come often and fill the gullies, they would say after good hunts when the meat boxes were full. We will fill our bellies with meat and the evenings with stories.

As the summer camps broke up and the people split into smaller groups and headed for the winter encampments, word came from the south about the settlement on the Shell River where it curved south toward the end of Elk Mountain. The whites had started wintering there. Some of the Sahiyela who were friendly to whites learned that some, to enrich themselves, made other whites pay to use the river crossing to haul the big canvas-top wagons across. Many of the old men shook their heads and sighed in disbelief. First, the trading fort west of Horse Creek had become a soldier fort and thus had been repeatedly a cause of trouble. Then, the little settlements came along the river, like the one near Deer Creek; these were overlooked by the Lakota because there were only one or two whites. And now this—one more place where the whites were putting up their square houses and looking at the land around them as if it all belonged to them.

Worm said as much to his sons. Crazy Horse said that perhaps in the spring a few good men should ride south to have a look. His father and mothers were glad to hear his words. It meant that he was putting something behind him.

A wound on the outside can be watched to see that it heals well, as everyone knew. Wounds on the inside could not be seen but for the pain in the eyes. Several months had passed since Black Buffalo Woman had taken No Water as her husband. Soon after, they had moved away from the Hunkpatilas, for, as everyone knew, No Water was afraid of Crazy Horse. The old women knew that best of all. But if their young man, as they called Crazy Horse, bore any ill will, it could not be seen in the way he conducted himself or heard in any words he had spoken. So they hoped that the wound inflicted by Black Buffalo Woman was healed, though some didn't blame her. She was, after all, only sixteen, and how could one so young stand up to the powerful ambitions of her father and uncle?

There were many realities in life that could not be avoided, the old women reminded one another, and two most of all: heartbreak falls into every life as surely as snow falls in winter, and life moves in a circle.

Reflections:
The Call to Adventure

From two worlds the future came calling long before Crazy Horse was given his adult name—first from the world he was in and then from the world of dreams.

Several bands of the Oglala and Sicangu Lakota were encamped south of Fort Laramie (in what is now southeastern Wyoming) in August 1854, waiting for the army to distribute the annuity goods promised in the 1851 treaty. The annuities were late, the weather was oppressively hot, and the people were impatient. White emigrants on the Oregon Trail, which cut through the southern part of Lakota territory, didn't exactly help the Lakota state of mind either. Fort Laramie was a stop along the trail, which was an irritant at the very least and an outright intrusion at the most. Many of the older Lakota leaders were afraid that trouble would develop because of the emigrants. Their fears came to pass when an old cow strayed away from its Mormon owner and wandered into a Sicangu encampment.

In his complaint to the officer in charge at Fort Laramie, the cow's owner alleged that it was stolen outright by "thieving Indians." How the cow actually ended up in the village of Conquering Bear is up for debate. Playful Lakota boys might have frightened it, causing it to run into the village, or the owner might have simply let it wander off since it was reportedly old and gaunt. Nevertheless, it was fresh meat and it was quickly killed and butchered. After all, the annuities were sitting in wagons waiting for someone to give permission for them to be distributed, and the people were hungry. That much is certain.

The dispute over the Mormon's cow led to the Grattan incident, which in turn led to General Harney's retaliatory attack on Little Thunder's camp one month shy of a year later. The Mormon cow incident, then, was a pivotal event in Lakota-white relations. It was probably *the* pivotal event of the Holy Road/Oregon Trail era because it tipped the balance toward conflict and confrontation and away from honest negotiation. It set the tone for life on the northern Plains for the Lakota—as well as other indigenous nations—and the Euro-Americans. These events shaped the attitude of many Lakota males, from the elder counselors and leaders to the fighting men and their leaders, down to the older boys on the verge of manhood—those who, as adults, would fight the fights in the ensuing forty years. One of those older boys, who actually witnessed the Grattan incident that August and saw firsthand the horrible aftermath of Harney's annihilation of Little Thunder's village, was, of course, Light Hair. Light Hair became Crazy Horse four years later.

Light Hair and his young friends were somewhere outside the Sicangu village, but close enough to have an unobstructed view, when Lieutenant John Grattan, a professed Indian-hater, brought his contingent of thirty soldiers and two mountain howitzers to the village. Like everyone else, Light Hair and his friends watched with a mixture of amusement and apprehension, expecting nothing more than for Grattan to strut around and make threats. Everyone was surprised when the soldiers opened fire with their rifles and the howitzers.

Light Hair looked to his father, Crazy Horse, and his mentor, High Back Bone (aka Hump), for guidance—not that he asked for it, but he simply observed and listened. That was his way. Not only was his father a healer, he was also a thoughtful man whose opinions were respected. The main topic of discussion centered on the Grattan incident, but there was also the broader issue of white people. There were varied opinions, of course, just as there are today with issues facing the Lakota. Most of the opinions expressed were antiwhite because they were the "boogey-man." There was a small but vocal group of Lakota who were known as "coffee coolers" and "loaf-about-the-forts" that advocated close ties with the whites. While they might have been welcome as guests in the Crazy Horse lodge, their opinions would have been met with stony silence.

History told from the viewpoint of those who consider themselves the winners in the so-called "clash of cultures" casts the indigenous people as the bad guys because they stood in the way of progress and "manifest destiny." The whites, so far as the Lakota—and many other Plains tribes were concerned—were the bad guys. They were not considered honored enemies, such as the Crow, Shoshoni, and Pawnee. The newcomers were arrogant intruders and loud, brash interlopers whose movement into Lakota territory was like a prairie fire consuming everything in its path. As one old man put it, ". . . if they were like the wind, we wouldn't mind, for the wind passes, bends the grass and breaks a branch here and there, but it passes and becomes a bad memory." That same old man likely chided his grandchildren by saying, "Be good or the white man will get you."

So far as those who witnessed the Grattan incident were concerned, the whites were more like a bad toothache than a bad memory. Even as an older boy, Light Hair lacked the perspective of experience to draw on, so he listened to people he respected and trusted. What he heard coincided with what he had seen. To understand his reaction, think of the emotional impact if suspicious and pushy people suddenly drove an armored troop carrier into your quiet suburban or rural neighborhood, deployed men with guns, made unreasonable demands that couldn't be satisfied, and opened fire, killing and wounding your friends, neighbors, and relatives. Any who witnessed such a horrific incident would be suspicious and distrustful of such intruders forever.

If that wasn't bad enough, the attack on Little Thunder's camp—located at the time in what is now northwest Nebraska—by General William Harney would certainly have solidified the idea in young Light Hair's mind that the whites were indeed "boogeymen." After the Grattan incident a year earlier, he had the benefit of adult perspective to help him sort it out. After the Harney attack, however, he was as alone as he could be as he returned from a hunting trip to find a burned-out village, and, worst of all, dead and mutilated bodies.

Most of us can only imagine the searing, gut-wrenching impact the sight of a horribly mutilated body would have on us. Such an experience would—and does—assault all of the physical senses. It burns indelible imprints into the memory that may fade a little through the passage of time but will never go away. As young Light Hair wandered, probably somewhat dazed, through Little Thunder's camp finding one dead body after another, he certainly must have yearned for someone to lean on emotionally. Understanding the emotional shock he felt at that moment in his young life will give us, in the here and now, some insight into the feelings he had about white people thereafter. That raw and ugly episode set the stage for his later interaction with whites. It was likely the single most compelling reason he could not bring himself to think of whites as caring or nurturing people, or as anyone to be trusted.

One wonders what Crazy Horse would think of the modern-day irony associated with General Harney, dubbed "Woman Killer" by the Sicangu Lakota: In the middle of the Black Hills is the highest of all the granite peaks. Like Bear Butte to the north, it was a favorite location for vision quests and other ceremonies. It was, and is, considered by the Lakota to be the spiritual center of our world. That highest and holiest of places was named

Harney Peak by the whites. I have seen old Lakota men simply shake their heads at what they considered to be the most grievous of insults, because they could find no words to adequately describe their feelings.

Few of us would consider using the word "adventure" in the context of our lives. Those of us who would narrate our lives to others may use words like ordinary, routine, or even mundane. Many of us might admit to occasional episodes of unexpected excitement or heart-stopping news or occurrences, but by and large most us would probably say we lead fairly quiet lives. Those of us who place ourselves in this category are the prime market for novels with larger-than-life heroes who perform almost impossible deeds. We gladly pay the going price for escapism on the movie screens that transports us to places and circumstances we think we are certain never to encounter in our ordinary, routine, and mundane lives. Furthermore, we would probably scoff at any statement that suggests life itself is an adventure, and turn our attention to the pile of bills on the kitchen table or look for the television remote control.

If you subscribe to the definition for the word "adventure" as "exciting undertaking or enterprises," it would be understandable that, for many of us, our daily lives do not live up to it. If one searches further, however, there is a definition that does describe life itself: "a bold, uncertain and usually risky undertaking." It is, in my opinion, entirely appropriate for all of us to think of our journey on this Earth in those terms. Of course, whether we make our lives into an adventure is entirely an individual choice. On the other hand, adventure as life itself does come calling every now and then, most often when we least expect it. Like it or not, life came calling that day along the Blue Water River, and young Light Hair would not have been able to disregard it even had he wanted to.

The gut-wrenching experience in Little Thunder's camp compelled Light Hair to reveal to his father a dream he had had almost a year earlier, shortly after the Grattan incident. His earlier reticence was probably due to the fact that the dream did not come to him in the usual process of a *hanbleceya,* or "to cry or call out for a vision," otherwise called a "vision quest."

The seeking of a vision is a serious, highly ritualized process undertaken respectfully, prayerfully, and under the guidance of a medicine man. To seek a vision is to seek guidance for one's life or an answer to a problem or predicament. Young Light Hair was probably afraid that the dream he had that night he spent atop a sandstone butte would not be taken seriously, because he had not followed all the rules. But it came nonetheless.

The dream, that vision, has been told and retold thousands of times since. The fact of the matter is we cannot be certain of the exact description Light Hair later gave to his father. Furthermore, it is critical to understand that much of the discussion and interpretation of the vision has occurred—and is still occurring—since Crazy Horse's death.

There are those who see the vision as a foretelling, almost a blow-by-blow revelation of what lay ahead for Light Hair. It depicted a powerful Lakota warrior rising out of a lake during a thunderstorm on a horse that changes colors, riding unscathed through a hail of arrows and bullets until he is eventually pulled down by his own kind, grabbing and holding back his arms. The vision might have been as much a consequence of wishful thinking as it was a glimpse into the future, for every Lakota boy grew up with dreams of being a warrior and winning glory and honor on the battlefield. Light Hair was no different. One elderly Lakota storyteller was of the opinion that Light Hair and his father chose not to tell everything about the vision, speculating that a warning was part of it—a warning that the boy would die as a young man in his prime.

Such a warning could explain Crazy Horse's daring and often

reckless exploits in combat as a younger fighting man. Perhaps he believed, each time, that he was about to perform the last act of his life and wanted it to be powerful and meaningful.

The vision was most certainly a consequence of the uncertainty of the times, since a new force had pushed squarely into Lakota territory and life. The passage of so many white emigrants along the Oregon Trail was such a spectacle that young Lakota men and boys would sit atop the ridges and watch the frenzy of activity that was usual for a wagon train. Part of the trail cut through the southern part of Lakota territory in what is now northwest Nebraska and southeastern Wyoming. In a relatively short span of time, the flow of whites into the northern Plains had grown from a trickle to a flood, and the impact went far beyond the narrow corridor of the Oregon Trail itself, which followed the North Platte River. Carcasses of dead livestock were left to rot, household goods were discarded, rivers and streams were polluted, migration patterns of bison herds were disrupted, and human graves dotted the landscape along the trail. Initial curiosity gave way to suspicion on both sides. Near confrontations terrified white immigrants primed with horror stories of Indian depredations, prompting them to call for help from the army and the United States government. The first treaty council in 1851 was convened as a result of such fears. The primary objective of the government's "treaty men" or "peace talkers," as the peace commissioners were labeled by the Lakota, was to secure assurances that white emigrants could pass unmolested, so long as they stayed on the Oregon Trail. "We need land only as wide as our wagon tracks," was the assurance given by the peace commissioners, "because we are only passing through." To win the promise of safe passage from the Lakota and other tribes, the commissioners promised payment in the form of annuities.

Like it or not, the future had arrived for the Lakota and for Light Hair. The whites and their promises were part of Lakota life forever. Even if the Lakota could have guarded their borders and prevented intrusion, and even if they had said no to the conditions of the 1851 Fort Laramie Treaty, the whites still would have flowed around them like water around an island in a river. By the power of numbers alone, the whites were, and would always be, a force for the Lakota to contend with.

From the Lakota perspective the whites were arrogant and land-hungry. The Lakota weren't specifically aware that the United States government's inability to solve serious economic issues in the east was a prime factor in the movement of whites along the Oregon Trail. They could only see, and try to contend with, the reality that the whites were intruding on their lives and their lands and were quite willing to take both at any cost.

The future did come calling during those troubled days after the attack on Conquering Bear's camp as Light Hair tried to sort out his feelings. His vision was connected to the difficult circumstances of the moment—the same circumstances that drove him to seek the comforting embrace of solitude and silence that would be part of his life's work, fighting against the threat of unwanted change.

Light Hair was born into a Lakota world that was already feeling the intrusive presence of Euro-Americans. In the late 1720s, a Frenchman, the Sieur de la Verendrye, led a small contingent of belligerent and heavily armed explorers northward along the Great Muddy (Missouri) River through Lakota lands. Lewis and Clark made their incursion through the northern Plains seventy-five years later in 1804 and were regarded as somewhat of a confusing oddity. Owing to the lack of language interpreters, the reason for their journey was never very clear. They were simply a group of nervous, heavily armed white men traveling north on the Great Muddy River. Other whites followed after that, however, and not without dire consequences for the Lakota. In 1837 a steamboat from St. Louis steaming up the Great Muddy unloaded materials and trade goods at the Whetstone landing, near the present site of Fort Randall Dam in southeast South Dakota. Unfortunately it unloaded smallpox as well. Between a thousand and two thousand Lakota died in the summer epidemic (further north, the Mandan people were nearly wiped out).

Trading outposts became military installations, such as Fort Yankton—at present-day Yankton, South Dakota—and Fort Pier (aka Fort Pierre)—at present-day Fort Pierre, South Dakota—thereby asserting Euro-American presence on the fringes of Lakota lands.

So the future came long before Light Hair was born, in a manner of speaking. But it singled him out in the summers of 1854 and 1855. It beckoned most compellingly in the dream wherein a warrior rode toward his enemies against the backdrop of lightning and thunder. As the record shows, the boy answered the call.

Part III

The Warrior
Leader

✦

Twelve

Crazy Horse, like so many Oglala, had no desire to go near the Holy Road or Fort Laramie. Since Woman Killer Harney had attacked Little Thunder's camp on the Blue Water, he had seen no white men, but he understood the concerns of those who warned that the absence of whites in the Powder River country didn't mean they had gone away. The Holy Road was still crowded each summer. That fact alone was an unsettling indication that there seemed to be an endless supply of them. How many more summers? some wondered.

The old men reminded their sons and grandsons that whites had been part of Lakota life for three and perhaps four generations—since a group of them had come from the south by boat on the Grandfather River and then north up the Great Muddy. They had wintered along the Knife River to the north, it was said, saved from cold and starvation by the People of the Earth Lodges. Years later, others came alone or in small groups. As more and more came, they put up trading posts and forts for soldiers to live in. Whites were not going away, the old men warned. How to make them go away was not the question; rather, they advised every council of old men in every encampment in Lakota country to talk about how to keep them from completely taking over Lakota lands. And when someone thought of the plan that would work, it would then be carried out by every Lakota man, woman, and child. Otherwise, they warned, there would be fighting at our very lodge doors.

"The Snakes, Crows, and Pawnees have been our enemies for longer than anyone can remember," said a very old man. "So we know them, where they live, how they fight, and how they think. When we meet them on the field of battle, sometimes their medicine is stronger and other times ours is. That's how things are. The whites don't understand war. They don't understand that the power of an enemy is a way to strengthen our fighting men. They are killers. A killer does not respect something or someone he knows he can kill, or must kill. Therefore he does not measure victory by the strength of his medicine. He measures his victories by how many he has killed. If we are to defeat this kind of people, we must come to know them in every way. It is not a pleasant thought, but it is necessary."

Crazy Horse decided to see for himself how things were at Fort Laramie. He found the Loafer camp a short way from the fort and stayed with them a few days to hear what they knew. Annuities were late again, they complained, and the longhorn cattle were skinnier every year. They noticed, not without some degree of envy, that while Crazy Horse carried a rifle and a pistol and a farseeing glass, he was not dressed in white man's clothes, as they were. He reminded them that he was a hunter. Though some took his remark as an insult, others knew that living off the promises of annuities was not really living.

The white man named Bordeaux could speak Lakota very well and he was surprised to see someone from the northern camps among the Loafers. He told Crazy Horse that more soldiers were coming to be posted at Laramie. He knew this because the whites had a way of talking over great distances that was much faster than the letters carried by stagecoaches and the pony riders: they had a tapping language by which they sent messages along a wire faster than even the prairie falcon could fly. Crazy Horse had noticed the tall poles planted in the earth in a long line, with a thin rope that seemed to connect one with the next. A message from Fort Laramie, Bordeaux told him, could be sent at sunrise and cross the Great Muddy River before the sun was halfway in the morning sky. Such a thing was not hard to believe since they had made the farseeing glass and the flint striker that made sparks to start fires.

On the way home, Crazy Horse followed the Shell but stayed well north of the Holy Road. He wanted a look at the settlement around the Reshaw Bridge where the immigrant wagons were said to cross the river on the way west. He happened on another camp of Loafers led by a man named Two Face, an acquaintance of his father before Two Face came to Deer Creek. Two Face was a gracious old man known for his friendliness to the whites. He told Crazy Horse that there was a camp of a few soldiers where Deer Creek emptied into the Shell. So Crazy Horse gave the camp a wide berth after he watched them through his field glass.

The river crossing used by the wagon trains was a half day's ride west of Deer Creek. Elk Mountain rose suddenly to the south and the Shell meandered below its ridges and then turned east. Crazy Horse stayed to the rough and rolling open hills north of the river, and from a distance he spotted a bridge, though he could see no whites near it through his field glass. He watched for most of an afternoon but saw no activity. Whites were known to bustle about even when they had nothing to do, as at Fort Laramie. A thin column of dust a little further to the west prompted him to have a look before he went north.

He saw over forty soldiers among the assortment of wooden buildings, as well as a few canvas tents inside a sharp bend in the river, as he sat among the tall sagebrush on a ridge to the north. The distance was too great for the field glass to provide a clear image, but the activity in the settlement near yet another bridge was easy to see—activity that was cause for worry. A few wagons were standing in line to cross the bridge, showing the whites as busy as ever. This was a part of the Holy Road not seen by many Lakota. On the Lakota raid into Snake country, they had traveled southwest toward the Sweetwater River and passed far to the west of the end of Elk Mountain, though they could see it in the distance. They had not seen the bridge.

The activity at the bridge and the settlement was annoying. Like Fort Laramie, there was an air of permanence. The presence of soldiers always bothered the old men because soldiers were brought in to protect the other whites against the Lakota, or any other people through whose lands they dared to travel. Soldiers always meant that more whites were not far behind.

With the day growing short, Crazy Horse headed north through the broken and dry hills. Bordeaux had said more soldiers were coming to Laramie. And more soldiers did come. The Loafers sent word to the northern camps that these soldiers were anxious to fight and kill any Lakota that got in their way. Some of the young men like Little Hawk were also anxious to prove to the new soldiers that carrying a big rifle and wearing a blue coat didn't make a man skilled as a fighter, or give him a brave heart. But the old men cautioned against going south against them. "If we kill them all, they will only send more the next time," they said. "They will send a hundred Woman Killer Harneys against us and fill the land with their stink. Wait; we must choose our battles as much as we can."

Word came from near the Black Hills that made the young men even more eager to go chasing after whites. Some Sicangu were three days out of Fort Laramie when they spotted a group of white hunters with their long shooting rifles. The Sicangu stayed on a hill to watch. The hunters were killing buffalo from a very long distance. The buffalo didn't run as one after another fell until the entire herd was killed, totaling over a hundred. Then the hunters skinned the dead animals by using horses to pull off the hides with ropes tied to the dead animal's nose. Fresh hides were then scraped and loaded on several big wagons, each piled very high and the team horses straining to pull the load. No meat was taken, except for what the hunters sliced off to cook and eat as they worked. When the Sicangu rode in after the hide hunters left, the flies, worms, ravens, buzzards, and coyotes were already at work.

Crazy Horse and Little Hawk went with a group of young men to the high meadow country west of the Black Hills, a land of tall grass and blue sage and the white-bellied pronghorn. They found buffalo bones scattered in several places, indicating that large kills had been made. All they could do was turn the skulls to face the east, to make the final sign of respect that the hide hunters knew nothing about. The Hunkpatila had struck their camp and caught up with them, and the old men decided to pitch their lodges north of the Black Hills to hunt and make meat for the winter. Perhaps they would find some white hunters, they thought, but didn't come across any.

They made much meat again that autumn and wintered within sight of the Black Hills. After the hunts, High Back Bone and Crazy Horse led a small group of warriors north to the edge of Crow lands, mainly to do a little scouting and give a few inexperienced boys the opportunity to know a little of the warrior's trail. A strange thing happened when they came to a narrow creek in a little valley and saw a like group of Crow approaching from the other side: the two groups stopped to watch each other from a distance, just beyond bowshot but within the range of a rifle. The man riding at the head of the Crow lifted an arrow into the air and it landed a stone's throw from the Lakota. High Back Bone rode forward to retrieve it and studied it closely. Then he strung his own bow, notched an arrow on its string and sent it toward the Crow. The Crow leader took the arrow and inspected it. After a wave from their leader the Crow rode away. High Back Bone showed the arrow and said it was from a man known for his reputation as a courageous fighter. On this day, mutual respect was more important than anything. High Back Bone took the arrow back and placed it in his own quiver and later hung it up in his lodge among his warrior accoutrements.

After the spring thaw, they moved back to the Powder River

country and heard news from far to the east and from the south. Their Dakota relatives near the lake country had fought a long war to drive the whites from their country, and had lost. The whites had trampled on their own promise to honor boundaries that were to protect Dakota lands from encroachment. Old men nodded gray heads knowingly. It seemed whites everywhere were the same when it came to land and promises. But there was worse news from the Dakota. Thirty-eight of their men had been hanged at once, on orders from the "great father" in the east. That bit of news brought a long, deep silence to the council lodge, causing even the wisest old man to stare long into the coals of the fire, trying to find the sense in such a thing. There was none to be found.

From the soldier settlement on the Shell below Elk Mountain came word that more soldiers had arrived and put up dwellings near a bridge so they could guard the white emigrants as they crossed. But it seemed there was no end to the strange things the whites could do. One was reportedly marking a trail north from Fort Laramie across the Powder River country to the lands of the Crow, staying east of the foothills of the Shining Mountains. It was said that he was marking the trail by pounding stakes in the ground. The strangeness of it was that he was doing this alone, with only a horse and a pack mule. Out of curiosity, young men searched the country and some did find him by the time he was near Crazy Woman Creek.

Worm, as usual, asked why and the answer came. The man had a purpose, although many Lakota thought he was crazy. He soon returned with other whites, including women and children, leading pack trains and wagons and following the trail marked with stakes. News came from the fort that the whites had found gold to the west and north of the Elk River, west of Crow lands, and the stake-planting man had found an easier trail to the gold fields. Gold or not, men like High Back Bone said, our land is our land and no one, especially a white man, should be allowed to make a trail through it. If it isn't stopped, the land on either side of it will die from the stink of their passing, like the Holy Road. Saving the Powder River country from becoming a dumping ground was a strong and necessary purpose, and hundreds of young men flocked to the staked trail.

After several days' travel north of the Shell River, the people in the gold-seeking train awoke to an unexpected sight. They were surrounded by hundreds of mounted Lakota and Sahiyela fighting men positioned on the hills and ridges around them. The trail north and south was blocked. The blockaders stayed out of rifle range and didn't make any aggressive moves, simply maintaining their positions as the day wore on—a ring of men and horses seeming to have risen out of the rocks. After nightfall, a ring of small fires burned. Morning light revealed the blockaders were still in place.

During the night, scouts had slipped up close to the wagons. Women and children were frightened and crying, they reported, and their men could do nothing but stare at the distant ring of fires. During the second night, two of the white men made an attempt to slip south. Warrior leaders told the young men to let them pass, guessing they were going for help.

Days and nights passed into five, and then six. After the fourth day, a Lakota messenger rode up from the Shell. Soldiers were coming to the aid of the gold seekers. The warrior leaders decided to wait to see if there would be soldiers, and if so, to see what they would do.

There were only two ways for the whites to go: continue north or return south. If the soldiers came and tried to take the gold seekers north, the Lakota and Sahiyela would attack, it was decided. If they turned back south, they would be allowed to return, hopefully with the knowledge that the Powder River country would not be another trail for the whites whatever their purpose or destination.

Crazy Horse and Little Hawk, along with Lone Bear, stood

watch on the ridges. The whites could do nothing but stay near their wagons and work hard at keeping their animals close to them. The overwhelming sentiment in the minds of the young men and warrior leaders on the ridges was singular and straight-forward. Crazy Horse agreed. What did they expect? He told Little Hawk about some of the things that had happened at the fort when the little soldier Grattan came with his men and wagon guns. They had killed a venerated old man over a cow. Thirty of them had died for that same cow, as he saw it. Now they were willing to risk their women and children for the soft iron called gold. There was no sense in it.

Soldiers came, perhaps fifty of them. They were allowed to pass through the line of warriors to the south and the line closed again when the soldiers reached the gold seekers. Their purpose was almost immediately clear. After the wagons were hitched and the pack mules loaded, they turned the train south.

The soldier-escorted column was allowed to pass, although several scouts shadowed them all the way to the Shell. How-ever, a small group of men from the train slipped away from the soldiers and headed toward the Elk River. Gold must be very important—perhaps a kind of medicine so valuable to the whites that it drove them to take such risks, some presumed. But they had left their group alone, knowing that it was likely they would meet their deaths some other way than at the hands of Lakota warriors.

Crazy Horse would always remember the strange episode on the staked trail, especially in light of all that was to follow. He carried a lesson from it that he would use as a measure every time he took to the trail as a fighting man: all the warriors on the ridges surrounding the gold seekers had invoked a feeling by virtue of simply coming together, a feeling of strength that comes from pursuing the same purpose. Several hundred had re-sponded, some of them Sahiyela and perhaps a few Blue Clouds married into Lakota families. He knew several by name, but most were unknown to him. On those windswept ridges for six days, however, they had shared the kinship of purpose.

More soldiers were coming to Laramie, it was said, and with them came many Pawnees, old enemies of the Lakota. Having never seen a Pawnee, Crazy Horse went to the fort and took Little Hawk with him. Along the way, several other young men joined them. They camped north of the fort and found a high place to settle in and watch with the long field glass before venturing any further.

They watched a long column of soldiers return to the fort, and instead of taking their mounts to the horse barns, they turned them loose in the open area in the middle of the buildings after unsaddling them. Long ago, the soldiers had stopped posting sentries, perhaps lulled into thinking that no one would dare attack them, especially in daylight. The sight of so many horses loose and unguarded was like waving a blanket in front of a buffalo bull and daring it to charge, especially since all the whites were in their dwellings out of the hot summer sun.

The plan was made in an instant. Blankets and robes were unfurled. Two men were sent to wait north of the fort while everyone else would go after the horses. With Crazy Horse leading the way, they circled to the west staying out of sight in the gullies and rode up out of the creek to the south, just past the stone building where the soldiers had a large wood-cutting apparatus of some sort. By the time the raiders gained the open area, they were at a full gallop, yelling and waving their blankets and robes and firing pistols. Panicked immediately, the big Long Knife horses bolted and broke past a large building on the northeast corner as groups of wide-eyed soldiers emerged from the buildings, but all they could do was watch helplessly. The Pawnees were sitting in the shade of some trees, watching.

The two Lakota waiting north of the fort helped point the horses in the right direction and then were joined by Crazy Horse as a rear guard. The herd and their new, gleeful owners were several hills and creeks away before the soldiers organized a pursuit. On into the afternoon and night, the raiders kept the horses moving, but the soldier pursuit was nothing to speak of. Sometime during the following day the soldiers turned back toward the fort.

In the Powder River camps, the horses were given away mostly to the old and the widows for packhorses or to pull the drag poles. They were not suited for much else since it was well known that they had difficulty in the rough country. First, the curved iron shoes nailed to their hooves were removed—they were too noisy.

Worm welcomed his two sons home. The older one, as usual, said nothing of his particular part in the horse raid—only that it had been done. Little Hawk, however, was not at all bashful about providing the details, to which his mothers and father listened with no small amount of pride, and amusement. Worm was especially pleased that Crazy Horse seemed to have put the disappointment over Black Buffalo Woman behind him. More than a few available young women had cast hopeful glances in his son's direction, especially since his reputation as a fighting man was rising rapidly. Yet it was difficult to know if he had any interest in any particular one. Now and then someone would deliver a gift of moccasins from Yellow Woman, the Sahiyela girl he had helped after she had lost her husband and child. But she looked on him as a younger brother and nothing more. There was time. Crazy Horse was still a young man. Meanwhile, while they waited for grandchildren, Worm and his wives would bask in the knowledge that few households had two such fine, strong sons.

But there was another reason for a little fatherly pride. Several of the warrior societies had approached him seeking to make Crazy Horse not only a member but to offer him positions of leadership. His exploits as a fighting man were well known even though he did not participate in the accepted ritual of telling victory stories. His uncle Long Face had made a fine staff for him covered with red trade cloth and attached the eagle feathers given to him to commemorate his achievements. Already there were nearly twenty. As a proven warrior, he was entitled to carry the staff in any ceremony or occasion, but he chose not to do so. Perhaps it was his way, Worm surmised, to honor the calling of the Thunder Dreamer. Worm knew that it was simply not in his son to brag or show off, but he also knew that his son understood that a Thunder Dreamer had to live his life as an example to others. Humility was a good example. A Thunder Dreamer was also called upon to do the opposite of what people expected. So it made sense that he would not carry the eagle feather staff or talk publicly about his exploits in the victory ceremonies, which was expected from an accomplished warrior. All in all, Worm was pleased to see his oldest son honor his calling.

Summer passed lazily, and people talked of making presents to the buffalo scouts and sending them out looking, so the planning for the autumn hunts could be made. So it was done, and once more the Lakota renewed the bond they shared with the buffalo, careful to observe all the rituals of honor and respect and keeping in mind the sacrilege of the white hide hunters. The meat was good and plentiful once again for the coming winter.

As the first heavy snows fell, troubling news came from far south, from the Sahiyela who lived along the southern fork of the Shell River: soldiers—it was always the soldiers. Three hundred people had been killed at a place called Sand Creek, most of them Sahiyela and some Blue Clouds led by Black Kettle and White Antelope. Both leaders were regarded as wise and always working for peace. The killing was bad enough because those killed were mostly women and children, but the soldiers who attacked did more than kill.

The white agent trusted by Black Kettle and White Antelope had advised them to find a place to pitch their lodges that was away from the main trails, it was told. There were many whites in that part of the country, many living in a large town called Denver, and there was a hatred among them for the Sahiyela and any people of the Earth. The camp was to fly the white banner of peace as well as the striped banner of the Long Knives to signify they were peaceful. But the soldiers found them and the banners meant nothing to them.

The messengers could barely tell the story, trying to keep back the anger and the tears as well as the bile that rose in the throat from remembering. Women and children were butchered after they were killed, it was told. Parts of their bodies were cut away, such as a woman's breasts and genitals, a child's hand or fingers, and boys' genitals. Brains were bashed out with gunstocks, and eyes were gouged out. Some babies not yet born were cut from their mother's stomachs. The final insult came when the soldiers attached body parts to their blue coats and rode in a victory march through the streets of the large town as the other whites cheered.

The Lakota did not want to believe the news—not because they wanted to deny the truth of it, but because it was much too difficult to believe that anyone could do such unspeakable deeds. Some asked after friends or relatives, fearing they might be among the dead, and the messengers would speak ever so softly the names they knew.

Crazy Horse walked away to his mothers' lodge and quietly sat against a chair near the back. From a painted rawhide box he slipped out a pair of moccasins he had yet to wear. They had been brought several months ago with a message.

"She who made these smiles at the sound of your name."

Yellow Woman. It was the last name the Sahiyela messenger had spoken.

With his rifle over one arm, he went out into the cool air and walked to the slopes past the horse herd. On the crest of a hill that looked out over a small valley, he stopped to breathe in the good air that rose from the land.

The old men had said it: We must stop them or we will be fighting them at our lodge doors.

Crazy Horse hefted his rifle and slid it from its decorated case, then laid it over the crook of his arm to aim it at all the enemies coming.

Thirteen

The old men had said it: We must stop them or we will be fighting them at our lodge door.

Crazy Horse hefted his rifle and slid it from its decorated case, then held it over the crook of his arm to aim it at all the enemies coming.

The strength of a tree, the old ones say, comes not from growing thicker in the good years when there is water, but from staying alive in the bad, dry times.

The winds howling across the prairies from the lower fork of the Shell River to the Powder River carried the wails of grief for the Sahiyela and Blue Clouds. Soon the hollow sobs of pain turned into angry growls for revenge. The Sahiyela sent messengers north to the Lakota that lamenting the blood spilled at Sand Creek was not enough. In the Moon of Frost in the Lodge, the camps of the Sahiyela and Blue Clouds moved north carrying their righteous anger, gathering more and more the further north they came. Many fighting men from the northern camps of the Lakota rode south to meet them, crossing the frozen Shell and the strangely quiet Holy Road.

Like a snowball rolling down a slope, they grew stronger by the day and gathered north of the south fork of the Shell. To the east was the soldier stockade near the trading post called Julesburg. Fighting men were selected by the various war leaders and sent against the soldier post. Hundreds of men hid themselves in the sagebrush as decoys drew the soldiers out and into the open, but the younger, inexperienced men couldn't hold themselves back. They rushed past their leaders too soon and the ambush was spoiled, with only a few soldiers killed or wounded. Their misguided zeal took them on to the trading post. Ransacking it, they rode away and tore down the poles that held up the singing wires. But most of the soldiers had retreated into their stockade and watched their attackers taunt them from inside the safety of their walls. The older leaders among the Sahiyela, the Blue Clouds, and a few Lakota with them grumbled their disappointment. It was a victory not worth the dancing.

Crazy Horse heard the grumbling and listened. Once more, the older men said that the whites were not honorable enemies, that to defeat them was not an act of honor but one of necessity. Therefore, the young men must understand that fighting them was not for honor or victory stories, but to wipe them out. For that to happen the young fighting men must understand that victory for the people must come before individual glory.

All whites were the enemy now and that thought was carried with the guns, lances, war clubs, and bows as angry men rode out from the great camp. The Lakota swept to the northeast, the Sahiyela to the northwest, and the Blue Clouds swirled like hornets in between. Way stations, soldier posts, and any travelers along the Holy Road or any trail frequented by whites were the objectives. Young men took the admonitions of their elders to heart as they hardened themselves to mercy and remembered Sand Creek. The spirit of revenge rolled with the thunder from the hooves of warhorses across the frozen prairies. Prominent among the leaders was Spotted Tail, who had returned from the prison at Leavenworth. No one had expected him to return alive from the place where whites punished their enemies and their own lawbreakers. The Oglala had heard that he had returned with a new fear of the whites, but it was not a fearful man that fought with the Sahiyela and Blue Clouds. Once more, he was like the wounded grizzly and fighting men followed him without hesitation.

Crazy Horse joined the second attack on Julesburg. But the whites were reluctant to meet them face-to-face in the open, so there was no fighting to speak of. They left the post ablaze after taking all they could carry from the storehouses.

The combined encampment moved north, reaching the upper Powder River in the Moon of Snowblindness. They had brought with them herds of cattle and horses taken in their raiding. After the initial gathering, and since it was still winter, the people broke into smaller encampments along the river.

Victories in the south and the coming together of the three nations brought a new sense of power not known for years. Horses were traded, marriages were arranged, and the councils of old men made plans to put the new power to good use. The avenging of Sand Creek would never end, some said.

Word came from the Loafers along the Holy Road that the soldier leaders were planning to drive all the nations of the Plains north beyond the Great Muddy. Now that the war over the black-skinned men was over, the whites could turn their attention to other things, the Loafers cautioned—which surely meant that more soldiers would be sent to fight the Lakota and their allies. One called Moonlight was in charge at Laramie, it was said, and he had five hundred new soldiers. Let them come, said many young men. Let them come.

Winter slid into spring. There was some excitement because the Crow could not pass up the opportunity to help themselves to some of the captured horses in the camps along the Powder. Most of them were not successful. In the Moon When Horses Lose Their Hair, the camps came together once more to make the warrior ceremonials before the planned attacks for the summer were carried out. Crazy Horse hung back in the shadows watching with great interest, listening with great amusement to Little Hawk's excited descriptions of the goings-on.

The old men had decided that the soldier settlement at the Shell River bridge crossing should be attacked and the soldiers driven out. Crazy Horse was picked as one of the scouts to ride south to watch the settlement. Soldiers had already crossed and were well on their way to the Wind River, guarding a line of wagons. The scouts attacked just to harass them and managed to take several horses before they broke off. A spring snowstorm stopped them when the soldiers couldn't, so they returned north with their captured horses.

Messengers came from the Loafers at Laramie. Two old Lakota who were friendly to the whites had been hanged after returning a captive white woman. The one called Moonlight had ordered it. One of the men was old Two Face, and Crazy Horse remembered the warm welcome in his camp along the Shell. He had been for good relations with the whites. Now he was dead. The two bodies were left hanging until they had rotted and fallen from the tree in pieces, the messengers said. Now the soldiers were sending all the Loafers to a place called Fort Kearny, because the whites at Fort Laramie couldn't trust them not to exact revenge. The soldiers led by one called Fouts had already taken to the trail, driving the Loafers like cattle.

Fighting men were quick to respond and a plan was made for a rescue. High Back Bone, along with Crazy Horse and several others, rode south. Several young men had ridden ahead and caught up to the captives, and, at night, they sneaked in to mingle with their friends and relatives, waiting for the attack they knew was coming so they could fight from inside and confuse the soldiers.

On the opposite shore, past the point where Horse Creek flowed into the Shell, a camp was made for the night, with soldiers posted around the ragged lodges of the Loafers. The next morning when the soldiers were ready to move on again, the women had not yet taken down the lodges. Angry and impatient, Fouts himself charged over to shout orders. The waiting warriors who had sneaked in opened fire, killing the soldier. A few others with him whipped their horses to get away, and all around the warriors waiting under cover opened fire. High Back Bone, Crazy Horse, He Dog, Spotted Tail, and even Red Cloud himself, among many others, broke from cover and attacked.

For a time, there was utter confusion. The young men who

had sneaked into the camp helped the women and children back across the river while the mounted warriors engaged the soldiers to enable the crossing. The soldiers could do nothing but defend themselves and watch their former captives scatter into the hills to the north. In frustration, they set fire to the lodges still standing and killed a crippled old man who had been left behind.

The warriors took the people north and then east to the sand hills, scattering into several small groups to confuse any pursuers. Moonlight and his column did come and stopped where several trails crossed. After the soldiers unsaddled their horses to rest them, Crazy Horse and a few young men swept in and ran them off. Instead of trailing the horses, Moonlight positioned his men to form a protective circle around himself. Crazy Horse led the young men and their new herd away. Clearly, this enemy was not worth the effort to kill him. Later, they watched from hilltops as the soldiers walked back toward Fort Laramie carrying saddles.

On the way back to the Powder River country, the former captives had stories to tell. Fouts's soldiers had tied boys to wagon wheels to watch them turn helplessly as the wagons rolled. Small children were thrown into the Shell still running high from the spring snowmelt. And some of the young girls had been dragged into the soldiers' tents at night. If a man's heart didn't turn cold toward the whites after hearing such things, then he didn't have one, was the sentiment among the rescuers. And one opinion they spoke low and among themselves. Perhaps some lessons had been learned about being friendly to the whites.

Word spread like wildfire that the Lakota were on a killing rampage. Whites living in strange little sod houses built into hillsides, or in log houses here and there along creek bottoms, sought safety at Fort Laramie and the various outposts along the Shell. But the old men leaders kept to their plan to attack the soldier post north of Elk Mountain. As the days rolled into the Moon of Ripening Berries and then the Moon When the Sun

Stands in the Middle, they waited in the camps along the Powder grazing the horses and letting them grow strong.

The Lakota had their Sun Dance and the Sahiyela did their Medicine Lodge ceremonies, and ancient warrior rituals were invoked to give strength to the fighting men. Crazy Horse was given a stone dreamer medicine—a small pebble to tie into the tail of his warhorse—from his friend Chips. Scouts returned with news of more soldiers gathering at the bridge on the Shell, and the old men sent the fighting men south, like the sudden storm turns loose the hailstones.

The Gathering of Warriors was done as hundreds of men circled the great camp. At the head of the Sahiyelas rode their great fighters Big Nose and High Back Wolf, while the Lakota were led by Red Cloud, Big Road, and High Back Bone. Ahead of them all rode the old men pipe carriers.

As the scouts had reported, the settlement at the river crossing had grown with straight rows of canvas tents and corrals full of horses and mules. The leaders decided to lure the soldiers into an ambush. Crazy Horse was one of twenty Lakota and Sahiyela picked as decoys. The main body of fighting men hid themselves in the broken hills to wait.

Crazy Horse and three others went ahead, while the other decoys waited back. The four rode for the horses and mules, drawing out a column of soldiers from across the river pulling a wagon gun. The decoys fired on them and withdrew slowly, staying just within rifle range, knowing their constant movement would make them hard targets. Far past the bridge, the soldiers stopped and fired several rounds from the wagon guns, the blast of the big gun echoing through the hills.

Hearing the wagon guns, many of the young men waiting in ambush rode to the tops of the hills before the signal to attack was given, and were spotted by the soldiers who immediately withdrew back across the bridge. Another ambush had been spoiled by youthful impatience. Crazy Horse was angry but could do nothing. The remaining decoys joined him, and they decided to go after the horses and mules on their side of the river.

The leaders decided to disengage for this day and make new plans for the next, and sent High Back Wolf to bring the decoys back. The decoys were already scattering horses and engaged in an intense exchange of gunfire with the soldiers. High Back Wolf rode into the river to join some of the decoys charging directly at the soldier settlement. A concentrated volley from the soldiers knocked the great Sahiyela fighter from his horse. The rest of the decoys disengaged thereafter, returning to face the stern words of the leaders and deliver the sad news to Blind Wolf, the father of High Back Wolf.

Crazy Horse knew that all of the decoys should have broken off after the ambush had been spoiled, but the heat of the moment was hard to turn away from. Such an excuse was of no use to Blind Wolf. Before dawn, Crazy Horse and several Sahiyelas took the old man to the river to recover his son's body.

After sunrise, Crazy Horse rejoined the decoys. Ambushers were hidden south below the bridge, and a large group of Sahiyelas waited in the hills to the west. To Crazy Horse's surprise, the mounted soldiers rode out once more when he thought they would be more cautious. Instead of chasing the decoys, the soldiers stayed on the Holy Road once they crossed the bridge. The ambushers below the bridge waited for a signal, then circled the soldiers from behind, and the battle was joined. Foot soldiers then came running over the bridge with a wagon gun, took up a skirmish line to open rifle fire, and then began firing the wagon gun.

Crazy Horse joined the main body of Lakota warriors and saw that some of the mounted soldiers had been cut down. Then the firing abated as a few Lakota recognized the soldier leader who was trying hard to control his horse. He was the one called Collins, who had hunted with some of them in the north. By now his soldiers were close to the hills where the Sahiyelas waited, anxious to avenge High Back Wolf. Seeing them charge, Collins ordered a retreat. As his soldiers turned back for the bridge, he stayed back alone to protect the rear. Meanwhile, the foot soldiers were sending shells from the wagon gun into the midst of the Lakota.

Some of the Lakota held their fire, Crazy Horse among them, as Collins faced the charging Sahiyela while trying to control his frightened horse. Wild with fear, the horse took him directly into the oncoming Sahiyelas, who cut him down quickly.

The Lakota had to turn their attention to the fire coming from the foot soldiers as they lowered the aim of their wagon gun and sent warriors scurrying away from its exploding shells. So most of the mounted soldiers were able to gain the safety of the bridge as the foot soldiers also withdrew back across the bridge.

Many of the Lakota and Sahiyela leaders were angry that the soldiers had been able to escape though outnumbered. The fighting had evolved into the two sides sniping at each other from long range, and neither was gaining any advantage. Crazy Horse rode into the hills to rest his horse and found a large group of Lakota watching a cloud of smoke to the south along the Holy Road. A large group of the Sahiyela had broken off in that direction, he had noticed earlier, so he rode to see for himself what might have happened.

He was close enough to smell the smoke when he met a number of Sahiyela leading mules and packhorses. They had found five wagons, the men told him, and soldiers already dug in for a fight. The warriors had run off a herd of mules, then attacked the circled wagons. Big Nose sent men in on foot to draw fire while the mounted warriors charged. It was a hard fight, they said, but they had killed all but two or three soldiers and took all of their supplies.

Now Crazy Horse understood why Collins did not follow the decoys. He was heading out to help the approaching wagons likely returning from the Sweetwater station.

The day wore on and many of the warriors rode back to the

camps. The Sahiyela, eager to avenge High Back Wolf, went down the Holy Road looking for soldiers. Crazy Horse turned his horse northward.

During the next few days, he sat on the fringes as old men talked about the fight near the bridge. They had not succeeded in wiping out the soldiers because a few impetuous young men couldn't hold themselves back for the right moment. It was a problem that had to be corrected if they were to defeat the whites, they all agreed. And one way to solve the problem was to find strong young men to lead the others. For that, they said, perhaps they should renew the tradition of the Shirt Wearers.

Some people scoffed at such talk. No Shirt Wearers had been selected for a generation because the purpose behind the tradition had been forgotten. A Shirt Wearer was to be a young man of strong action and good ways, one to set the example for others. Instead, the tradition had become the father choosing his son to wear the Shirt next. Better to let it be, some said, instead of dishonoring a good thing again.

After the fight against the soldiers at the bridge, the great gathering began to break up slowly; a few of the Blue Clouds and Sahiyelas returned to their own country. Crazy Horse and Little Hawk returned home to news of a large column of soldiers heading north led by a man named Connor who was promising to punish the Lakota for the soldiers killed at the Shell River crossing and those killed at the wagon fight. Preparations were made and scouts sent to watch the column of angry and vengeful whites. Warriors picked a good spot for an ambush and waited but were surprised when the soldiers turned aside and attacked a small encampment of Blue Clouds along the Tongue. The Lakota rushed in to help and recovered many of the horses run off by the soldiers. Instead of engaging the Lakota, the soldiers hurried away to the north and crossed over the Wolf Mountains. Perhaps they were not so angry after all, some young men said. But another column appeared.

When the Lakota and Sahiyela found them they were hiding behind their circled wagons along the Powder, not very anxious to fight, it seemed. The warriors surrounded the wagons and watched them for days. Finally, two whites walked from the wagons to talk with the Lakota leader, Red Cloud, and Dull Knife, who was leading the Sahiyela. For a wagonload of provisions, the soldiers would be allowed to leave, it was decided. So they went south toward the Shell, not knowing that the Lakota and Sahiyela didn't have much powder and shells for a long fight.

On the heels of their leaving, yet another column was found, this time further north, close to where the Powder empties into the Elk River. The Mniconju had been fighting them, helped by a sudden strange turn in the weather. Though it was early in the Moon of Leaves Turning Brown, a rainstorm had turned to ice, killing the big Long Knife horses. So there were many soldiers, the biggest column yet this summer, with many wagons and not enough horses to pull them all. They came up the Powder anyway. So the Lakota and Sahiyela, still low on powder and ammunition, went out to meet them.

The best the Lakota and Sahiyela could do was make the soldiers use up their ammunition, so they charged up close. Once more, the Sahiyela Big Nose showed his strong medicine by riding back and forth in front of the soldiers until his horse was shot. Strangely, however, the soldiers were reluctant to come out and fight. Someone's medicine seemed to be on the side of the warriors. Another cold, hard rain came and killed most of the remaining wagon horses of the Long Knives.

The warriors stayed close, harassing the soldiers, sometimes charging in to send a few arrows. Crazy Horse, Lone Bear, He Dog, and Little Hawk did this often, keeping the soldiers pinned behind their wagons. If the warriors were hampered by the lack of powder and bullets, the soldiers had a more serious predicament. They had no food and began eating their dead horses. Finally, after piling all their goods from the wagons they couldn't carry or burn, the soldiers walked away and the warriors let them go. They followed them over a few hills just to remind them to keep walking, but the soldiers seemed to be in no condition to turn back and fight, some stumbling and dropping their rifles. Crazy Horse picked one up, a back-loader that fired a very large bullet; a man didn't have to pour powder down into the barrel first.

A new rifle seemed to be the beginning of things that suddenly turned in his life. Deep into the Moon When Leaves Fall, he rode up into the foothills of the Shining Mountains to ponder all that had transpired, especially in the days that had just passed.

The strange incursion of the soldier columns that didn't seem to want to fight seemed long ago. Yet the news of the death of Yellow Woman felt as though it had come only the day before. Little Hawk was growing into a daring fighter, already winning several war honors. But the most perplexing and heavy change was symbolized in a shirt made from the hide of a bighorn sheep, now rolled in a decorated case and waiting in his parents' lodge. Also waiting were the duties and responsibilities that came with it.

The old man leaders had indeed decided to revive the old tradition of the Shirt Wearers. And as expected, the shirts were given to young men of important families. The choice of Young Man Whose Enemies Are Afraid of His Horses, Sword, or Long Knife Horse (aka American Horse) surprised no one. But when the name of Crazy Horse was announced, a gasp went through the gathered crowd, and the shouts, the whoops, and the trilling that followed were the loudest of all. He felt truly honored and yet was uncertain that he was a good choice. Later, two more Shirt Wearers were chosen and he was pleased that his friend He Dog was one. The other was Big Road, a good, strong, and honorable man.

"To wear the shirts you must be men above all others," said an old man chosen to speak. "You must help others before you think of yourselves. Help the widows and those who have little to wear and to eat and have no one to help them or speak for them. Do not look down on others or see those who look down on you, and do not let anger guide your mind or your heart. Be generous, be wise, and show fortitude so that the people can follow what you do and then what you say. Above all, have courage and be the first to charge the enemy, for it is better to lie a warrior naked in death than to be wrapped up well with a heart of water inside."

Crazy Horse's vision had told him he would be a fighting man, and, thus far, he had honored that foretelling, and would do so for as long as he could. But the vision had shown nothing about shouldering the cares and the welfare of others. Even in the best of times, it was difficult to do the right things for oneself; now he must do the right things to show others how it must be done. Perhaps that was why the Thunders were in his vision, his father and others had suggested. His would be a life of sacrifice, to live it for the good of others when all he wanted was to walk his own road. As his father had said during a quiet evening after the making of the Shirt Wearers, such a man does not belong to himself; he belongs to the people.

Something else was new also. His enemies, until now, had been the Crow and the Snakes. Now he could also count the relatives of Red Cloud among them. Everyone thought that Red Cloud himself, or certainly one of his relatives, would be chosen. After the ceremony, they had moved their lodges, and one of those riding away with a backward scowl at the son of Worm was Woman's Dress, known as the Pretty One when he was a boy. Crazy Horse knew that an enemy from within was the most dangerous of all.

As he sat on a slope looking over the rough, broken lands of the Powder River country, he pondered all that had happened, and then smoked his pipe and prayed for the strength to follow the path that had chosen him.

The makers of the Winter Count had chosen to call this year

the Winter When the Men Were Hanging at the Soldier Fort. An early snow came before all the berries were picked, a sign that did not escape the notice of the old ones. Things would happen backwards, they warned.

A messenger came from the north, from among the Hunkpapa Lakota. He was of the camp of Sitting Bull. Soldiers were running around everywhere, he said. And at the same time a man was traveling up the Great Muddy with a peace paper from the "great father." First they send the soldiers, then they send the peace talkers. If they can't kill us, perhaps they will try to harangue us to death, some suggested.

But in spite of the laughing, everyone knew that sometimes the peace talkers were more dangerous than the soldiers. The Hunkpapa visitor said that already some Loafers along the Great Muddy had signed the paper that said they gave permission for the whites to make roads through Lakota lands. Perhaps I should sign a paper to give away my brother-in-law's lodge, said one man. The laughter was a little bitter this time, for everyone knew what the man meant. Who among the people had the power to sign a paper that bound everyone? It was not the Lakota way, but the mark of one Lakota by his name was taken as agreement or permission given by all Lakota, as the whites saw it. So no one among the Oglala would expect to see the peace talker visit their camps soon. The Loafers were easier to persuade, already liking and needing the things of the whites as they did.

Perhaps the early snowfall had been a sign, some thought. Early in the Moon of Frost in the Lodge, when the new cycle of moons began, came news that brought a narrowing to the eyes of old men: Swift Bear of the Sicangu had signed the peace paper giving permission for the whites to make a road and build forts in the Powder River country.

Fourteen

Swirling breezes from several directions collided at the summit of the ridge and circled the two men watching the tiny spots of white against the still green background of the meadow far below them to the north. The spots were soldiers' tents.

To the west were the jagged ridges of the Shining Mountains. To the east, the foothills played out and then opened onto the broad expanse of prairie stretching all the way to the Great Muddy River. All of it was Lakota territory, none of it with room for the whites, so far as Crazy Horse was concerned. Lone Bear stood beside him watching the activity in the meadow through the farseeing glass.

The whites had been warned, yet here they were. Last month, in the Moon of Ripening Berries, Red Cloud had gone to the peace talkers at Fort Laramie to speak for the Oglala. There were to be no new roads, he said, reminding them of the Horse Creek Council fifteen years past. But it was not a new road they wanted, the smiling peace talkers had replied, but simply to use an old one. All the old roads were made by drag poles and moccasins, and, before that, the hooves of the buffalo, said Red Cloud, and they are only for us to use.

As the peace talkers listed the wagonloads of presents they were offering for the use of this "old" road of theirs, new soldiers had come up the Holy Road. They brought with them many loaded wagons pulled by mules—and, of course, wagon guns, too. A Loafer, who was something of a speaks-white, wandered in among them as the new soldiers set up their camp near the fort. Carrington was the man in charge, he learned, who forthrightly announced to the Loafer that he was going up to the Powder River to put up forts.

Hearing this news, Red Cloud and Young Man Afraid left the peace talkers with the warning that no road was to be opened, no forts were to be built, and no whites were to travel through the Powder River country.

Now Carrington had come to Buffalo Creek beneath the jagged ridges of the Shining Mountains with his seven hundred walking soldiers, after they had stopped to build a small fort on the Dry Fork of the Powder.

By the middle of the Moon When Calves Turn Dark, the pine log walls of the Buffalo Creek fort were up so the soldiers could be safe inside with their families and animals. And, as at the fort on the Dry Fork, the Lakota had harassed the soldiers. But they held themselves back, saving their energies for the all-out fighting they were expecting Red Cloud to lead. Even before the fort on Buffalo Creek was finished, some of the soldiers were sent north. Near the mouth of the Big Horn, very near to Crow lands, they built yet another fort. By the time summer was over and the leaves were starting to turn, three forts were standing in the middle of the best Lakota hunting grounds. And whites were traveling along a trail where once a man pounded stakes to mark the way to the gold fields west of Crow lands beyond the Elk River. Every line of wagons that came up the trail was attacked with High Back Bone, Young Man Afraid, and Crazy Horse leading raids as far south as the first fort. In the meantime, the fort on Buffalo Creek, which they learned had been named Phil Kearny, was constantly watched and attacked as often as opportunities allowed. But there was little the Lakota could do until the soldiers were caught out or lured into the open.

The Lakota camps along the Tongue and the outlying valleys numbered several hundred lodges altogether, mostly Mniconjus and Oglalas and a few Sicangu. There were Blue Clouds, but not many, and of course the Sahiyela. Early in the Winter Moon, the Lakota tried to lure the soldiers out to fight them in the open. But they were wary from the constant harassment, and reluctant to pursue the attacking warriors, though two soldiers were killed and a few wounded in a brief encounter. The failure was partly on the shoulders of the decoys because they did not work together—they were after guns and scalps first and not overly worried about a successful ambush. But too many young men could not hold themselves back until the right moment. The old men leaders were angry and distraught, remembering the trouble caused by impetuous and glory-seeking young men at Julesburg and again at the bridge fight on the Shell. They turned to High Back Bone for guidance.

Calling the young men together, High Back Bone scolded them for causing the ambush to fail. The young men listened without protest as he reminded them that fighting the whites was not a war for glory but a war for survival. He reminded them of Sand Creek. When he finished there was a loud affirmation, but even a louder one came after he announced his plan for another ambush.

Most of the fighting men would hide themselves and their horses in the ridges and gullies on either side of the wagon trail up from Prairie Dog Creek to Lodge Trail Ridge. A small group would attack the wood gatherers who always went out from the fort by wagon in the morning. When soldiers came out to drive the attackers away, ten decoys would show themselves and lead them toward Lodge Trail Ridge, and then north down to a slope ending in a meadow before Prairie Dog Creek. When the signal was given, the hiding warriors would attack, and not before or the ambush would be spoiled. The soldiers had to believe that only the ten decoys were fighting them.

Most important to the plan were the decoys. If they failed, several hundred fighting men would be denied the opportunity for a victory. Therefore the decoys needed a strong leader, one skilled in warfare, with proven judgment in battle. The leader of the decoys would be Crazy Horse.

The cries and shouts of affirmation rang through the camp, and fighting men—young and old—crowded around the Hunk-patila to put their names in as one of the other nine. The decision would be made in the morning, they were told. Crazy Horse and High Back Bone would smoke on it and make the choices.

Far into the night, Crazy Horse sat with He Dog, Lone Bear, and Little Hawk as they prepared themselves and their weapons. Watch yourselves, they told each other; we are many, but the soldiers have many more bullets.

They began gathering at dawn, starting from the farther camps. By the time they reached the flats around Goose Creek they were over five hundred strong. Just past Prairie Dog Creek—below Lodge Trail Ridge—the Sahiyela were given first choice to pick their ambush spots. They chose the northern gullies so they could stay out of the wind, for this was one of the coldest days ever in the memory of old men and women. The Lakota groups dispersed as well, mostly to the east of the wagon trail. Now the responsibility for success or failure fell on the decoys.

The Mniconjus called on a medicine dreamer among them. With his holy robe tied over his head, he rode among the hills in a back and forth pattern and returned to announce he had caught a few soldiers. He was sent again and returned to report a few more. The third time, he reported that he had so many, a hundred in the hand, that he couldn't hold them all.

Crazy Horse had selected two Sahiyela and seven other Lakota as decoys. Each rode one horse and led a good warhorse for this day. One of the Sahiyela was Big Nose. They, and the group of twenty or so that were to attack the wood wagon, swung around to the west, staying below Lodge Trail Ridge and out of the line of sight from the fort and the soldiers' farseeing glasses.

The main gate of the fort was on the west side and the trail to the pine slopes started there. Crazy Horse and his men found a good thicket, mounted their warhorses, and waited beneath warm robes while the others went to wait near the wagon trail. At midmorning wagons left the fort and headed west along the well-worn trail.

The attack came well away from the fort but still within sight, so the Lakota could be seen surrounding the wagons. After an initial charge the attackers kept the wagon men and escort riders engaged. The gunfire sounded especially sharp in the frigid mountain air. Soon the western gates swung open and a column of mounted and walking soldiers appeared. The Lakota attackers kept up the firing, making sure the rescue column was well out of the fort. As the soldiers passed their thicket, Crazy Horse and his decoys charged.

Fortunately, enough of the decoys had a few bullets so that they could fire several shots to make it seem like an all-out attack. Crazy Horse shot a few arrows when he was close enough to see the hairy faces of some of the soldiers. For some moments, the soldiers seemed confused. Then they finally opened fire.

Uneven snow cover over frozen ground and dangerously frigid air were the decoy warriors' first obstacles, and bullets humming and buzzing past them like angry bees reminded them that they had a daunting task ahead and a long way to go to finish it.[1] The first few mounted soldiers turned off the trail to pursue them and the rest of the column fell in slowly behind them.

Feinting head-on charges, the decoys would swerve at the last moment, well within range of the soldier guns. They took the soldiers north over the frozen snowfields. At one point, some of the decoys, including Crazy Horse, had to ride down a treacherously steep, frozen slope. The soldiers took the gentler slope of the south face and kept pursuing. An open valley with a thick stand of trees on either side of a creek lay ahead with no serious

---

1. It was nearly five miles from Fort Phil Kearny to the battle site.

obstacles to impede the soldiers' advance. Once across the creek, the warriors turned straight north and came in sight of Lodge Trail Ridge.

The walking soldiers were slowing down the column. Crazy Horse dismounted well within rifle range, pulled out his knife, and calmly scraped ice from the bottom of his horse's hooves. When the bullets began to ricochet closer and closer, he remounted and loped away. The other decoys, to infuriate the soldiers, used similar tactics. One of them stood on the rump of his mount and calmly watched the soldiers before he retook his seat and galloped away. Each time the soldier column seemed to be slowing, the decoys charged at them to draw their fire. On and on they took them, ever closer to Lodge Trail Ridge and the warriors hiding in the cut banks and gullies beyond. Many of the walking soldiers grabbed stirrups or saddle skirts to hang on and run a little beside the horses.

Now they gained a gradual slope that ended on the mostly east-west crest of Lodge Trail Ridge. To the south, the fort was partially visible through some trees. The breath of the big soldier horses formed puffs of misty clouds that dissipated quickly. On and on the soldiers came, some of their big horses slipping, some of the walking soldiers slipping and falling.

Movement gave a searing edge to the frigid air. Faces of the decoys were numb and fingers could barely hold weapons and reins. Now and then, one of them dismounted to stand against his horse to get warm. Crazy Horse ran up the slope leading his horse and then stopped to build a fire, fumbling with the flint and striker. He was barely able to coax flames to life from the small pile of tinder and kindling to warm his tingling fingers before bullets began erupting in the snow around him. Calmly, he mounted and galloped up the slope, leaving the warmth of the little fire.

He gathered the decoys on the back of Lodge Trail Ridge for a quick parley, deciding to stay on the wagon trail since it was familiar to the soldiers. A few rounds passed overhead with a high-pitched whine. Those that were closer had a lower, angrier hum. They waited and waited as the bullets sounded closer and closer before they slid their mounts down the north-facing slope. Gathering at the bottom, they waited for the soldiers to gain the ridge.

On the ridge the soldiers hesitated, perhaps waiting for some to catch up. The decoys renewed their efforts, coaxing their tired horses partway up the slope, moving dangerously close. One pretended to be shot off his horse and immediately bounced up, running behind the horse before skillfully remounting from the back. Crazy Horse had picked the right men for the task at hand. Here, the decoys opened fire, sending the heaviest volley so far at the soldiers. Down off the ridge came first the mounted soldiers. The decoys loped to a slight rise that was the wagon trail and milled around, as if uncertain what to do. Like a dark blue stream, the soldiers reached the bottom of the slope and those on horses went hard after the decoys.

For Crazy Horse and his decoys, this was the decisive moment. If the waiting ambushers attacked prematurely the soldiers could still escape. The decoys looked right and left as they proceeded north along a very narrow part of the ridge, but could see no movement. Below the slope of the ridge falling away before them was the winding Prairie Dog Creek, and the end of their task.

Now the soldiers were pressing harder, increasing their gunfire, obviously certain that the decoys comprised the entire enemy force. Crazy Horse formed his men into a skirmish line, and those with bullets to spare fired at the oncoming soldiers. Drawing heavy return fire, the decoys raced their horses down the slippery slope, forming two lines as they rode. They crossed the flats leading to Prairie Dog Creek, each line of riders swinging out wide and then crossing each other on the opposite side of the creek. This was the signal to attack.

From out of the very Earth itself came the waiting ambushers.

Horses and men burst from the gullies, cutbacks, and what little winter shrubbery there was. In a heartbeat, several hundred fighting men rode south, some from the east and some from the west. Those closest to Lodge Trail Ridge quickly shut the soldiers' escape route back to the fort.

The soldiers' advance stopped. Then they instinctively began their fight to reach the safety of the fort. The walking soldiers were strung out far to the back, closer to Lodge Trail Ridge. They were the first to fall as gunfire blasted up the slopes below them.

There was no end to the guns firing. The soldiers fought hard as they retreated up the ridge, but there was nothing to be gained. They were cut off with nowhere to go. Wave after wave of mounted warriors fought their way up the treacherous slopes. Those with guns used up their bullets and then resorted to their bows. Some had only bows and arrows. Arrows flew up the east slope and from the west. The sky was dark with them and some found their mark in the body of a Lakota or Sahiyela. Toward the end, the warriors waded in among the dead and dying soldiers, killing them with a pistol shot or a hard, skillful swing of a war club or the deadly thrust of a lance. And then all was quiet. All the soldiers were dead.

It began with the Sahiyela, as they remembered Sand Creek and what had been done to their relatives. When the frenzy ended, the soldiers were stripped naked, fingers were chopped off, bellies slashed open, eyes gouged out.

Many warriors were wounded, but fewer than fifteen had been killed. Crazy Horse found a pouch with bullets for his gun, suddenly remembering that he had not fired one of the four bullets he had for his back-loading rifle. He had used only his pistol and bow.

Little Hawk, He Dog, and High Back Bone found him, and then they began looking for Lone Bear. Even as someone warned that more soldiers were coming, they found him on the east slope below the wagon trail, face down in the snow. His body was cold but he was still alive. A bullet had torn through his chest and only the brutally cold day had prevented him from bleeding to death immediately.

Crazy Horse turned his friend over and watched his eyes flutter. The dying man grimaced, or perhaps it was a smile at this last bit of bad luck. Then he was gone.

Crazy Horse held him close for a time, tears freezing as they fell out of his eyes. For Lone Bear, the victory had come at the highest price. Little Hawk and the others stepped in and helped carry him up the slope.

Later, he was told that there had been eighty soldiers, so the Mniconju medicine dreamer had known the true outcome when he saw one hundred soldiers in his hands. Almost before the warriors reached the warmth and comfort of their lodges, it was known among them as the Battle of the Hundred in the Hand. Sometime in the night, word was brought to Crazy Horse that among the dead was one of his decoy warriors, Big Nose, the stalwart and fearless Sahiyela.

The soldiers stayed in their fort for the rest of the winter. The wood wagon did not venture out and no whites traveled along the wagon trail to the gold fields, due mostly to one of the hardest winters in memory. It was so hard, in fact, that many Lakota camps were dangerously low on meat.

Snow was deep and hunters wore out horses or injured their legs traveling in it. Many went out on snowshoes looking for elk and buffalo. A month after the battle, Crazy Horse and Little Hawk went east and then south to Crazy Woman Creek to sheltered areas and cottonwood groves. Elk, like horses, fed on young cottonwood trees in winter.

Days of scouting brought no results and they were forced to seek shelter in a sudden blizzard. As the wind whipped the snow sideways, they could do no more than huddle beneath their buffalo robes in the lee side of boulders in a narrow creek bed.

When the wind abated somewhat, they saw shapes in front of them through the veil of snow, a small herd of elk also seeking shelter from the wind. Stringing their bows, the brothers crawled through the snow and managed to shoot several before the others fled. The next morning when the storm ended, they found their elk, some already being torn apart by hungry wolves. They managed to rescue most of their kills and gathered wood for a large fire. Crazy Horse stayed there to guard the meat against the wolves as Little Hawk returned to camp for horses. Back at the encampment, they distributed the fresh meat first to those who had nothing to eat but kept only a little for their family. There was no hunger in the lodge of Worm, however, because with each scratching at the door, someone handed in a buffalo horn filled with elk soup or a skewer of roasted meat.

Travelers returned to the wagon trail in the late spring after the runoff from the mountain snows had receded. The Lakota harassed or attacked every wagon they could, hampered by a lack of ammunition for the various assortment of pistols and rifles they owned. Nonetheless, they managed to take horses practically at will. Occasionally, however, the people in one of the wagon trains would be well armed and prepared to fight. Crazy Horse frequently joined a raiding party, sometimes going all the way to the first fort on Dry Fork, called Fort Reno.

In the Moon When the Sun Stands in the Middle, the peace talkers at Fort Laramie requested a council, so the Oglala chose Old Man Whose Enemies Are Afraid of His Horses to speak for them. But they also sent Red Cloud along. Their terms were simple: no one would sign the paper unless the whites abandoned the forts, stopped using the wagon trail, and paid the Lakota with a worthwhile supply of ammunition. The peace talkers, of course, refused, so Old Man Afraid and Red Cloud left the council.

With no agreement in place, the soldiers and the forts stayed. Whites continued to travel up the wagon trail, known to the

Lakota as the Powder River Road and the whites as the Bozeman Trail. Various headmen from the camps met, deciding they should keep attacking all three forts. But they couldn't agree which to strike first, however. The warrior leaders stepped in and decided among themselves that the Sahiyela would attack the fort near the mouth of the Big Horn and the Mniconju would lead against the fort on Buffalo Creek. Crazy Horse returned from a raid in Crow country to join them.

The attack against the wood camp west of Fort Phil Kearny turned into a hard-fought battle, one the Lakota didn't expect. For Crazy Horse, it was a lesson in fighting the whites. Waging war against them, he learned, had to be done with a cold heart.

Thirty soldiers behind a circle of wagon boxes detached from the wheels and frames had poured continuous rifle fire into each wave of Lakota attackers, whether mounted or on foot. For most of a day, the fighting went on. Though a few soldiers were killed in the initial attacks, Lakota casualties were higher. Bravery on the part of the Lakota was not the issue—some had died because they were foolishly brave. A good man named Jipala had walked in the open toward the wagon boxes with his shield before him, and was shot dead. The outcome of the battle had to be just as important in the minds of the Lakota as demonstrating bravery during it. The whites didn't fight a battle to show how brave they were, they fought to kill as many of the enemy as they could. Killing enough of the enemy would lead to victory. Crazy Horse said as much to High Back Bone, Little Hawk, and He Dog. Their reply was a philosophical one: then we must learn to jump from one horse to another in the middle of the rushing river.

Crazy Horse learned later that the soldiers behind the wagon boxes had new back-loading guns. They could be reloaded and fired much faster than muzzle-loaders. In fact, as one soldier fired, a second behind him reloaded a second rifle.

They had won the Battle of the Hundred in the Hand because they outnumbered the soldiers, though each had a rifle and a pistol and plenty of bullets. But faster-shooting rifles would sooner or later enable one soldier to fight like two or three. Warriors outnumbering the soldiers would not always be the answer. Acquiring more and better guns and putting aside foolish acts of bravery in the face of an enemy that didn't care were the ways to win against the whites. There was no choice but to jump from one horse to another before the rushing river became stronger.

The Lakota and Sahiyela went hard against the travelers on the Powder River Road until only soldiers or a wagon train with plenty of guns and ammunition to put up a good fight dared to use it. Crazy Horse and Little Hawk joined the raiding, but as the autumn was passing, they joined the hunts to make meat for the winter.

Snows came and the winter passed, and the camps along the Tongue waited to see what the new cycle of seasons would bring. The soldiers in the forts along the Powder River Road kept themselves inside, watching through their farseeing glasses and ready to fire off their wagon guns at the first Lakota that came within range.

Then a strange thing happened. The soldiers left. In long columns of riders and wagons piled high with their goods, they set off south toward the Shell. Almost before the soldiers were out of sight of the fort on Buffalo Creek, the Sahiyela and Oglala went in to claim what had been left behind. Then they set fire to the fort and watched the great leaping flames reduce the walls and buildings to ashes, vowing they would never let another be built on their lands.

In spite of the cruelty of the soldier leaders at Fort Laramie (Fouts and Moonlight), new Loafer camps were pitched around the fort. And it was a Loafer that brought word from the peace talkers. They had come with more presents, kettles, blankets, knives, and now guns. And they were asking for Red Cloud to come and sign the paper so that all the Lakota could share in these gifts—so there could be peace in the Powder River country. The peace talkers had come with a new offer as well. All the country from the Great Muddy River to the Shining Mountains would be Lakota land, so long as the rivers shall flow and the grass grows.

Where did the whites get the power to give the Lakota lands they already control, Crazy Horse heard many old men ask.

Summer came and passed into autumn. The things of life went on. The people gathered at Bear Butte so the old men leaders could decide that Red Cloud should touch the pen on the peace paper for all the Oglala. Crazy Horse rode north to raid the Crows.

He returned with new horses, and to news that his uncle Spotted Tail had his own lands to live on, given to him by the whites. Agency, it was called. Perhaps he was influenced by the kindness one soldier leader gave him when his daughter had sickened and died. Nevertheless, the Sicangu was advising that Red Cloud should touch the pen. From the north came different news. Sitting Bull was still defiant, and his Hunkpapa were still fighting the soldiers in the north and chasing buffalo. But there was a new worry, he had warned. The whites were making new kinds of roads, strips of iron laid across rows of wood so that a new kind of wagon could travel on it—an iron wagon that breathed smoke like the houseboats on the Great Muddy and dragged houses on iron wheels. The "iron horse," he called it.

Crazy Horse pondered this news even as Red Cloud rode south to Fort Laramie with a new power of his own. The old headmen had given him the power to sign the peace paper for the Oglala. Late in the Moon When Leaves Fall, he made a mark next to his name on the white man's peace paper.[2]

---

2. Fort Laramie Treaty of 1868.

Life in the Powder River country was rather like the pale shadow made by a thin cloud. Something had changed, but the whites were still telling the Lakota what to do. Some of the younger men wondered if Red Cloud knew all the things written on the paper he had marked on behalf of all the Oglala.

Spotted Tail, meanwhile, had been arguing to move his people to a different agency even as Red Cloud was told he would have to move to one. Crazy Horse and He Dog stayed north, close to the Tongue, and raided into Crow country. More and more Lakota were moving south closer to the Holy Road, wanting to trade for goods they had grown to depend on—butcher knives, kettles, buckets, and bolts of cloth, and so on. The black medicine, coffee, was another favorite. So, too, was whiskey.

As Crazy Horse stayed to the north, more and more people came to pitch their lodges with him. Though he had no wife and no lodge of his own, he found himself suddenly the headman among many families. Many fighting men attributed the victory of the Battle of the Hundred in the Hand to his bravery and skilled leadership—not because he told other men what to do, but because he showed them how to do it. And, in him, they saw the quality of good thinking that was just as important in the quiet times as daring action was in the time of battle.

High Back Bone moved into the Crazy Horse camp and the two were considered the most powerful fighting men among the northern camps of the Lakota, perhaps of all the Lakota. Crazy Horse waved aside such words and said nothing of this new responsibility of headman that had been put at his lodge door. But he was, after all, a Shirt Wearer, his father reminded him gently. He must live up to the responsibility and be careful of the power and influence that often comes with it. It was the path of the Thunder Dreamer laying itself out in front of him, and he must walk it.

So the Crazy Horse people flourished in the north country.

They rode across the Elk to keep the Crow from becoming too bold. They hunted and observed the rituals that made them who they were, and the seasons passed. Crazy Horse saw to the duties of leadership he had not sought to have. The old ones would smile as he walked through the camp asking after their needs, often with his brother Little Hawk at his side.

Returning from a hunt, he stopped in the camp of No Water to rest. Since the great gathering below Elk Mountain two years past, he had spoken to Black Buffalo Woman several times. Whatever had been between them had long passed. She was the mother of three now and it seemed entirely proper for him to ask about her children. But each time they talked, they lingered longer, something that did not go unnoticed by some who knew what had happened before. So now Black Buffalo Woman waited discreetly for the gift of elk teeth Crazy Horse had lately been leaving for her with someone. But as he was preparing to leave she approached openly and brought him food, and they stood together talking. He left, not lingering too long, but as he rode away some noticed that she watched until he was out of sight.

His father was still awake that night as Crazy Horse returned, long after his mothers and Little Hawk had fallen asleep. The old man had been waiting to share a smoke and a few words. Two men had come from the camp of No Water, he announced carefully. There was no need for more words. Crazy Horse understood why the men had come. But Worm spoke nonetheless because much rode on the shoulders of his son, much that was important to the people.

"They will not let her go," he said quietly.

Crazy Horse said nothing about the visitors. He smoked with his father and then took his anger to his bed. There was no one else to talk with. High Back Bone had left to visit among his Mniconju relatives to the north. He had long been angry over Red Cloud being given the power to put his mark on the paper for all the Oglala, saying that it would lead to trouble down the road.

But Crazy Horse already knew High Back Bone's thinking where Black Buffalo Woman was concerned. The power of a woman over a man is sometimes the greatest mystery of all, he had said.

At such times the warrior's trail seemed to open new ways of looking at one's troubles, so Crazy Horse decided it was time to fight the Crows again. When He Dog heard his friend was calling for young men to ride north, he suggested it should be done in the old way, many men taking the trail with their women along to add their strength. The Crow Owners Society agreed and invited Crazy Horse and He Dog to join them as lancer bearers. But more than that, they were made caretakers of the two warrior lances of the Oglala, which had been given to the people in the time before horses. No one could remember exactly when, only that the spring grasses grew thick and tall when brave men carried the lances into battle. So it was done. Crazy Horse and He Dog carried the old lances into Crow lands.

The raiders returned undefeated with many Crow horses and scalps to show that the power of the lances had not diminished. He Dog and Crazy Horse had been the first to attack and the last to withdraw. During one fight, they had chased the Crows to the gates of the fort of their soldier friends. Though they made camp close by to rest, the Crows or the soldiers did not come after them.

Women from the No Water Camp helped with the victory feasts, since their old men and warriors had gone south to the fort along the Holy Road. One morning after the victory dances, whispers flew through the camp. Black Buffalo Woman had left her children with relatives and rode out beside the light-haired one. The hot sun of the Moon When the Sun Stands in the Middle shone brightly on them as they had ridden away openly and with friends along. No two people could agree over this new turn. Some said it was coming for a long time, since her father had made the choice of a husband for her when her heart belonged to the shy, quiet young man who was now the most powerful warrior among them. Others said there would be trouble;

though she was a good Lakota woman free to choose, her husband was not one to let her have that choice. Besides, the reasons
her father and uncle had influenced her choice of a husband
were even more important now, some said cautiously. And they
were right.

The couple and their friends came to a small camp in a narrow
little valley, and, there they rested. Little Shield, He Dog's brother,
and Little Big Man were along and made a feast. As night fell,
there came a commotion and a man tore into the lodge where
Crazy Horse and Black Buffalo Woman were guests, a man worn
from a hard trail and driven by the anger of a jealous heart. No
Water stood above them, a pistol in hand.

As Crazy Horse leaped to his feet, the pistol boomed.

Fifteen

He awoke in a lodge unfamiliar to him, but he knew the strong, old face that appeared as his eye cleared and he could see. One eye was still swollen along with the left side of his face. Old Spotted Crow, his uncle, the brother of Long Face, nodded a greeting and held him down as he tried to sit up.

"She is back with her people," the old man said in answer to the question on his face. "My cousin Bad Heart Bull made it so. No one will harm her."

He had been in and out of sleep for three days, he was told. The swelling on his face had gone down a little, but he would have a scar where the bullet had opened his face from the corner of his nose down to the jawline. There will be black powder in the scar from the pistol, Worm had indicated.

Two very fine horses were tied outside his uncle's lodge, sent by No Water as a gesture of peace. Take them, his father advised, to soften the anger of those who would take revenge in your name. So he did, and the young men who wanted No Water turned over to them set aside their anger and put away their bows and guns. Now the only worry was Little Hawk, away on a raid into Snake country. Worm sent a young man to find him and give him the news—that his brother wanted peace among the Oglala most of all, and that that was why he had given back the woman who had been in his heart since boyhood.

When the fever caused by the wound finally broke, Crazy

Horse rode back to his mothers' lodge and put himself in their care. One cleaned his wound with her special medicine and the other fed him good buffalo stew to make him strong again. And when he slept, they sang the soft lullaby only a mother can, for they wanted to heal the wound in his heart as well.

The man returned from the Snake country saying he had not found Little Hawk and some wondered if he had tried at all.

Day by day he grew stronger as his face regained its narrow shape and the wound was not as tender to the touch. Finally came the day when he was strong enough to ride along on a hunt, even if all he did was watch a buffalo chase from a hill. Young men came to exchange a few words of greeting, glad to see him well again. But no one said anything at all about Black Buffalo Woman and the trouble that almost caused Oglalas to spill each other's blood. Then one night the young men who had gone into Snake country with Little Hawk slipped back into camp. The raiding against the Snakes did not go well. On the way home, Little Hawk was killed by whites in an unexpected attack.

The news was like a war club to the stomach. As his mothers began to weep softly, Crazy Horse went out to stand alone in the night. His brother had been killed while he had been chasing after his own selfish needs.

The next day he saw No Water unloading meat at the lodge of a relative. Seeming to sense Crazy Horse's anger, No Water jumped on his horse and galloped out of camp. Perhaps unable to contain his anguish over both the loss of the only woman he wanted and the death of his brother, Crazy Horse grabbed the nearest horse and gave chase. Across the broken land, he kept up the chase until No Water plunged his horse into the Elk River and escaped to the other side.

Not many days after that, the council of old men met, influenced by the relatives of Red Cloud and No Water. Crazy Horse was to return the Shirt, they decided. His actions over the woman endangered the peace of the Oglala like no outside enemy could, they said, and could not be overlooked. Though there was anger in his own lodge—and from the young men—at this trickery, Crazy Horse gave back the Shirt. Soon after that, the lodge of No Water moved far south to another camp and whispers were made behind the hand that Red Cloud was to be given the Shirt.

But the angry whispers that flowed from camp to camp opened the ears of the council of old men. It would be just as dangerous to name another Shirt Wearer since the people didn't agree that it should have been taken from the light-haired one, and the old men didn't want to be the cause of bad blood by their actions. So they solved the problem by letting it lie, never to pick it up again. Never again would the Oglala have new Shirt Wearers.

High Back Bone returned from the north two months later and listened with hard eyes to the news of Little Hawk. News of the trouble over Black Buffalo Woman had already reached him, even far to the north. But there was other news as well. Old Spotted Crow and He Dog had talked to the family of Red Feather, a young man who thought well of Crazy Horse. There was a strong woman in that family, the older sister of Red Feather, who was still unmarried well past the time when women were. It was her choice to say yes or no to the offer made, and so Black Shawl became the wife of Crazy Horse.

The old women who had watched the light-haired one grow into a good man were satisfied that such a match had been made. So they pitched a new lodge close to that of his mothers, and it was good to see the wife of their headman set the red willow tripod to the right of the door and hang his warrior things from it. Such a thing showed the people that he was walking the path of life with a good woman.

Soon after the new lodge had been pitched, the new couple had ridden off together south toward the Sweetwater. It was a long and arduous journey, dangerous too, into enemy country.

But everyone knew that Crazy Horse was riding to find what might be left of his younger brother. They returned more than a month later and Black Shawl quietly told Red Feather that they had found the bones of Little Hawk and put them on a scaffold hidden from any enemy. Behind them came stories of Lakota raiding against miners sifting for gold in the cold creeks. Many had been killed but not scalped, and each body had a Lakota arrow impaled in the heart.

Crazy Horse said no words in response to those stories as he sat smoking his short-stemmed pipe, the sign that he had lost a place of high honor. But the young men in his camp noticed that he walked straight again with the sure step of a man who knows where he is going and where he has been. He did not sit in the council lodge with the old men, however, so he was not there when Red Cloud came to speak to them. He had been to see the "great father," riding for many days in the houses pulled by the iron horse. He talked of the rows of square houses in the towns of the whites, towns so large that a man would need a good horse and half a day to ride across one. It was easy to see that he was deeply impressed by the ways of the whites and of the things he had seen, among them buildings so large that a man with a strong bow could not send an arrow across from one side to the other. These things the old men heard with raised eyebrows. But when he talked of the treaty paper, they all leaned in close.

The land has a new beginning and a new ending, he said. New pictures of the land had been drawn and new territory had been set aside for all the Lakota to live in for as long as the grass grows and the rivers flow. Where, they asked, might be this new territory? East from the Great Muddy to west of the Black Hills, was the reply, and north from above the Running Water to a line that crosses east and west below the Knife River.

"What of the Powder River country?" a young man wanted to know.

The Powder River would always be Lakota hunting grounds,

was the straight-faced reply, but "we must move our camps to the new territory that the whites call the 'great reservation.'"

Throughout the Oglala camps, as in the Hunkpatila council lodge, there was anger and much debate. Clearly Red Cloud had agreed, in the name of the Lakota, to the whims of the peace talkers written on their paper. In return, he had been given his own place to live, his own agency. The young men felt that the paper had no power over the lives of any Lakota. They said, We are Lakota and these are our lands and we will not move our lodges here or there because one man made a mark on a paper, a paper with words that could not be known or understood by even the wisest Lakota. The white man can use those words, change those words, to fit his truth and his needs, was the angry sentiment.

The council at Bear Butte had given him the power to make his mark for the Oglala, Red Cloud reminded those who questioned him. That was true, some agreed, but in looking back, it was not the right thing to do.

Red Cloud returned to his own camp but kept away from Fort Laramie until the whites called him in to take charge of the distribution of wagonloads of goods. Many of the northern Oglala camps came to see what things the whites were giving in return for the power to tell the Lakota what to do and where to live. Ignoring the threats and ridicule of some young men, Red Cloud gave orders and the goods were placed in four very large piles—three for the headmen that he knew would stand behind him, and one for himself. So Long Knife Horse, Man Afraid, and Red Dog came forward to claim the goods for their camps. It was said there were over five thousand Lakota there.

There was one headman who had not brought his people down, and his absence was a loud message. Crazy Horse is doing the right thing, many of the young men said to one another. His power has grown the old way, in the hearts and minds of those who follow him. Perhaps, some said, I will take my family north and pitch my lodge in his camp.

Sitting Bull sent a message from the north when he had heard the white peace talkers say that Red Cloud now spoke for all the Lakota. *No one speaks for my people but me,* Sitting Bull had said, *and even then only in words they tell me to use.*

In the Moon When Leaves Fall, after the autumn hunts had been made and the meat containers were full, High Back Bone gave in to restlessness and invited Crazy Horse on a raid into Snake country. They rode over the passes of the Shining Mountains and crossed the Wind River into enemy lands. Here a rain came and turned the land into an endless bog. Horses were sliding and falling to their knees. Cold, wet moisture seeped beneath the robes and dampened the powder, and worse, made the bowstrings lose their tautness.

The scouts returned, having found a large camp—one that would not expect enemies to attack in this rain, High Back Bone thought. But Crazy Horse advised caution. There were only three rifles among them and bows were useless in the rain. For the first time in their friendship, High Back Bone scoffed at the younger man. If anyone was afraid, they could wait, he said; he would go on alone.

They split their force in two, High Back Bone leading one, Crazy Horse the other. But as they approached the camp, Crazy Horse held back because the horses had no good footing. High Back Bone rode to him angrily with a scolding.

"If you do not want this, you can go back, but I will stay and fight!"

They attacked, but the Snakes were too many. The two Lakota groups were too far apart to regroup and the mud was too deep, their horses tired. Somehow they managed to hold back the determined counterattack. Crazy Horse, High Back Bone, and Good Weasel, with their rifles, were the rear guard as the others retreated. First one fell back, then another, managing to keep the Snakes at bay. But several Snakes on fresh horses suddenly were able to surround High Back Bone, and Crazy Horse saw his old friend take a bullet in the chest. Still, the old warrior pulled out his pistol and emptied it at the onrushing enemy until they over-ran him. Crazy Horse rode in to rescue him, but his horse was too tired from pulling himself out of the mud and the enemy fire was too much. Good Weasel finally intervened, grabbing the rein to his horse.

The rain turned into snow as they rode toward home. Some-time in the night, they found a sheltered place and built a warm-ing fire while the horses rested. Crazy Horse sat huddled beneath his robe, alone with thoughts of his old friend and teacher. Their last words to each other had been in anger. And the one who had taken him from boy to man, the one who had given him the skill to be a fighting man and the heart to be a good man, lay dead in the mud.

Crazy Horse rested, and when their horses had regained strength and the snows stopped, he and his brother-in-law, Red Feather, returned to recover the body of his old friend. Coyotes had already scattered the bones about. They wrapped them in a good elk robe and took him home to his family.

Crazy Horse smoked his pipe and pondered all that had hap-pened since he and He Dog had carried the lances against the Crow. Much had been taken away, it seemed. First, Black Buf-falo Woman, then his place as a Shirt Wearer. Now his younger brother and his oldest friend were gone. He took little comfort in knowing they had died on the path they had chosen. There was only emptiness where they had been. Perhaps these things had come to pass because he had not fully honored the calling to be a Thunder Dreamer. Though he had learned the importance of honoring the old ways from his father and uncles, and his mothers, he was not one for ceremonies or standing in front of the people. But if he must live a life of sacrifice, he would. As a Thunder Dreamer, he did not belong to himself, he belonged to the people. It was not what he wanted for his life, but it was what life wanted from him.

The old men suggested they move to Rosebud Creek because the buffalo were moving in great herds, and it was always good to make more meat since the old weather women were fearful of deep snows coming. South of the Tongue, it seemed, there were fewer and fewer buffalo, which worried some of the old men. So they moved and camped close to the Mniconju and Itazipacola. The snows were deep and the winter winds did howl, but there was plenty to eat and there were many long visits in the lodges of relatives and friends, and long nights of storytelling from the old ones.

In the spring, they moved back south a little to find good grazing for the horses to grow fat and strong. An old woman, a relative of Black Shawl's family, had come to live in the lodge of Black Shawl and Crazy Horse. Many people came to visit in the lodge of the headman, and all needed to be fed, and, for this, the woman of the lodge needed help. Especially since she was expecting her first child.

In the south, Red Cloud was still arguing with the Long Knives and peace talkers because he wanted a different place for his agency. Some of the young men from the Crazy Horse camp rode south to see for themselves, Little Big Man among them. There were many Oglala camped around the fort, they saw, all waiting for the annuities from the whites while the women made soup from the meat of the longhorn cattle. With the annuities came a new agent, a "little father" not known to Red Cloud and one not so turned by his words. Perhaps, some suggested wryly, Red Cloud should travel east and speak with the "great father" about this.

But when the goods were distributed again, even some from the Crazy Horse camp struck their lodges in the night and went south. They returned before the summer was over, trying not to make a big thing over new skillets and white-man clothes. But they also brought disturbing news of hide hunters coming up from the Grandfather River with their wagons and far-shooting guns, bragging that each man could kill a hundred buffalo in one day.

The geese were starting to fly south when Black Shawl returned from the woman's lodge with a small bundle in her arms and a shy, uncertain smile on her face. Inside the bundle was not the future warrior son her husband had been yearning for, but a daughter. Crazy Horse lifted the tiny bundle gently and looked into the black eyes already trying to open.

"Good!" he said. "She shall be the mother of warriors and she shall be called They Are Afraid of Her."

A hard winter came on the heels of a short autumn, almost as cold as the Winter of the Hundred in the Hands, five years past. Many Oglala camps had moved north away from Fort Laramie, bringing smiles to the faces of the Crazy Horse people. Perhaps the power of the white man's annuities faded quickly, some women said. Until more come, others reminded.

Crazy Horse and the old men passed the winter worrying over all the things that those do who have the welfare of the people to carry on their shoulders. The Holy Road had caused the buffalo to move their trails. There were still a few herds in the Powder River country, a few more along the Tongue, it was said. And the Crow seemed to have plenty in their country, so perhaps it was time to think about moving and staying closer to the Elk. The Crow would have something to say about that, cautioned some. Yes, but life isn't worth living unless you have to defend it now and then, others replied.

And so the camps moved north and the Oglala joined the Mniconju and Hunkpapa south of the Elk for the Sun Dance in the Moon When the Sun Stands in the Middle. In the Moon When Calves Turn Dark some Hunkpapa found a large column of soldiers near a small tributary of the Elk. Warriors were sent out but Crazy Horse stayed behind a few days, worried that his young daughter seemed to have the white man's coughing sickness. When he joined the warriors, he saw that the soldiers had dug themselves in and they seemed to be shooting the same back-loading rifles he had seen at the wagon box a few years back. And, as then, a few Lakota had already been killed trying to be foolishly brave. Crazy Horse talked with Sitting Bull and the warrior leaders of the Hunkpapa and Oglala. The soldiers had too many guns and bullets, enough to defend themselves. It would be wise to withdraw and watch them. So long as they stayed away from any encampments, they should be left alone. So the Oglala and Hunkpapa rode away, though many thought it was not the right thing to do. One good Lakota lost left a bigger hole than one dead soldier, the older warriors said. Scouts caught up with Crazy Horse on his way back south to tell him that the soldiers rode away fast as soon as the Oglala and Hunkpapa were out of sight.

As the leaves were falling news came from the south. There had been some trouble over whiskey, and soldiers were sent to chase some Lakota. Red Cloud was also growling at the agent, but no one was certain what he was complaining about this time. Crazy Horse took this news with a smile.

They Are Afraid of Her was growing quickly, and the most powerful warrior among the Oglala was turned into a willing playmate with only a curl of her tiny mouth or a sparkle in her large dark eyes. Both her mother and father worried that she caught the coughing sickness often, and even her grandfather's medicine couldn't help. Nonetheless, she filled the lodge with the spirit of innocence and hope and mystified her parents.

Though the weather was not as harsh, the camps had to move far to find buffalo for the autumn hunting. Another lean winter passed. But spring has a way of chasing away the memories of even the bitterest of winters, and so it did. Summer came with good grass and just enough rain, and once again the people came together in the Moon When the Sun Stands in the Middle for the Sun Dance.

They clashed with the Crow, a little raid that turned into a hard fight lasting for several days. When it was all over, some good Lakota had been lost, but it was good to fight an honorable enemy, some said—though we still despise them, others laughed.

In the Moon When Calves Turn Dark, soldiers came up the Elk again, this time guarding canvas-topped wagons like those that traveled the Holy Road. Fearing that another Holy Road was being made, Crazy Horse and his young men rode out. But as they watched from a distance through their farseeing glasses, they saw no women and children, only men busy doing puzzling things that white men had a way of doing. One of the Sahiyela among them recognized the little markings that the soldiers wore on their blue coats and became angry. He was sure they were the same soldiers that had killed many of Black Kettle's people camped peacefully along a river called the Washita, down in the flat prairie country. The man was so angry he charged across the river after the soldiers, and the fight was on.

Though some joined the Sahiyela, they were fired upon heavily by the soldiers and had to return. Crazy Horse pulled his men back when he saw the soldiers preparing to fire a wagon gun. They moved away, leaving a few scouts to watch. They returned to report they had counted nearly a hundred soldiers.

Though Crazy Horse had more than twice as many fighting men by then, there were not half as many guns among them. The next day an ambush was tried, but the soldiers didn't chase the decoys, so Crazy Horse decided to simply harass them, hoping they would make some mistake the Oglala could take advantage of. They followed along the river for days, shadowing the soldiers, but the soldiers kept to their column and wouldn't chase them. One morning, the Oglala decided to try the ambush again; they charged across the river in a large group this time and drew the soldiers out once more. Back across the river they scattered into small groups, but the soldiers ended the chase before they could be led into the ambush. Their ammunition running low, Crazy Horse gave up the chase.[1]

1. This group was the Stanley railroad survey expedition of 1873, escorted by the U.S. Seventh Cavalry commanded by Lt. Col. George Custer.

The autumn winds were too cold, the weather women warned—a bad winter was coming. They were right. Hunters had to roam far to find the buffalo, and when the snows came, the meat containers were not full. So they had to probe along the river for elk and deer, but young cottonwoods were thin this year, so even those four-leggeds were hard to find.

News came up from Fort Laramie that Red Cloud's agency had been moved to the White Earth River, far north of where he had wanted. But his complaining to the agent fell on cold ears, and he was forced to move.

These things Crazy Horse listened to with deep concern. If the whites wouldn't listen to Red Cloud, then no Lakota had words that would open their ears, he thought. During a break in the weather during the Moon of Frost in the Lodge, he went alone south to the Medicine Water to fast and pray—to seek guidance so that he could carry all that fell on his shoulders. But though the winter seemed to pause to give him days of silence to be alone with his thoughts, no vision came to him.

He returned to his lodge still troubled by many things. One big concern was the buffalo becoming fewer and fewer since the one good year up on the Tongue. But he was most concerned about the coughing sickness that had now come to his wife. First his daughter and now his wife. He watched them sleep as he rubbed the scar on his face, remembering that so many changes had happened so quickly in only a few years. He prayed that the hard winter would be chased away by warm winds, and that the spring would bring strong new life.

Sixteen

Hunters returned empty-handed time after time to the encampments along the Powder River, with worn-out horses and the same frightening news: the buffalo were harder and harder to find. Many reported seeing nothing at all. A few saw only old bulls and let them go, knowing their meat was tough and stringy. Old meat was better than no meat, others said, but the elders kept their counsel, knowing there was something bigger to worry over. Their way of life was changing.

True, there was still elk that could be found anywhere—the black-tailed deer in the mountains and the white-tailed deer on the prairies. But the buffalo had always been the mainstay of life. They had covered the prairies from horizon to horizon only within the past generation. Now hunters had to ride for days to see just one. There was good reason for worry.

Crazy Horse hunted as often as he could. Like other hunters, he pursued elk or deer, often taking two packhorses with him far up into the foothill slopes of the Shining Mountains. Hunters were almost constantly in the field because the meat of seven or eight deer and four or five elk was equal to the usable meat of only one buffalo. Furthermore, lodge coverings could not be patched or repaired without fresh buffalo hides. It was out of the question to make new lodges since about twenty or more hides were required. Word came from the agency Lakota that the white man's canvas was very good for making lodges. Some of the old ones said, however, that canvas lodges rattled in the breeze and were outright noisy in a wind. Buffalo-hide lodges didn't make any noise even in the strongest wind.

Crazy Horse pondered all of these new and unwanted realities as he sat in his lonely hunting camps, the burden of a leader's responsibility heavy on his shoulders. Were the Lakota facing a future of living in noisy canvas lodges? It seemed unavoidable when hunters had to travel for days before they could find one or two buffalo.

No one but Wakantanka could replenish the buffalo. First the whites had to be driven away, completely out of Lakota country. That was for the Lakota to do, not Wakantanka. Within the span of his lifetime, they had always been around. Who could forget the day twenty years ago now that old Conquering Bear was killed, and the loudmouthed soldier Grattan who caused it? The cold hard truth was that white men brought trouble. The hide hunters killed buffalo in numbers that were hard to imagine, for example. One hunter with a powerful gun could kill hundreds in one day. Hundreds of hunters over hundreds of days over many years were most of the reason the buffalo were gone in this part of the country.

There was another cold, unbending truth: driving out the whites would take more fighting men than Crazy Horse had, and more guns, bullets, and powder than all the Lakota fighting men had together. To make matters worse, more and more Lakota were slipping away to live at the agencies, yearning after the material goods of the white man. His uncle Spotted Tail had taken his Sicangu Lakota people to an agency. And a goodly number of Oglala Lakota had followed Red Cloud out of the Powder River country to his own agency near the mouth of the White Earth River to the southeast. Who was left to resist? Who was left to say that the Lakota way of living was still good? Who was left to fight, if it came to that? Not many, Crazy Horse knew. Not even the buffalo, as it turned out.

As far as he could tell, Crazy Horse had about 150 fighting

men. Most of them were hardened veterans, all of them skilled and committed. He would lead them without hesitation against any enemy, Crow or white. And they would follow without hesitation. But what could 150 men, as good and brave as they were, do against a people whose numbers were like hailstones in the sudden thunderstorm? It was a bothersome sign of the times that he had to always think of fighting and resisting the whites. It was a sign of the times.

Undeniably, the whites were like the two-faced giant in the childhood stories the grandmothers told during the long winter nights. With an endless hunger, the giant ate anything and everything and trampled the land as he did, smashing all that lay in its path. The more it ate the larger it grew until it could leap across lakes and shake the Earth when it ran. For Crazy Horse, the giant was real. It had eaten all the buffalo.

He knew the two hundred or so families in his encampment could adjust to life without the buffalo in order to keep their free-roaming ways. At least most of them would. Life was always changing, after all. But this was different. This was unforeseen, unwanted change. Perhaps they were destined to live in noisy canvas lodges. If he had to, he would—so long as it meant staying free of the agencies, though he could not speak for everyone. Messengers came now and then from the agencies with stories of the easy life, stories that would have anyone believing that the new life with the whites was good, with the agency Lakota not wanting for anything. Soon after such visits, a few families would take down their lodges in the night, as if leaving at night would make their departure less painful for the relatives and friends left behind. The buffalo were becoming more and more scarce and so were the "wild" Lakota, as the agency people called the Crazy Horse camp as well as the Hunkpapa Lakota who were with Sitting Bull to the north.

The buffalo were almost gone, unbelievably, and more and more Lakota began living on the agencies. Such realities plagued

Crazy Horse as he sat alone at a dying fire in a shadowy gully far below the craggy peaks of the Shining Mountains. As a more-than-proficient hunter he could provide for Black Shawl, They Are Afraid of Her, and his parents. For any given year, every family needed fresh meat equal to one buffalo and perhaps the hides from twenty to thirty deer and elk for clothing and items for the household, such as sleeping robes and rawhide clothing and food containers. If survival depended only on hunting, life would be good. But even if there were enough elk and deer to feed the "wild" Lakota, there was always the problem of the whites. Survival also meant doing something about them.

That was one of the problems that haunted Crazy Horse, sometimes not letting him sleep. He was a worrier as it was, though he rarely voiced his concerns to anyone, not even to Black Shawl or his father, Worm. It was his place to worry because the people depended on him. Worrying came with responsibility. But he was not good at thinking and weighing all the factors of a situation when others were around. Strange that it was easier to function on the battlefield in the face of the enemy and in the midst of noise and chaos. One simply acted and reacted seemingly without thought. Facing the overall problems of life, however—especially as the one to whom the people looked for answers—was far more difficult.

People were constantly coming to his home to talk and the old men called him frequently to the council lodge. Consequently, it was difficult for him to be alone with his thoughts. And solitude had always been one of his best allies. So he sought out the solitude of the prairies or the mountain slopes. He needed the reassuring silence broken only by the passing breeze or the distant howl of a wolf. In such places, he could gather his thoughts and pile them up like stones and then examine them, one by one.

His friends and relatives thought he shouldn't wander off alone as much as he did. They worried after his safety, but also in their minds was the feeling that a leader's place was with the people. Many wondered what pulled him, what drove him to the solitude of a cave or a hidden camp, or to the shadowy place just below the crest of a ridge. They didn't know what he felt. They could only watch him ride away yet again.

Black Shawl wondered most of all, even as she silently prepared and packed food for him to take along. But she kept her fears to herself. They Are Afraid of Her would smile as he swept her into a close embrace and played with her—especially when they played with her favorite toy, the stuffed doll made of deer hide with a face painted on it. She smiled and giggled in great delight as her father pretended to rock the doll to sleep. But the smile would fade quickly from her little face as she watched him lead his horse away through the circle of lodges. Crazy Horse worried that she was so thin—that she sometimes didn't have the energy to play and would fall asleep in his arms.

They watched him in painful silence, his wife and daughter, as he would ride away, their eyes fixed on his back. He could see their faces in his campfires. But he could also see the pile of stones that were his thoughts, the burdens he carried, the many problems he had to solve. When a man belonged to the people, he no longer belonged to himself. How does one explain that to a four-year-old?

One of those stones was larger than the others. It was a giant growing larger with each passing year—a giant that had forced even Sitting Bull, the powerful Hunkpapa leader, away from the Great Muddy, pushing him west toward the Elk River country. Sitting Bull had refused to travel to the last treaty council at Horse Creek near Fort Laramie in the year the whites called 1868. He had sent word that he would never touch the pen to any treaty paper the white man had.

Sitting Bull knew what would happen, Crazy Horse was certain. The whites would use that treaty as a way to control the Lakota. They drew lines on a paper to outline the picture of the land, something not unknown to the Lakota. But the idea that an imaginary line could define where the land begins and ends was laughable—as if the line would somehow show up on the land. Even more laughable was the rule that the Lakota had to live in one part of the land and obtain permission from the whites to hunt in the other. Their thinking was laughable but it was their thinking and they had the power of numbers, many soldiers with many rifles, many wagon guns, and plenty of powder.

Part of the answer was to fight. There could be no other way, and it was coming to that. The whites understood force, how to use the threat of it effectively. Soldiers were always part of the treaty talks, prominently displaying their weapons and firing their thunderous wagon guns that splintered trees. Those wagon guns could obviously knock over several men at once. Therefore, behind the words of the white peace talkers was the killing power of the soldiers. As a whole, whites were willing to kill to get what they wanted. That had always been obvious to Crazy Horse. To put up a strong resistance and defeat them, Lakota fighting men had to meet force with force. They would have to kill as many Long Knives as possible, as many as it would take until they understood that coming into Lakota lands would always be dangerous. There could be no other way. But there was the unsettling probability that too many Lakota men would die before they could kill enough soldiers. If that happened, who would protect the women and children, and the old ones? Who would provide for them?

Some of the younger men were getting restless, anxious for some type of action. But most of them didn't understand that fighting the whites would be different than going against the Crow or the Snakes. The young ones barely into manhood couldn't remember a time when the white men were not a constant threat and the objects of animosity, or the topic of heated conversation in just about every lodge among the "wild" Lakota. Perhaps it would be wise to shape the young men into different kinds of fighters, some of the older men said to Crazy Horse.

The Crow and the Snakes understood the philosophy of being a warrior, that defeating an enemy didn't always depend on taking his life. Defeating one's enemy meant being better on a given day, overpowering his mind and spirit with the strength of your own being and the power you carried in your own spirit. Such victories were honorable. That certainly wasn't the philosophy of the whites. So perhaps it would be best to teach the young men, the new crop of Lakota fighting men, that whites didn't understand honor, that they only understood killing. He had said as much to the old men in the council lodge. His words were received with silent, somber nods because they all understood the kind of adversary they were facing in the white man.

Crazy Horse returned home to resurgent rumors that miners were going into the Black Hills in violation of the rules set down in the Horse Creek treaty. Gold was the reason. Ah, yes, gold, the white man's god. It was because of gold that the man called John Bozeman had laid out a trail for wagons from Deer Creek, just north of the Shell River to the south, northward through the Powder River country east of the Shining Mountains and on north into Crow lands.

The whites were willing to risk their own lives to get gold. Gold was the reason for their interest in the Black Hills, the heart of everything that was to the Lakota. The center of their world was apparently now coveted because of the misfortune of gold. It was the heated topic in the council lodge. The consensus was that something must be done. But the Lakota were too scattered—too scattered over the land and too scattered when it came to the issue of the whites. One of the old men suggested sending word to the agencies, a call to young men to join the "wild" Lakota under Crazy Horse and Sitting Bull. Everyone agreed, so it would be done. Meanwhile, Crazy Horse would lead a raid against the Crow to give their young men something to do, and to keep their edge as fighters. Doing nothing wasn't good, because it took away the edge, the sharpness. A good fighting man needed to remain taut, like a good bowstring. Without a good string that could remain taut, the best-made bow was useless.

Crazy Horse invited a few young men to go north into Crow country. Most of them were inexperienced and untested. Some of them probably wondered why the greatest fighting man among them, probably among all the Lakota, would invite them to accompany him. They soon deduced Crazy Horse's rationale, but were still grateful for the opportunity to learn from him.

The raiding party left the encampment in the Greasy Grass valley and went north toward the Elk River. This time of the year, the Crow moved away from the sheltering slopes of the mountains, usually to hunt buffalo. Surprisingly, however, the Lakota had to cross the Elk before they picked up fresh sign of human movement. They had seen several buffalo, so perhaps the Crow had a few more to hunt than they did. Keeping a wary eye on their back trail to the south, they kept moving north, staying east of the foothills of the mountains, looking for an encampment with enough horses to make a little raiding worthwhile. Not far from a bend in the Elk, they finally found a sizeable but well-guarded herd in a small box canyon. There was an encampment beyond it, a small one. The Crow always had more horses than they really needed. But as Crazy Horse studied the Crow camp through his farseeing glass, something caught his attention. The meat racks were empty and no women were busy scraping fresh hides, which was always a sure sign the hunting was good. In fact, not only was the camp just a few lodges in size, there was not much activity overall. Most of the people in sight were the boys and young men guarding the large horse herd grazing in the thin meadow of the box canyon. Something wasn't right.

From all outward appearances, the Crow camp was small and poor, with few women and children and only a few boys and young men guarding the herd. What *wasn't* in the camp was the more bothersome fact. Crow men, like the Lakota, were in the habit of picketing their best warhorses next to their lodge doors. There were none here. Where were the older men? Were they out on the hunting trail, on a raid, or simply hiding in the foothills all around?

Crazy Horse explained that they might have walked into a clever trap. He sent the young men in twos back to their horses, cautioning them to move silently and stay out of sight. They had to call on all the skills they had to move unseen and silently through the gullies and dry creek beds, using every stalk of the sparse brush for cover. He was the last to leave, scanning the terrain around his hiding place as he waited. Soon after, he rejoined his raiding party, where their horses were hidden in a pine-choked bowl below a ridge, and his suspicions were confirmed. Scanning through his farseeing glass, he spotted several groups of armed Crow, waiting and watching their own encampment.

The young men were worried and anxious, nervous to be so deep in enemy country and outnumbered. But they waited for darkness, taking their cue from the calmness of their leader. Crazy Horse devised a plan and whispered it to the young men as they waited for dusk to turn into deep, friendly darkness.

Each man would take his turn at scouting a path in the darkness for the distance of a good bowshot, then return and lead everyone to the farthest point he had gone. After that, the next would go and so on until they were well out of danger. Crazy Horse did the first scout, returned and led them through the darkness. When he called for volunteers, he was encouraged that all of the young men tossed down a stick as a sign to go next.

Dawn found them out of danger. Slipping away from under the noses of the enemy was no small feat, a solid victory in itself. The young men had done very well. They voiced no fear, nor did they complain. In among this group very well could be the man who would succeed in leading the Lakota to drive out the whites once and for all. Crazy Horse knew it would be that kind of fight, one that would test the resolve of good men for years, perhaps generations, to come.

A day later they spotted an old, crippled buffalo cow. How she had managed to escape the wolves or human hunters was a mystery. But in spite of her lean flanks and the dragging front leg, she had not lost her dignity. Knowing she couldn't run, she turned and faced the hunters as they approached her on horses. As their arrows drove into her sides, she bellowed and charged the nearest horse and rider. Her pursuit was so persistent the young Lakota had to whip his horse into a gallop to stay away from her. The cow finally gave in to her age and loss of blood, collapsing among the sagebrush.

It was a subdued feast after they butchered and skinned her. Drag poles were cut and tied together, the meat wrapped in the hide and loaded. The raiders, briefly turned hunters, set out for home. They had not battled the Crow or taken horses, but they had learned important lessons and were bringing home a little meat as well.

The encampment had moved from the valley of the Greasy Grass, leaving signs pointing in the direction they had gone, off to the southeast toward the Tongue River. There, along the bluffs above the floodplain, was the new encampment. Smoke from the cooking fires rose like wavering thin lances on a calm late afternoon. Riding into camp, the raiders noticed the first people to greet them smiled thinly, almost afraid to look in their direction. Worm emerged from his lodge and moved deliberately to meet his son. He was haggard, appearing as if he hadn't slept. His shirt hung in tatters, a sign of mourning.

"This is a time for you to be strong, my son," said the old man.

The village was unusually quiet. Worm pointed to the lodge next to his own. "Go," he said, "go comfort your wife. Be strong for her."

Inside the lodge, Crazy Horse found Black Shawl, her hair

loose, her dress torn, her forearms gashed, her eyes swollen from weeping.

Like many Lakota after a certain point in life, Crazy Horse was prepared for his own death. But no one could ever prepare for the death of one's child.

Reflections:
The Legacy of Leadership

Honest self-awareness should be an ingrained characteristic in a leader. Crazy Horse had many positive characteristics as a person and as a man, but I believe that the stepping stone to his rise and his growth as a leader was that he knew himself as well as he could. It was a direct consequence of the mentoring process that began at the age of five or six and continued for ten to twelve years. Its methodology was simple: one teacher (at a time) for one student, so the focus was entirely on the student. The lessons, the exercises, and the information were directed at developing the skills and abilities to be a hunter and a fighting man. At the end of those ten or twelve years emerged a young man who had all the requisite physical skills and basic knowledge necessary to begin fulfilling his role as a hunter/warrior.

Young Crazy Horse, while he was still known as Light Hair or *Jiji*, had a superb mentor by the name of *Tanitahu* or Backbone (of a buffalo). He was called Hump (also mentioned as High Back Bone), a Mniconju Lakota married into an Oglala family. Hump took a liking to the quiet, light-haired boy and became not only his mentor but his lifelong friend as well.

Hump taught the boy all the requisite skills, of course, but the ultimate lesson was self-reliance. The standard by which any boy was measured was, of course, the teacher. A good teacher didn't make things easy. A wise teacher taught the student to handle failure rather than to revel in the momentary euphoria of success. A wise teacher taught the student that what he held in his mind and heart were more powerful than any weapons he might carry in his hands—in other words, that knowledge and character win the battles more often than the bow, the lance, and the gun, that in the end the most powerful weapon a warrior takes into battle is himself. Therefore, each warrior must know honestly what he can and can't do and always strive to learn more from every experience.

It would be safe to assume that Crazy Horse, like all his peers, was eager to take his place as a fighting man, the warrior. When his dreams of becoming a warrior were fulfilled, they were replaced with dreams of being as good a warrior as he could be. There were certainly dreams of glory, of performing deeds that would bring individual recognition and honor to one's family. But dreams of glorious deeds invariably are crushed by the unexpected realities of war and combat. (One of the best non-Indian books on this topic is *The Red Badge of Courage* by Stephen Crane.)

The mentors that guided the young Crazy Horse and his peers through their learning process didn't say "don't dream of glory" or "reality is different than dreams." They knew that experience was the best teacher of all, so they simply placed young men into situations that would teach them the realities of being a warrior. There was glory to be had, of course, if one was willing to take the necessary risks, but young men soon learned that achieving glory was a small part of the path of a warrior. Dreams of glory dissipate with light speed when one catches sight of a live enemy intent on harm and mayhem, when the first shots are fired, and when one realizes that one's life is measured in mere heartbeats. Dreams then become plain unbridled hope that one will survive from one heartbeat to the next. Difficult situations obviously make or break one. At these moments the untested warrior battles his own inexperience while he endeavors to face the enemy. But if he somehow remembers even some of what he has been taught, he will live through the moment, and learn something about himself.

There will always be the philosophical question: Are leaders born or made?

While he was still a boy, Crazy Horse and some of his peers were taken on raids and patrols into enemy country. They were generally given menial but necessary chores to perform, such as gathering firewood for the camp or holding the horses. But in return they had the opportunity to observe experienced warriors in action, whether it was a scouting patrol or actually facing an enemy in the field. Over time and several outings they learned resilience, endurance, good judgment, courage, and perseverance—all the qualities that would keep them alive and enable them to fulfill their roles as protectors and providers. Just as important, they learned about their own strengths and weaknesses.

Most boys, therefore, basically learned the same lessons and were given the same opportunities to perform as fighting men. So how does a Crazy Horse emerge from a broad cultural blueprint and set himself apart? Perhaps he is testimony to the premise that some things cannot be taught. Perhaps there is something innate that some have and others don't. Men and women who coach young athletes point out that, while skills and methodology can be taught to any athlete, the physical attributes of speed and quickness are frequently the difference between a good athlete and an outstanding one.

Many people dream of becoming leaders, while others shun the opportunity even when it falls into their laps. General George Patton, of World War II fame, certainly sought the responsibilities of leadership and reveled in its rewards and prestige when he was successful. Crazy Horse, on the other hand, was not as quick to grab the opportunity when it came and literally had no desire to talk about his exploits. But both were exceptional leaders, and their accomplishments could not have been achieved without a certain amount of basic ability, as well as the experience of winning and losing. What is less obvious is that both of them also had inherent characteristics only a few of us have. Those characteristics enabled them to perform daring and reckless deeds and make bold decisions, and to inspire others to follow them. What those characteristics are by name or label is often difficult to identify, but the consequences they enable are not difficult to see.

There were many turning points in Crazy Horse's life. The Grattan incident of 1854 and General Harney's retaliatory attack on Little Thunder's village a year later shaped his attitude as a Lakota toward Euro-Americans. His ascension, if you will, to leadership began on a bitterly cold day in December 1866. That day and, more to the point, his actions on that day set him apart from other men. His actions, of course, were motivated by those characteristics not easily perceived on a day-to-day basis but which can and do rise to the top when it is necessary.

On that December day, Crazy Horse was not aspiring to rise to leadership heights; he was simply doing his best to perform the critically important task given to him by his elders. But because he performed his task so well, from that day on the responsibility of leadership was his, whether he sought it out or not. The lesson we can all take from this episode in Crazy Horse's life is that leadership is as much based on performance—actions—as it is on anything else, perhaps more. If a leader can demonstrate that something can be done, others will likely attempt to do it. Furthermore, the opportunities for leadership can come at any time, sometimes from directions and out of circumstances least expected, such as the construction and occupation of a log wall fort.

Fort Phil Kearny was built in the summer of 1866 in direct violation of an agreement between the United States government and the Lakota relative to roads and white military installations in Lakota territory. Neither was to happen without Lakota permission. The garrison was to protect Euro-Americans using the Bozeman Trail, which was laid out from southeast Wyoming north to Montana through the Powder River region, which was

Lakota territory. The fort was situated on Buffalo Creek at the foot of the Big Horn Mountains (halfway between the present towns of Buffalo and Sheridan, Wyoming), and was one of the few (contrary to Hollywood portrayals) military forts that actually had log palisade walls all around. The soldiers faced constant harassment by the Lakota from the moment they arrived to begin construction.

Although Lakota warriors outnumbered the soldiers in the fort, they were not as well equipped with firearms. When facing a heavily armed enemy, the obvious tactic is to use superior numbers to the best advantage, not to mention knowledge and familiarity with the terrain. But at least two attempts to draw soldiers into a fight away from the fort failed because younger, inexperienced men attacked prematurely. Consequently, the soldiers were doubly cautious. The council of old men in the Lakota camps advised Hump to make a final attempt. Knowing the soldiers wouldn't leave the safe confines of their fort to face a large force, Hump's plan was to decoy them with only a few warriors. Thus he chose Crazy Horse to lead and he in turn selected two Cheyenne and seven Lakota, ten in all.

A wood detail of one or two wagons and a small escort of soldiers regularly left the fort in the early morning to foray into the "pinery," the thick stand of pine a few miles west of the fort, for fuel and lumber. An attack on the wood detail would immediately bring soldiers out of the fort to effect a rescue. The objective was to lure those soldiers into the ambush and defeat them, thereby convincing the whites that the wise move would be to leave the Powder River country and stop using the Bozeman Trail.

No one among the Lakota and Cheyenne knew it was December 21; to them it was the Month of Popping Trees, with the air so cold that tree limbs cracked. But it was cold, very cold, and there was a patchy snow cover.

The wood detail left the fort, it was attacked about a mile from the fort, and, according to plan, a column of soldiers emerged from Fort Phil Kearny. The rest of the plan was simple: lure the soldiers into the ambush. That meant leading them across at least one creek, numerous gullies, steep, slippery snow-covered ridges and slopes, and frozen ground—a distance of five miles. There-after, it was up to Crazy Horse and his decoys to win the day.

Crazy Horse was in his midtwenties and his abilities as a fight-ing man were widely known; his reputation was well established, perhaps even surpassing that of his friend Hump. After Hump announced his choice for leader of the decoys, Crazy Horse was approached by tens of dozens of young men, all wanting to be picked as decoys. Hump was hoping that would happen. (Amer-ican Horse, His Enemies Are Afraid of His Horses, He Dog, and Little Hawk [Crazy Horse's younger brother] were the Lakota decoys that most of the old storytellers agree on. The names of three remaining Lakota have been forgotten. The two Cheyenne were Big Nose and Bird Ash.)

Crazy Horse was confident in and realistic about his own skills and abilities and his experience, and he was aware of his limitations as well. Most of the men who wanted to be picked were more than qualified as far as physical skills and abilities were concerned. But Crazy Horse was the only one who could have led the decoy warriors at this particular time for this partic-ular mission. By picking him, Hump had won the battle before the first shot was fired.

The soldiers had two opportunities to prevent the eventual outcome. The first came at the moment the field commander of the eighty-man column saw the decoys. The opportunity was only fleeting, however, lost forever the moment he gave the com-mand to pursue, because from that moment on his fate and that of his soldiers were in the hands of Crazy Horse. There are two kinds of people most dangerous in combat: the lucky one and the battle-hardened fighter supremely confident in himself. On this frigid morning in the Month of Popping Trees, Crazy Horse was both.

To the soldiers, the small force of attacking Indians likely seemed disorganized and uncertain. Some were on foot and running for their horses. Probably feeling certain of a quick victory over such a small group, the soldiers left the wood road and turned north in pursuit. The decoys were like the mother sage grouse with the useless wing that prevented her from flying, so she could barely manage to stay a few jumps ahead of the pursuing coyote. Such a ruse hardly ever failed the sage grouse.

The apparently frightened and disorganized Indians moved north, staying just ahead of the soldiers. Lodge Trail Ridge stood four miles north; beyond it was the waiting trap. And here was the soldiers' second opportunity to save themselves. Unknown to Crazy Horse, the fort's commander had ordered the field commander, Captain William Fetterman, not to proceed beyond Lodge Trail Ridge under any circumstances. That second opportunity disappeared the moment Captain Fetterman ordered his soldiers to move off Lodge Trail Ridge in pursuit of the decoys.

Euro-American history labels the battle as the Fetterman Massacre. Every man in the Fetterman column was killed when the trap was successfully sprung in a fight that lasted perhaps forty-five minutes. The Lakota and Cheyenne call it the Battle of the Hundred in the Hand. A seer had a vision of catching a hundred soldiers in his hands, a prediction of victory. But it was not an easy victory. It was a ferocious battle with the soldiers acquitting themselves well and inflicting heavy casualties. Many Lakota and Cheyenne were wounded, although probably not as many were killed as is believed. Analysis of the Fetterman Massacre/ Battle of the Hundred in the Hands has been predominantly from the viewpoint of it as a defeat for the Eighteenth Infantry. Indeed, the army branded the fort's commander, Colonel Henry Carrington, as the scapegoat and relieved him of duty. Rarely is any analysis done on the factors that brought victory for the Lakota. Such a study will reveal that the primary factor was the leadership of one man: Crazy Horse.

Crazy Horse had been given a formidable task: to draw the soldiers away from the fort and then entice them to pursue his decoys for five miles. To make matters more interesting, the air temperature was well below zero and the ground, if not covered with snow or ice, was frozen. Footing for unshod horses was treacherous.

Crazy Horse set the stage by riding back and forth in front of the advancing soldiers, drawing their fire. Others, like Big Nose the Cheyenne, followed his lead. All the decoys carried firearms but were woefully short of ammunition. Crazy Horse had four rounds for his breechloader. All were armed with bows and carried thirty to forty arrows. They fired on the soldiers or launched arrows with enough frequency to draw them into a running fight. The fact that about half of the soldiers were mounted (they were mounted infantry and not a bona fide cavalry unit) and half were on foot slowed their progress. But they were drawn into the ruse.

Amazingly there were no casualties among the decoys, except for one who was blown off his horse by the concussion of the earlier howitzer round. He remounted and joined the fray. (Big Nose was killed in the subsequent battle.)

Crazy Horse and his decoys pulled out all the stops. Amazingly they were able to lure the column of eighty soldiers nearly five miles. Just as amazingly, the warriors waiting in ambush attacked only when the signal was given. These factors were a consequence of the dynamic leadership of the young Crazy Horse and his mentor, Hump. True victory is rarely achieved without it. Both of them, as well as the older leaders, realized there was a bigger purpose at hand than winning one battle. They were defending their territory and their way of life against an imperialistic enemy.

The Battle of the Hundred in the Hand was a turning point for Crazy Horse. His leadership obviously shaped the eventual outcome and lifted him head and shoulders above other fighting men. It forever identified him as a man who could inspire others.

But just as important, he learned something about the enemy. The soldiers were an extension of a people who were willing to exterminate whatever obstacles lay in the path to their objective. Defeating them would require nothing less.

Non-Indian historians and writers are fond of postulating the observation that Crazy Horse wanted to emulate the "superior" tactics of the soldiers. But the Lakota, in their own environment, had the superior tactics and were better trained as fighting men. Crazy Horse realized that the definition of warfare was different for soldiers and the society they represented. Therefore tactics were not the issue, methodology was. The soldiers fought to inflict as many casualties as possible and thereby reduce their enemy's numbers. However, like many indigenous people of the Plains, the Lakota, while realizing that war was often part of human interaction, regarded it as a proving ground and not always necessarily a means to achieve national objectives or an instrument of policy. To put it bluntly, Crazy Horse realized that the only way to defeat the soldiers was to kill them as opposed to dazzling them with feats of courage. Warfare of attrition was the whites' own methodology and it would be necessary to use it against them in order to successfully defend Lakota lives and territory.

But in spite of the victory at the Battle of the Hundred in the Hand, Crazy Horse was not yet in a position to broadly affect the thinking of the older leaders. And when the forts along the Bozeman Trail were abandoned, many of those older leaders regarded it as a victory, a direct consequence of military action. However, the fact of the matter was the Bozeman Trail was no longer necessary as a route to the Montana gold fields. A rail line to the north along the Yellowstone (Elk) River shifted the U.S. government's focus and Red Cloud and the Oglala were allowed to think they had won a war. When the whites ceased to be a consistent presence in the Powder River region, the Lakota shifted their focus as well: out of sight, out of mind. Crazy Horse stayed in the north, refusing to go near Fort Laramie and relieved at not having to see or contend with white people on a regular basis.

As much as Crazy Horse wanted to avoid contact with whites, however, Fort Laramie and the Oregon Trail were still both unwelcome intrusions because they meant the whites were not going away. As much as he and the people who flocked to him hung on to their own nomadic, hunting life, there was always much discussion about the whites overall. News flowed constantly from the Lakota camps near the fort and the trail, so the northern camps were never out of touch. It was during this period that Crazy Horse made a critical error in judgment in his personal life. He tried to take another man's wife.

Black Buffalo Woman, Red Cloud's niece, was the love of his life. Politics, however, influenced her choice for a husband. She married No Water only because he was also of an influential family and their union enabled a broader influence and a stronger political power base. Crazy Horse was, of course, heartbroken. In time the wound seemed to heal, but, as is often the case, a true love is never completely forgotten. A few years later when the opportunity arose, Black Buffalo Woman followed her heart and left her husband. Lakota women could make such a choice because societal norms allowed it, but in her case a jealous husband did not.

Crazy Horse had put himself in harm's way many times as a fighting man. But he probably never came as close to dying as he did when No Water showed up with a borrowed pistol and shot him in the face. It was No Water's intention to kill Crazy Horse, and he thought he did. The subsequent furor brought several factions to the brink of bloodshed. On one side some wanted to defend No Water and on the other some wanted to avenge Crazy Horse. To prevent any violence, Crazy Horse gave up the love of his life for the second time.

Those who were jealous of him were quick to influence the old men leaders to strip him of the position of Shirt Wearer. Crazy Horse willingly gave up the shirt, but the status he had achieved circumvented the loss of influence. Many people, though not totally overlooking his mistake, still regarded him as a strong leader and remained loyal to him. It was a lesson not lost on him. Never again did he put his own desires above the needs of the people. That was yet another example for others to follow.

True leadership is rarely the consequence of election, appointment, dictatorship, or inheritance. Good leadership overall is much too critical to be left to elected politicians, monarchs, managers, administrators, supervisors, and directors. Having authority does not make anyone a leader. True leadership is exercised when someone performs a necessary or critical task and accomplishes an objective, thereby setting an example. Leadership by example, then, is the truest and most effective kind. We are more likely to follow someone who has done it before he or she asks or tells *us* to do it. Most of us will never face the daunting task of leading men and women into combat, but we will likely have the opportunity to set an example. We may not carry titles such as president, governor, mayor, general, or even chief, but we can be leaders simply by demonstrating that effort can be made, tasks can be accomplished. Furthermore, setting an example means that one has the benefit of firsthand experience. Personally, I would rather follow someone who has been through the swamp than someone who has only a map as a guide.

Leaders are in every walk of life, waiting for the opportunity to unlock the intangible characteristics that will set them apart, if but for a moment. But having had that moment, one will always know that one can be a leader when the need or the occasions warrants. Once a leader, always a leader, because we can only be true to what we are and have done.

Long ago a hunter heard strange noises somewhere on the prairie. He cautiously searched for the source, pausing to listen to growls and roars of pain and rage, and to the sound of trees and shrubbery apparently being torn apart. Then there was silence. Curious, the hunter continued to search until he came to a scene of mayhem and death.

A grizzly bear and a badger lay dead. The ground, trees, and grasses all around them showed signs of a great struggle, a battle to the death. But it was the dead combatants that fascinated the hunter. The badger's jaws were still clamped to the bear's snout; thus they were locked together forever. The hunter could only surmise that, although the bear had shredded the badger's body, the smaller animal did not relinquish his hold. In turn, the badger had torn out the bear's eyes and inflicted deep wounds on his head, causing the bear to bleed to death.

The hunter walked away, impressed by the tenacity of the badger and vowed to emulate him. To the very last the badger had remained true to what he was.

Part IV

The Road to
Camp Robinson

Seventeen

He found her scaffold at the top of a little hill overlooking a small valley north of the Big Horn River. That he was on the borderlands of the Crow did not concern him. He stopped at the scaffold, no higher than his chest. The buffalo-hide bundle tied to the top of it was so small. From the support poles hung a dewclaw rattle, a small wooden hoop, and the stuffed deer-hide doll with a face painted on it.

Death was not new to him. He'd been taught that it was part of life and that sooner or later everyone dies, as his mother had. Lone Bear, High Back Bone, and Little Hawk were gone, too. Men died in battle sometimes—and he was not surprised that they were gone, or at the way they had died as fighting men. But the bundle atop this scaffold was a harder reality. It was a reality that challenged the goodness in life. He fell across it and wept uncontrollably.

Days passed. There was thunder, some wind, and a little rain. When he could no longer stay awake, he slept beneath the scaffold curled up under a robe. He ignored hunger and thirst. Worm had told him a kind of coughing sickness, unknown before the whites came, had taken her. Though he had tried, he could find no medicine to help her.

Finally, when no more tears would come, Crazy Horse took his leave.

The news that awaited him fanned his anger even more. Soldiers had gone into the Black Hills—a large contingent, according to the sketchy reports from a few Lakota who had the misfortune of being in the wrong place at the wrong time. A group, friendly to the whites, had been watching the column of wagons and soldiers when they were attacked. One of the Lakota was killed and another wounded. They somehow managed to escape to tell their story.

The Black Hills in the hands of the whites was the culmination of one of the worst Lakota fears. It was for the gold—so much so that the whites deliberately sent a large and well-armed column of soldiers. But there was another equally galling fact that gnawed at Crazy Horse: the Lakota were not in a position to throw up any significant resistance.

Lakota fighting men should have been there to attack in force. Every man in camp would have followed Crazy Horse, but they would have suffered heavy losses because they had few bullets and little powder. Soldiers were always well armed, and now the advantage of numbers was on their side. So they were able to travel through the Black Hills along their "Thieves Road" in relative safety to accomplish whatever task they were sent in to do. Every Lakota knew the soldier's task was to find the gold, something the whites had always been willing to die and kill for.

A few visitors from the agency brought word that confirmed this news. But the soldiers weren't alone. Behind them came the miners.

News of gold in the Black Hills had spread through white towns to the east, the visitors said, faster than a wind-whipped prairie fire. The feeling among the Loafers was that the Black Hills were lost and nothing could be done. So many gold-hungry whites were coming into the Black Hills that there weren't enough warriors to keep them out.

Crazy Horse mulled over all the disturbing news and the implications for the future of the Lakota as he sat secluded in his lodge, a pile of brush outside the door to show he did not wish to be disturbed. The gashes across Black Shawl's forearms had not yet scarred. She would always mourn, as he would. She was coughing less and had more of an appetite. She knew that he was preparing to leave again.

Black Shawl fixed a meal for them and prepared the dried meat he would need to take along. He carefully inspected enough arrows to fill two quivers and counted his few bullets. Sometime after they had eaten, he took her hairbrush and gently brushed her hair, though it was not as long as it once was. In mourning for their daughter, she had to cut it to her shoulders. She accepted the gesture in the same spirit that it was given. From his paint bag, he prepared a little mixture, and, with the tip of his finger, colored the part down the middle of her head. He had painted it red. Tomorrow, after he had gone, she would walk among the people and they would see the coloring and know that she was a woman greatly loved. But for the coming night, they would hold off tomorrow and sleep beneath the soft, comforting buffalo robe. They would hold each other close, perhaps pretending there were no troubles in the world.

The next morning, Crazy Horse and a small group of hardened veterans set out east toward the Black Hills. Feeling relatively secure in their own territory, they traveled swiftly. They carried an assortment of firearms, a few muzzle-loading rifles, a few cap-and-ball pistols, and some breech-loading single-shot rifles captured at the Battle of the Hundred in the Hand eight years earlier. Powder and bullets were in short supply, however, so as a backup each man had a bow, some two, and at least one quiver of forty or so arrows. Lances, knives, and hand clubs for close-in fighting rounded out their arsenal.

A few days out, one of them hid near a waterhole and lured an antelope to within bow range by waving a raccoon tail on a stick. The fresh meat tasted of sage but it was welcome fare. As usual, the men gorged on the trail, eating as much of the roasted meat as they could. Days later, they could just barely make out the summit of Bear Butte, and from there they turned southeast into the mountains.

Traveling into the Black Hills—even simply observing them from a distance—always evoked a moment of reverence, an unspoken acknowledgment of all that this sacred place meant. Such feelings were often hard to put into words, so one simply paused and looked and allowed images to have their impact. Now there was a dark feeling, an undercurrent of uncertainty mixed with anger over the blatant invasion by the whites.

One of the men suddenly spoke of his sister, a young woman who had been abducted by soldiers when the family had visited relatives near the post on Horse Creek years earlier during the height of white movement on the Holy Road. When she didn't come home, the family thought she was staying with a cousin. Days later she returned, so withdrawn into herself that she spoke to no one for days. When she finally did, her story broke her mother's heart and sent her father into a rage. Only the influence of her closest friend prevented him from taking revenge. Months later, the girl gave birth to a light-skinned baby with gray eyes. She would have nothing to do with the child and her mother finally gave it away to relatives who raised the boy. In the storyteller's opinion, what had happened to his sister was happening to the Black Hills. No one could disagree, and so they rode on in silence.

Not only were these mountains the place of Crazy Horse's birth, they were the center of the Lakota world, which carried far more meaning. *The heart of everything that is.* Sun Dances were done here near Bear Butte and on its summit; many boys on the edge of young manhood, and men seeking to rediscover their path, did the vision quest. No one knew how many Lakota were laid to rest here in these mountains—over countless seasons their flesh and bones becoming one with this most sacred of places. There was no way to own these mountains, not in the sense one owned clothing or a weapon. But this was a place to feel connected, truly related to *everything that is*. It was a place that owned the Lakota. Any of these truths were reason enough to protect the Black Hills at all costs.

No one could have imagined that years, no, generations ago— when the first trickle of whites edged their way into Lakota lands— that it could come to this. Crazy Horse played in these great mountains as a boy. He had hunted here as boy and man, and as much as he loved the Shining Mountains and the Powder River region, no place defined his sense of being like the Black Hills.

The rumors and fears were true. Whites were in the Black Hills and were not hard to find. Along just about every stream, groups of them had set up strange wooden boxes through which they ran water. They were young and old, bearded, unkempt, and busy. Many of them simply dipped flat pans into the water and swirled it around. Watching from hiding, Crazy Horse and his men marveled at how much danger the miners were willing to face, how much discomfort they were willing to endure to find the gold. Gold, it was said, could buy anything for them including horses, dwellings, weapons, clothes, food, and women. It was a strange way to live, the Lakota thought as they watched the busy miners. Most of the little camps had no one on watch as sentinels to look out for any kind of danger. Finding the gold was apparently more important than their safety.

The tactics Crazy Horse and his companions used were simple, yet effective. After observing isolated miners' camps to determine their numbers and weapons, they positioned themselves and swept in. If the terrain was rough and offered good cover, they sneaked in close on foot before they attacked. In open areas with little cover, they charged in on horses. In either situation, they used their lances and war clubs and the silent bow quite effectively. Rarely did any miner react quickly enough to fire a gun, which worked in the Lakota's favor. Without gunshots to warn anyone else in the area, miners in the next valley or watershed remained oblivious and thus vulnerable to attack.

It was only a matter of time, however, before the whites began to discover the bodies left behind by Crazy Horse's attacking force. But by then, the number of miners in the northern part of the Black Hills had been considerably reduced. After a wild shot by a terrified miner wounded a good man, Crazy Horse decided their foray was over. It was time to go home. With a string of pack mules they had captured, with many usable items still in their packs, such as butcher knives and iron cooking pots, they turned their horses westward. The most valuable booty, however, was rifles, pistols, and bullets. One of the men had given Crazy Horse a new kind of repeating rifle he had found, one that could be fired nine times before it had to be reloaded.

It was necessary to attack the miners and kill them. They were trespassers and thieves, not honorable enemies. The tactics they used were the only way to fight them, especially in the Black Hills. Strike hard and fast, inflict as much chaos and as many casualties as possible, and withdraw swiftly. That kind of fighting would play to the Lakota's strengths and skills as fighters good at close combat. Crazy Horse spoke these thoughts to his companions as they rode home, and they listened and agreed. They had seen firsthand what could be done. If enough Lakota fighting men could be persuaded to fight in the same way, and if enough bullets and powder could be obtained, the whites could be driven away.

"How many bullets would we need to drive all the whites away?" asked one of them. It was a difficult question to answer because no one knew how many whites walked the face of the earth.

Crazy Horse found the duties of leadership waiting at home. The council of old men wanted to hear about the raiding, and so he told them. The pack mules, as well as the items in the packs, were given away to families who needed them. Crazy Horse spent long days in the council lodge with the old men; sometimes they talked far into the night. He felt a sense of restlessness at doing nothing but talking, especially given the sense of satisfaction from the successful raids against the miners in the Black Hills.

But he realized that he was at a turning point in this life, a time when his experience was broad and he had much to draw on. He wasn't ready to stop leading men in the field, but it was clearer that common sense and good thinking were as effective as dynamic, action-oriented leadership. He had a newfound appreciation for the wisdom of the old men. Yet the sense of restlessness wouldn't dissipate.

Worm came to visit and got around to urging his son to exercise more caution when facing the enemy. Crazy Horse's companions had told of their actions against the miners in the Black Hills and described how their leader was always the first to charge. Worm was concerned that his son was too reckless, admonishing that he had more than a family to worry over him. A leader had many families to think of and shouldn't forget there were matters to attend to other than leading fighting men. There were other men capable and qualified to do that. But the old man's underlying concern was his son's state of mind after the death of his daughter. Recklessness was Crazy Horse's way as a fighting man and it served to inspire other men to fight harder. Yet it was only natural to wonder if recklessness could now be a way to seek death, a way to challenge his boyhood vision, in a way, especially after the unexpected death of a beloved daughter. Worm understood only too well the confusing swirl that grief caused.

Crazy Horse listened to his father, taking no exception to the older man's words and concerns. Worm was right. The nation was split, the sacred hoop of the people was broken. There were now two kinds of Lakota, those living on agencies and the few still living the true path. Without good leadership, the two factions would remain divided and the situation would get worse before it got better, if at all. That was the reason the whites sent soldiers into the Black Hills. They knew the Lakota couldn't mount an effective resistance with most of the able-bodied men languishing on the agencies. Now the Loafers were suggesting the Black Hills were lost.

Crazy Horse knew what his father was trying to say. A leader had to consider issues bigger than his personal burdens. One of the old men on the council had suggested that the future of the "true Lakota," as he put it, rested with Sitting Bull and Crazy Horse. In the opinion of that old man, the Loafers were tainted, by and large more interested in pleasing the Long Knives so that annuities and food rations would be provided. Therefore, they could no longer be regarded as true Lakota, or trusted to act for the good of the nation. The old man, speaking for all the old men, was pointing out that a responsibility beyond the two hundred families in this encampment rested on Crazy Horse's shoulders. Of course, he could walk away from it if he chose. But now, perhaps more than at any other time before, the Lakota needed strong leaders.

Disturbing news came north from the Red Cloud agency, and perhaps within the story was the very reason for the need for strong leaders. The white Indian agent, a diminutive but brash man by all accounts, had insisted once again that all the Lakota living within treaty-designated territory be counted. When that notion had first been voiced, Red Cloud himself had answered with a resounding "no." When the agent decided to withhold food rations until the agency Lakota complied, Red Cloud refused again, warning that the agent was running the risk of fomenting unrest among some of the younger men. But to prevent hardship for the women and children and old people, two younger leaders—Young Man Afraid and Sword—complied and allowed their camps to be counted. Some of the "wild" Lakota who had been encamped closely to the north of the agency to visit their agency relatives broke camp and hurried away to avoid detection. The agent had his count: ten thousand Lakota, it was said. But, sadly, it was becoming clear that Red Cloud's influence was waning and his judgment was in question.

Ten thousand Lakota, and within that number just over a thousand fighting men, more than enough to wipe out the whites at the agency. Crazy Horse marveled at the power the white agent must have, or the power Red Cloud no longer did. If a thousand Lakota warriors had overwhelmed the soldiers at and around the agency and taken control, the message such an action would have sent across Lakota country would have been loud and strong. But the agency Lakota, apparently seduced by the rations of poor longhorn cattle and a few blankets, let the opportunity pass.

Crazy Horse was sickened by the implication that the Loafers empowered the white Indian agent to that extent. It was hard to believe that so many grown and capable men would stand by while a small group of whites—surrounded like a small island in a river—held sway over them. As the months went by, the circumstances indicated that perhaps the agency Lakota would have been wise to take some kind of action when there had been the opportunity.

Because the buffalo were few, the "wild" Lakota hunted during the autumn for deer and elk to make meat for the winter. When the snows came, they were prepared because the old ones warned of hard times; the horses grew their winter hair early, the bears were unusually fat, and the geese flew south early. When the howling winds came, the Crazy Horse people tightened their doors and ventured out into the deep snow only when absolutely necessary. Overall, they were more fortunate than the agency Lakota.

Deep snow kept the freight wagons at the railway stations with the annuities and food rations intended for the agencies. No white herders would risk life or limb to drive the longhorn cattle from the rail terminals to the agencies. The "wild" Lakota were at least free to hunt if their meat ran low; at the agencies, the people living the "good life" under the care and protection of the whites had to eat their horses to survive, and they shivered throughout the long winter.

Spring came, but the only improvement was in the weather. Miners poured into the Black Hills as soon as the snow melted.

Messengers arrived from Sitting Bull. The Hunkpapa holy man was suggesting that the people gather to talk before it was too late. As if underscoring his concern came news that Red Cloud was going east to speak to the "great father" in Washington.

Crazy Horse and the old men agreed that they should keep an ear to the ground. Red Cloud's trip east would certainly affect everyone because the whites didn't understand, or simply ignored the fact, that there were different opinions among the Lakota. The camp moved south, with some of the young men going directly to the agencies to remind the agency Lakota, especially the Red Cloud people, that there was still another way to live.

Red Cloud, it was learned, was making the trip to persuade the powers in Washington to remove the little agent from his agency. Crazy Horse could only smile wryly at the news. He saw it differently. Going to the seat of white power was the same as saying that living on agencies was the future for the Lakota. Perhaps some did actually say that to the "great father." When all was said and done, it didn't matter who the agent was on the Spotted Tail agency or on the Red Cloud agency. As long as there was an agent and the Lakota accepted annuities, the whites were in control. But when Red Cloud and the others returned—and there were many supposed headmen who made the trip—the news they brought back incensed the "wild" Lakota. The "great father" wanted to buy the Black Hills.

Sell the heart of everything that is? Sell the dust of the ancestors? Crazy Horse was so disgusted at the news that he traveled north near Mniconju Lakota country to visit with Young Man Afraid. They had had their differences, but Young Man Afraid was a thoughtful man and rarely acted on impulse, and Crazy Horse wanted to hear what his friend thought about recent developments.

Young Man Afraid likened the situation to the people suddenly finding themselves at the edge of an approaching storm. The storm would come whether the people faced it or hid from it. The Lakota had two choices, and only two, in his opinion. Fight the whites or step aside and let them come.

The two friends agreed that something needed to be done and that in all probability a war with the whites the likes of which they had never known lay ahead. Crazy Horse left Young Man Afraid's camp with a heavy heart but at the same time with a sense of vindication. Not everyone was in agreement with Red Cloud and Spotted Tail's approach to dealing with the whites. They had all but stepped aside to let them come, Spotted Tail basing his position on the fact that there were too many to fight. There was a very difficult choice facing all the Lakota: one's life or one's freedom. *Better to lie a warrior naked in death than to be wrapped up well with a heart of water inside.* This was the creed by which he had lived as one whose calling was to protect the people and the Lakota way of life. Living on an agency under the control of whites was not Crazy Horse's definition of life or the Lakota way. It was Spotted Tail's right to make a choice, and Red Cloud's as well. Overall, he thought no less of them, but he was firmly convinced they were wrong, and because of who they were, they had the power to mislead many people. If war was on the horizon, as Young Man Afraid had said, then it was a war to defend all that was right and sacred; it was not a war to infringe on others and take their land. Such a war must be fought with all the skill and commitment possible. It was the only way.

Crazy Horse and the young men who accompanied him went home by way of the Black Hills and managed to harass a few miners. But they were low on ammunition, not to mention anxious to return to their families. So they reluctantly avoided further contact even though miners were easy prey. The news awaiting them made them wish they had carried out more attacks while they had the opportunity. The "great father" was sending his peace talkers to persuade the Lakota to sell the Black Hills. A solemn promise was sent ahead. They would bring with them wagon after wagon piled high with gifts to show their good faith.

More than ever Crazy Horse felt the weight of responsibility. He was afraid that armed conflict with the whites on a scale never before seen was imminent. They were determined to have the Black Hills and would pressure the old men leaders among the agency Lakota to give their consent. He knew most of the old men among the agency people understood that one or a few men couldn't speak for all the Lakota. More important, those old men understood what the Black Hills meant to the people. But most of those old men didn't have much influence with the whites. A refusal from them would mean little, unless Red Cloud and Spotted Tail stood with them. Perhaps, suggested some, Red Cloud and the headman who had gone east had already sold the Black Hills. The only hope was that the very real possibility of losing the Black Hills would at least philosophically unite the Lakota. It would serve as the one issue behind which enough fighting men could stand. Sitting Bull, it seemed, had already realized that, sending out his call to gather. Crazy Horse understood the rationale behind the Hunkpapa Lakota leader's message. Among the "wild" Lakota were not enough able-bodied men to put in the field against the whites. Most of the Lakota fighting men were on the agencies eating beef and pork and losing their edge as fighters. Meanwhile, the white peace talkers were coming to talk the Lakota into selling the Black Hills. Crazy Horse agreed with Sitting Bull's logic: no matter what the agency Lakota did, the Black Hills and Lakota lands were not for sale. If the land were to be lost, and since the buffalo were already disappearing, the last vestige of being Lakota would disappear. So Sitting Bull was right. The first battle was for the hearts and minds of Lakota fighting men, because anything that was still meaningful to the Lakota— land and the way of life—must not be given away for meaningless words written on a paper and wagon loads of trinkets. Therefore, enough fighting men had to join the side of right because the next and final battle would be to defend the land—because defending the land was to defend the true Lakota way of life.

Back at the camps in the shadows of the Shining Mountains, the routine of life went on as usual. Children played within the circle of lodges, the most reassuring sign of all. Within them were the seeds of reassurance that the Lakota way of life would go on. Whatever happened, they had to be given the opportunity to fulfill their lives as true Lakota.

A few older boys were playing the Arrows-in-the-Hoop game, trying to shoot arrows through a wooden hoop rolled on the ground. Not far from them several girls watched over babies strapped in cradleboards. One child was conspicuous by her absence. She would be approaching her fifth year if she were down there with the rest of them. But she wasn't. She ran and played in memory, where her scurrying footsteps raised no dust, only melancholy sighs.

More news came from the agencies. The white peace talkers had set a time and a place for their council. They would come in the Month of Leaves Turning Brown, the one they called September, to Red Cloud's agency. A few fine gifts had been sent ahead with the white messengers who brought the news to the agencies, including a silver-trimmed repeating rifle for Red Cloud from the "great father" himself. Many old men among the "wild" Lakota could do nothing but raise their eyebrows at that bit of news. Some reiterated the thought that perhaps the Black Hills had already been sold when so many Lakota headmen had gone east to Washington. That would mean, then, that the council set for the Month of Leaves Turning Brown would be nothing but a meeting to decide the payment, if that hadn't already been decided, too. Those fears were given substance with the arrival of a Mniconju band under the leadership of Crazy Horse's old friend Touch the Clouds.

Touch the Clouds' father, Lone Horns, had been one of the old headmen who had gone to Washington. He had come home with a broken heart, the son told Crazy Horse. Lone Horns had been practically the only Lakota voice in Washington to speak against selling the Black Hills. He had been so discouraged at all that had gone on regarding the Black Hills that he had fallen ill upon his return, and didn't recover. He had died a broken old man.

Touch the Clouds' fear and words echoed those of Young Man Afraid. There was a storm coming, and all the Lakota not taken in by the slippery words of the whites would have to stand together and prepare to fight to the end.

Eighteen

Old Lone Horns had been right. The issue of a price for the Black Hills was very much on the table at the council at the Spotted Tail agency.

Messengers flowed back and forth from the agency to the northern camps of the "wild" Lakota, especially to the encampment of Crazy Horse. Since the start of the talks, hardly a day went by that someone didn't arrive with a worn-out horse and yet another mouthful of significant news. And the news was never more than two days old.

Spotted Tail, now a proponent of diplomacy in dealing with the whites, had somehow convinced them to have the council conducted at his agency. Now the issues important to the agency Lakota apparently had to do with who could ingratiate themselves the most to the whites. The talks had begun under an air of tension. Many fighting men from the "wild" Lakota opposed to selling the Black Hills had traveled to Spotted Tail to make their presence and their attitude known to those among the agency Lakota who were in favor of selling. The talks were delayed almost immediately when an especially aggressive contingent, led by Little Big Man, threatened to kill anyone who spoke of selling. Only the calm yet resolute words of Young Man Afraid had convinced many angry young men to put away their weapons. He diffused the moment, and perhaps saved the lives of the white peace talkers as well. The whites were shaken to the point of insisting that negotiations be conducted within the pro-

212 The Journey of Crazy Horse

tective confines of the army stockade, out of sight and earshot of the militant young Lakota.

Crazy Horse had been within half a day's ride of Spotted Tail when he was told of Young Man Afraid's intervention. He could understand his friend's reasons for wanting to prevent bloodshed, but he wondered who it would help in the long run. When he heard that Red Cloud had named a price for selling the Black Hills, he knew that Young Man Afraid's earlier warning was true. War was inevitable.

Some called the meeting "The council to steal the Black Hills." Nothing was settled, or finalized, however. The white peace talkers didn't get their sale, but months later they were waving a piece of paper they called an "agreement" that, they said, gave them ownership of the Black Hills. The story of the paper was a galling thing to hear for the "wild" Lakota, but it was typical of the whites. A group of old Lakota, leaders far past the prime of their influence, had been called to the agency in the dead of winter and told to sign the paper. When those old men steadfastly refused, soldiers were positioned behind them with cocked rifles pointed at each of their heads. Still they refused. When the white peace talkers threatened to stop all the annuities for the agency Lakota and to immediately round them up for transport south to the Indian Nation, the old men signed. The agency Lakota had heard of that country, a place of hunger and disease. Besides, who would fault them for saving lives? No one did. The incident only served to further the resolve of Crazy Horse and Sitting Bull.

As the snows flew, young men who had gone to visit relatives at the Spotted Trail agency returned with news that coincided with the "agreement" story. The "great father" had issued an order that all Lakota must move to the agencies by the end of the moon they called January—sometime in the Moon of Frost in the Lodge—or risk being hunted down by soldiers.

Crazy Horse's people had broken up into smaller winter

camps along the Tongue River. Among them were He Dog and a few Sicangu Lakota families who had grown tired of the agency. Crazy Horse was glad to see his best friend, someone with whom he could speak freely about all that concerned them. In lodges up and down the valley, the news hung in the air like acrid smoke as the sun sank behind the western mountain ridges.

The order given by the "great father" was nothing more than an idiotic notion. As ridiculous as it was for anyone to presume to exercise such control, Crazy Horse knew that soldiers would likely be dispatched to round up people. So be it. Armed conflict and the anticipation of it was part of interaction with whites. The probability of it was constant because of their attitude. He knew what the old men were thinking. An order that the whites knew would be ignored was simply an excuse for them to take action against the Lakota.

Crazy Horse made plans to travel north to visit with the Hunkpapa Lakota and Sitting Bull, to discuss this latest foolishness unleashed by the Long Knives, and he asked Black Shawl to accompany him.

Sitting Bull had already gotten word of the order and he was not surprised by it, but he didn't like its implication. He would send out a call again, he said, to ask the people to gather and talk. Everyone needed to be of a like mind against this new threat, but, more important, nothing could be done effectively unless the agency Lakota would come to their senses. Somewhere in the area of the Greasy Grass valley, he thought, would be a good place for a large gathering. There was usually good grazing in the floodplain, especially if the snowfall was good over the winter. He would send out word in the Moon When the Geese Return that he would take his people to the Greasy Grass in the Moon When Horses Lose Their Hair. He hoped that the right people would come, mainly the men who could influence others. Time would tell.

After several days Crazy Horse and Black Shawl returned to their own camp.

The day when all Lakota had to report to the agencies had come and gone. The northern camps were nervous, watching the horizons for the first sign of the soldiers they had heard had been gathering at Fort Fetterman. Winter relaxed its grip and a span of warm days melted the snow and thawed the ice on creeks and rivers. He Dog took advantage of the opportunity to head for the agency; his contingent of eight Sicangu Lakota families were mostly women and children in no condition to outrun mounted soldiers. Before he left, Crazy Horse had ridden up into the hills, unable to watch his closest friend give in to the agency, though he understood all too painfully He Dog's reasons. The spaces vacated by eight lodges were not as big as the holes left in the hearts of the relatives who watched their loved ones riding away slowly and uncertainly, looking back frequently.

Winter came back, swooping across the Powder River country without mercy. When the blizzards stopped, an exhausted messenger leading a horse with legs gashed by crusted snow stumbled into the Crazy Horse camp. Soldiers had come north and attacked Two Moons' Sahiyela camp north of the forks of the Powder River. Crazy Horse immediately sent out scouts, and less than a day out, they found the Sahiyela struggling through the snow. With them were He Dog's Sicangu Lakota.

The soldiers had appeared suddenly out of a storm. Their mounted attack was well coordinated, coming from several directions at once. The Sahiyela had felt relatively safe because they were not part of the current difficulty involving the Black Hills. But they would never feel safe again.

Most of the fighting men were still asleep when the attack came, and most of them were armed only with bows and arrows. Many women and children managed to escape and hide in the gullies west of the camp. The Sahiyela and the few Lakota fighting men with He Dog retaliated swiftly and managed to slow down the soldiers long enough for their women and children to move out of harm's way. But the camp was burned and most of the horses were driven off. Food, clothing, and robes were lost. Miraculously, only a few were wounded and two killed.

The Crazy Horse camp received the refugees. Two Moons and He Dog informed Crazy Horse that Indian scouts—perhaps Crow—had led the soldiers. One of them was a man they all knew as Grabber, the son of a black-skinned man. He would know where the favorite locations were for winter camps. And so, it had begun.

Scouts who had stayed behind to follow the soldiers learned they were part of Three Stars' contingent. Three Stars was General George Crook, who was at Fort Fetterman. Crazy Horse, Two Moons, and He Dog decided to move their people north to join the Sitting Bull encampments. The combined force of fighting men grew to around three hundred. Sitting Bull's people had traded with the Gros Ventures for rifles and bullets. It was good news at a time when such news was needed. Let them come, was the sentiment among the fighting men. Let the whites come.

Sitting Bull sent out his carefully chosen messengers to announce that the people should gather near the Chalk Buttes in late spring, entreating them to speak wisely and clearly to the leaders among the Lakota as well as the Dakota and Nakota. He wanted his messengers to appeal to their sense of pride, especially to those who were surely disenchanted with life on the agencies.

Two Moons decided to keep his people with Crazy Horse's camp. He Dog decided it was better to die a free and "wild" Lakota. He advised Crazy Horse to send a message aimed at the young unmarried Lakota men languishing on the agencies. Unattached as they were, they could leave anytime, and their response to Crazy Horse's call could influence the agency Lakota to heed Sitting Bull's message. It made good sense.

Early in the Moon When Horses Lose Their Hair, Sitting Bull moved his people north to the Chalk Buttes. Shortly thereafter, the first arrivals from the agencies began trickling in. By the beginning of the Moon of Ripening Berries, the encampment was estimated at three thousand people, including approximately four hundred fighting men.

Warm weather seemed to improve Black Shawl's health and state of mind. As Crazy Horse's people prepared to break camp and move north, she sat with her husband on a hillside. The people, with no objection from Sitting Bull, thought he should be the overall leader of the Lakota. Few men in the past had ever held such a position—no one in recent memory, in fact.

Black Shawl knew it was a responsibility he already had. Not many men could walk through the circle of lodges and make people feel better simply because he passed by.

They both knew that difficult times lay ahead. The future was uncertain, and to help ensure the survival of the true Lakota way of life, the evil that had been nipping at their heels and flanks had to be driven back, if not destroyed. That evil was the Long Knives. A large part of the answer to that problem was for all the Lakota to think alike and combine their efforts. And Crazy Horse, Black Shawl knew, could bring people together.

More and more people arrived almost every day. The horse herd was growing and eating down the sparse grass around the buttes. Some young men said perhaps there were as many as seven thousand head. Sitting Bull was already at work, inviting the older leaders to his own lodge or to the roomier council lodge. He was an impressive and charismatic man. A slight limp from a gunshot wound to his hip during his days as a young fighting man served only to give him more credibility. He had earned nearly seventy battle honors, more than any man at the gathering except Crazy Horse. Now past the age of fifty, he had a solid reputation as a wise leader and counselor, enhanced by his status as a medicine man. He was immensely pleased at the response to his message and announced he would conduct a Sun Dance. Spiritually, as well as psychologically, it was the right thing at the time. It could only serve to unify the people and add to the feeling of strength and pride that seemed to be growing as quickly as the horse herd. It was that kind of insight that made him an influential leader.

The encampment moved west across the Powder and the Tongue into the valley of the Rosebud, and across it as well, turning at the northern slopes of the Wolf Mountains into the broken country near the Greasy Grass River. The long procession moved in the old way, with the holy men leading the way carrying the embers from the council fire, while the warrior groups rode on each flank and brought up the rear. Each day, the lodges were pitched before sundown and were ready to travel at dawn. They finally came to Ash Creek and followed it west. There the old men selected a place.

While Sitting Bull was hard at work for the hearts and minds of the people, Crazy Horse sent scouts in all directions. The feeling among the military leaders was that the biggest threat lay to the south, from Three Stars' army. Nonetheless, scouts went as far as a day's ride in every direction, a distant first line of defense. To the north were the Crow, but they were not stupid enough to attack such a large encampment defended by several hundred fighting men. Given the "great father's" order, Crazy Horse kept his eyes and ears—in the person of his scouts—concentrated toward the south.

Preparations were completed for the Sun Dance. Sitting Bull didn't lack for participants, stalwart young men offering their sacrifice of pain and flesh on behalf of the people. To set the tone, Sitting Bull himself offered one hundred bits of flesh, fifty from each arm—a real and symbolic sacrifice not lost on the people.

The effect of the Sun Dance, the most holy of Lakota ceremonies, was to rekindle a sense of unity and remind the agency Lakota that the true path of the Lakota way was still very much alive and viable. Sitting Bull fell into a trance, and after he awoke he described dead, wounded, and bleeding soldiers, and their horses falling headfirst from the sky into a Lakota encampment. Soldiers falling into camp became the watchwords for victory.

The growing encampment buzzed for days with speculation on the meaning of Sitting Bull's vision. Interpretations varied but the unmistakable message was definitely victory over the Long Knives. When scouts returned to camp one evening with word of a large column of soldiers heading north, the news was not unexpected and it was received as a precursor to the eventual validation of Sitting Bull's vision. Most of all, there was no sense of panic.

The scouts were taken immediately to Crazy Horse. By late afternoon, he took their report to the council lodge. Three Stars was bringing an army north, probably in keeping with the "great father's" order. The column was likely in the area of Goose Creek in the foothills of the Shining Mountains by now, Crazy Horse deduced. Riding with the Long Knives were Crow and Snakes, old enemies to the Lakota—over two hundred according to the scouts' estimates. Three Stars' army was three to four days away. Of course they couldn't know of the gathering on Ash Creek and must not be allowed to come close.

Crazy Horse told the old men he would lead the young men against the soldiers, any and all who wanted to follow. Runners carried the call to every lodge in the encampment.

Crazy Horse hurried to his own lodge as the entire encampment was alive with anticipation. Black Shawl had already heard and was preparing food and had filled his water flasks. He would ride the paint mare and lead the bay gelding; they both had stamina to spare and were hardened combat veterans themselves. Like all Lakota fighting men, he was in a constant state of readiness, his weapons always in easy reach and in good working order. So there was little other preparation to complete.

The moment came, as it frequently had for them, to face the parting. Crazy Horse tied his weapons and gear to the paint, then embraced his wife, covering them both beneath his elk robe. They said little. Whatever they felt came through in the strength of their embrace and the reluctance to let go. He took one of his lances and jammed it point first into the earth. Then he swung onto the mare and rode away.

The sun was near the jagged western horizon as she watched him head to the east opening of the great circle of lodges, riding the paint and leading the bay. There he turned right and began to circle the large encampment. Men hurried to join him as he continued around the outer edge of the camp. By the time he reached the opening again, a file of riders were strung out behind him.

As he finished the second turn around the encampment and began the third, the old ones watching realized what Crazy Horse was doing. He was invoking an old ritual known as "Gathering the Warriors." It had last been done eleven years past when the Sahiyela and Blue Clouds came north after the massacre at Sand Creek. Word spread quickly as more and more men joined the growing procession. It seemed as though everyone in camp stopped whatever they were doing to watch. Women began to sing the Strong Heart songs to encourage their fighting men.

As the fourth and final turn around the encampment began, it was difficult to see where the procession of fighting men started and where it ended. It encircled the entire camp. Sitting Bull's vision had brought a sense of confidence, and the sight of close to six hundred fighting men emphasized it. Drums pounded throughout the camp like the heartbeat of the land itself. Grandparents took their grandchildren by the hand to make sure they saw the awe-inspiring sight.

As he finished the fourth turn, Crazy Horse pointed his horses south and the great procession followed, feathers and banners streaming, the very image of strength and invincibility. Sunset's long shadows had stretched across the land by then, and when

Crazy Horse reached the western slopes of the Wolf Mountains, dusk had already settled.

Foremost in the minds of the fighting men was the attack on Two Moons' and He Dog's camp. That was a singular and specific motivation for the action they had embarked on, but also present was the awareness that an invasion into their lands and lives had been going on for longer than most of them had lived. For most of them, therefore, following Crazy Horse to fight the soldiers was necessary to repel that invasion. Many had yet to fire a shot in anger at the Long Knives. Righteous anger and a strong sense of resolve rode with them as they moved south into the deepening dusk and approaching night. Amid the occasional snort and the soft thud of hooves on dry ground, the younger men pretended to check their weapons or neck ropes as they tried to ignore their apprehension and thoughts of death.

Crazy Horse called on the men he knew who had detailed knowledge of the area to lead them over the Wolf Mountains. The terrain was rough, rocky, and covered with sagebrush. Two factors had prompted Crazy Horse to take the fight to Three Stars: First, his advance scouts probably stayed relatively close to the main body, perhaps no further than half a day's ride. Therefore, the likelihood of encountering any of Three Stars' scouts or soldiers was highly unlikely. And, if by chance that happened, it wouldn't be difficult to overwhelm them. Second, nights were short this time of year. To take advantage of the cover of darkness meant leaving the Ash Creek encampment no later than sundown. The advantage, of course, was that an enemy couldn't see the rising dust from an approaching force at night.

The trail guides were more than equal to the challenge. Except for three stops to rest the horses, six hundred men and a thousand horses moved quickly and without incident. As the dawn's light grew, Crazy Horse called a halt and sent scouts ahead. They were in the Rosebud Creek drainage and he wanted to scout the next drainages over on each side.

Final preparations were made and weapons were checked. Some men painted their faces for battle and prayed, or performed whatever ritual that seemed to help keep nervousness in check. Horse holders, older boys who had been brought along to stay in the rear and watch the spare mounts, were given final instructions.

Crazy Horse moved off by himself. He tied his medicine stone behind his left ear and draped the calf-hide cape over his shoulder. He left the mare with one of the boys and led the bay aside, tossing gopher dust over his back. Then he settled behind the ridge of a gully to check his weapons and wait.

The scouts returned after sunrise. Three Stars' army was below them, encamped on either side of Rosebud Creek, most of them still asleep. Crazy Horse was about to issue instructions for the men to lead their horses quietly down the slope when gunfire cracked from the valley below. He was later to learn that one of Three Stars' Crow scouts opened fire. The battle was joined.

The Rosebud Fight, as the battle came to be known, was the toughest combat Crazy Horse had seen. The Battle of the Hundred in the Hand ten years earlier had had its own set of circumstances that made it tough. But at the Rosebud, the Lakota faced a larger and more heavily armed enemy force. Three Stars' soldiers were both infantry and cavalry, forcing the Lakota to adjust to different tactics as the fighting progressed. Attack was met with counterattack as the day wore on. The valley of the Rosebud thundered with gunfire and dust hung in the air. Late in the afternoon it was evident that the soldiers were disorganized, fighting in scattered units, their effectiveness significantly reduced. Crazy Horse was notified that, even though nearly a hundred Hunkpapa had arrived at midmorning, the Lakota and Sahiyela were critically low on ammunition. Sensing that Three Stars wouldn't be able to mount any pursuit, Crazy Horse sent word to withdraw.

Crazy Horse rode with He Dog, Big Road, and Good Weasel,

among others, as they once again chased dusk into night. There was no pursuit from the soldiers to speak of. The feverish aftermath of combat slowly faded as the reality of the day began to take hold. Ten good men had been killed, and many wounded. In a day or two, the scouts Crazy Horse had left behind would report on the soldiers.

Crazy Horse was bone-tired, but as a leader of fighting men, he was satisfied with the way the Lakota and their Sahiyela allies had performed. They had engaged a numerically larger force and fought them to a standstill. Experience and fighting ability were not in question, only rifles and ammunition. He was convinced that, adequately supplied, Lakota fighting men would drive the Long Knives out.

Two days later, scouts reported that Three Stars had turned back south. The encampment was alive with excitement. Sitting Bull's vision had come to pass, many said. But others were circumspect. The vision was of victory over soldiers attacking an encampment. Rosebud was not that victory, some felt.

Sitting Bull worked harder than ever, knowing he would likely never have the opportunity to make his case to so many influential leaders gathered in one place at one time, especially with the impetus of victory to add credibility. New arrivals came on a daily basis, swelling the encampment's population to over seven thousand and horses to nearly ten thousand head. More important, the number of fighting men increased to around a thousand.

Many people compared the encampment to the one near the Shell River crossing north of Elk Mountain in the summer of the Battle of Red Buttes eleven years earlier. This one was larger, and people were still arriving. The patriotic fervor Sitting Bull had hoped for was alive and well in the young men, but a few of the older headmen were still cautious. One battle won against one column of soldiers may have inspired Lakota fighting men, but it would also serve to anger the "great father."

Crazy Horse left the diplomacy to Sitting Bull as he kept

scouts on the trail to the south in the event Three Stars decided to turn around and strike back. He had his own opportunity to convince his contemporaries—men like Big Road, Young Man Afraid, and Touch the Clouds—that organized resistance was the best answer to the problem of the whites. As large as the encampment was, there were as many or more people still at agencies, and the most notable absentees were Red Cloud and Spotted Tail. But most of the older leaders at Ash Creek understood why those two men were not here. Their presence would have meant an outright acknowledgment of the influence of Sitting Bull and Crazy Horse, not to mention loss of the status they both had so carefully cultivated with the whites.

Crazy Horse's reputation as a fighting man and combat leader was well known across Lakota country. He Dog had been right. Many young Lakota had joined the gathering simply because of Crazy Horse. Everywhere he went in the encampment people gathered to him. Simply checking on his horses was a chore that took half a day because everyone wanted to talk with him or invite him to their lodges to eat. So when the horse herders came to him complaining that the enormous herd, more horses in one area than anyone had ever seen, had grazed the meadows and gullies around Ash Creek practically down to the roots, he was glad to deal with the mundane aspects of leadership. With He Dog and a group of older boys, he rode northwest to the Greasy Grass valley to scout a new location for the herd. The floodplain west of the river was perfect for grazing.

Six days had passed since the Rosebud fight. Victory dances still went far into the night and the fighting men were asked to tell the stories of their involvement. The mood of the encampment had changed from an initial uncertainty to one of a comfortable sense of strength. Hardly anyone, no matter how old, could remember the Lakota ever gathering in such numbers for any purpose. At midday, Sitting Bull sent criers to announce a move to the Greasy Grass valley, and by midafternoon the first lodges were taken down and families began moving. By sundown most of the encampment was gone except for a few lodges and the Sun Dance arbor.

It was not a bustling mass move as one camp, but the marks of loaded drag poles left deep grooves in the earth. The horses were not moved as one herd because that would have been virtually impossible. Over ten thousand head were unmanageable except in small groups. Families caught their own horses because most of them were transport for lodge covers, poles, and household goods and as basic riding mounts. Horse herders did move the extra warhorses and buffalo hunters in several small manageable herds of a few hundred each.

As the sun went down, the new encampment was organizing itself among the big cottonwoods west of the meandering Greasy Grass River, and because of the river's bends there was no overall circle of lodges. The various groups staked out their own identifiable areas. Sitting Bull's Hunkpapa were on the southernmost end, while the Sahiyela, as guests, chose an area at the northern end beyond an old crossing that opened onto a wide gully given the name of Medicine Tail Coulee by the Crow. In between were the Sicangu, Itazipacola, Mniconju, Oglala, and a small band of Ihanktunwan Dakota.

The east bank of the Greasy Grass rose to high, undulating ridges overlooking the west side and the flat valley that stretched away to low hills. On the ridges, men sat on their horses and gazed down at the sprawling encampment, the mouth of Ash Creek now to the south. Among them was Crazy Horse. The sun was going down and cooking fires were lit, becoming flickering spots of light in the shade of the cottonwood groves. Some families, who were quietly anxious that the whites at the agencies not associate them with the Rosebud fight, had left. There was talk of some people moving to the north, closer to the Big Horn River. But he was dismayed to hear the consensus that it might be time to break up the gathering.

Crazy Horse knew that people would slowly begin to leave, but he hoped not for a few more days. Much of the talk around many campfires was that such a gathering would never happen again. He broke from the line of horsemen, rode slowly to the river and crossed it, and then rode from one end of the encampment to the other.

Long after sundown, a man with a limp crossed the river at the south end of the large encampment. He climbed the ridge with a long bundle under his arm. He wore a brain-tanned hide shirt decorated with plaited and dyed porcupine quills, leggings, and a breechclout. In his right hand, he held a short lance with a long, wicked-looking iron point. The lance was, for the moment, a walking stick. Reaching the top of a small knob, the man stopped and opened his bundle. Soon he had arranged various accoutrements that were the symbols of his calling as a holy man. He loaded his pipe, offered it to the Sky, the Earth, the Four Directions, to the Grandfather, and then prayed. He spent the better part of the evening sitting deep in thought and praying. Finally he gathered up his things, carefully rearranged them into his bundle, and left the hill.

The largest gathering of Lakota ever known would leave the Greasy Grass valley in three days, but not before the most defining event of all of their lives would occur. Dawn at the new site was cool, but shortly after sunrise, the air grew steadily warmer, a sure sign of a hot day coming. The big cottonwood trees released their white fluffy seedpods, giving the illusion of a thin fog up and down the river.

Crazy Horse took the gift of a horse to the Sahiyela camp for Buffalo Calf Road, the sister of the Sahiyela leader Comes In Sight. She had galloped into a hail of soldier gunfire at the Rosebud fight to rescue her brother, whose horse had been killed. He visited briefly in the Sahiyela camp and left. Big Road was waiting for him back at his own lodge, visiting quietly with Black Shawl. He mentioned that several families had taken down their lodges and were moving to the north. Midday was approaching and the air was hot and still, a typical day at the end of the Moon of Ripening Berries. The Moon Where the Sun Stands in the Middle was a day or two away.

A man paused at the edge of a hill east of the river above the encampment. He was alone, riding one horse and leading a second loaded with packs. He was leaving for the Spotted Tail agency some fifteen days to the southeast. After a last glance in the direction of the encampment in the valley, he urged his horses down a long gradual slope, and offhandedly noticed a long line of dust beyond Ash Creek to the south.

The sides of the council lodge had been rolled up to allow cross ventilation. A few men were waiting in anticipation of meeting with Sitting Bull. Women had already brought food. Sitting Bull had been busy through most of the night attending to a gravely ill woman. He arrived at the council lodge just as a slight din of commotion came from the south end of the encampment, where he had just been.

A lone Lakota rider splashed across the Greasy Grass, filled bank to bank from the heavy spring runoff from the mountain snows. Gaining the west bank, he began to shout: "Prepare yourselves! The soldiers are coming! The soldiers are coming!"

The sun was hot again just as it had been the day before. Crazy Horse rode up the long slope and stopped just below the top. Beyond, he could see the barricade of saddles, boxes, and dead horses. Behind it were the last of the Long Knives, many of them wounded. All around them, on the hills and in the gullies stretching to the river were nearly a thousand tired and angry Lakota and Sahiyela fighting men. Most of them wanted to finish the soldiers.

Whether those soldiers, perhaps three hundred of them, would live or die had been hotly argued through the night in the council lodge. Good Weasel, exhausted and dirty, the blood of a wounded friend dried brown on his hands and arms, saw Crazy Horse and limped over from his position, a captured Spencer rifle in his hands. Crazy Horse delivered the decision of the old men. The soldiers would live, a decision that was influenced by scouts hurrying in from the Elk River area. Another soldier column had been spotted and it was heading south toward the Greasy Grass valley.

The soldiers hiding behind the barricade in a grassy swale on a ridge above the bluffs overlooking the Greasy Grass River had been the first to attack the day before. They had crossed the river far to the south near the mouth of Ash Creek, and tried galloping their tired horses across the long, open floodplain toward the south end of the encampment. They had been quickly driven back and then chased across the river. Many were killed at the water crossing after heavy fighting in some trees near the river. As far as Crazy Horse and other leaders were concerned, that was the first fight. Gall of the Hunkpapa and the Oglala battle leaders Black Moon and Big Road were among those who had courageously led two hundred fighting men in that action.

The second fight started at Medicine Tail Coulee. More soldiers had tried to cross into the encampment from the north end but were stopped by a small but determined group of boys and old men armed mostly with old single-shot rifles. By then many of the women, children, and old people were fleeing to the northwest. Somehow word had reached Crazy Horse and Gall of the second attempted incursion. Gall immediately disengaged from the first fight and led a hundred men to Medicine Tail and crossed. The soldiers galloped away up a long slope to the north.

Crazy Horse had hurried to his lodge and found Black Shawl waiting with his second warhorse. The camp was in total confusion. Not only were women and children running away to safety, men were galloping through to hurry to the second fight. Shouts and screams filled the air; gunshots could be heard to the south and now thinly to the north. He took his second warhorse and gathered as many men to him as he could.

If a second group of soldiers were heading north, they could be circling to attack from another direction. It made sense to try to flank them. So he led the men who were with him to an old crossing. Guessing the soldiers would stay to the high ground, he had crossed the river and raced to meet them if they came off the end of the high north-south ridge he knew lay to the east. On the slopes across the river, they circled to the east and encountered twenty or so soldiers, whom they chased back to the main body.

The gunfire never stopped. He heard it as they crossed the river, a continuous sound, rather like someone tearing canvas. Gall and his men, Crazy Horse heard later, stayed in pursuit of the running soldiers even though they did gain a ridge. At first the soldiers were organized, even managing to dismount and form skirmish lines to fire at the oncoming Lakota. But Gall's relentless pursuit broke their lines and after that they were running away and their fire was no longer effective.

Two battles in eight days. The soldiers had retaliated after all. Sitting Bull's vision had come to pass. Runaway horses from the first attack had actually taken their hapless riders into the encampment, where they had been immediately killed.

The soldiers had come to the end of the long ridge and there was nowhere else to go. A bunch broke from the ridge and galloped west toward the river. Some were cut down immediately and others managed to find cover further downslope. By then, the Lakota and Sahiyela seemed to be rising out of the earth itself, avenging spirits flying through the dust that hung low over the slopes and ridges, and made the soldiers pay a terrible price.

Crazy Horse led a charge when the soldiers tried to push north off their ridge. By then the gunfire was thinning. It was sporadic and then there was silence. The second fight was over. As he rode through the dust, he could see how it had unfolded.

Dead horses and dead soldiers were strewn along the path they had taken.

❖

And now they were into the third fight, which had begun the early morning of the second day. The younger men were in favor of wiping out the soldiers behind the barricades with one final mounted charge. Grind them into the dust they came from, some said.

But the report of soldiers coming from the Elk River saved their comrades on the hill. Crazy Horse agreed with the decision. It was wiser to move the people to safety while they had the opportunity.

Good Weasel chose runners to spread the word. The Greasy Grass fight was over.

A very old Mniconju had said, sometime during the night, that if he still had the strength of arm and a good horse he would ride down the soldiers himself. It was a brief moment of levity during the heated arguments. He went on to say, however, that to let the soldiers live would be a message to the "great father" that the Lakota had compassion as well as strength. To the old man, it was a matter of what the whites were really willing to pay for the Black Hills. The cost couldn't be measured in their money. They should have been asked if they were willing to pay with their blood. That was the price that should have been put on the table at "the council to steal the Black Hills."

That old man should have been the one speaking for the Lakota at the Spotted Tail agency, some said. But now the whites would understand that the issue of selling the Black Hills had not been decided at the Spotted Tail agency with their "agreement." The heart of everything that is, would be defended as it had been at the Rosebud—and, now, as it had been at the Greasy Grass.

Nineteen

"When a rattlesnake crawls into your lodge, you crush it," advised an old man. "You crush it because it knows the way to your lodge."

Crazy Horse couldn't agree more. The threat to Lakota territory had to be stopped and at all costs. But the overall sense of unity that had prevailed at the Greasy Grass seemed to give way to complacency. Among the younger warriors, however, flowed a feeling of invincibility.

Around night fires throughout the camps along Goose Creek, they recounted their deeds in the Greasy Grass and Rosebud fights, one story leading to another, in an ancient ritual that served to strengthen the warrior brotherhood. The Sahiyela had identified the overall soldier commander at the Greasy Grass, known as Long Hair to some and Son of the Morning Star to others. The last was not a name of respect, as it was given because he had attacked a Sahiyela encampment just after dawn eight years past at a place called Washita. In the span of eight days, the Lakota and Sahiyela warriors had defeated two separate armies. Let them come, was the sentiment. We can defeat them all.

Crazy Horse knew the value of the sense of confidence earned from two hard-fought battles. It was the best weapon to take into a fight. Nevertheless, unless an overall plan was devised to anticipate and meet the threat of retaliation from the soldiers, all that confidence would be useless. To his dismay, however, there was no talk of planning. He heard, instead, the first indications of disagreement among the old men during the move south toward the Shining Mountains. It was the kind of fundamental disagreement that left little room for discussion.

There were two widely divergent opinions. One side felt they shouldn't pass up the advantage they had gained. Never had the Lakota so decisively defeated the Long Knives. Why, it was asked, did Three Stars retreat in spite of the fact he still had a large force unless he had a newfound respect for the fighting ability of the Lakota? Furthermore, the soldiers they had spared behind the barricades at the Greasy Grass would certainly report the fighting ability of the Lakota and Sahiyela to other soldiers. When an enemy was truly afraid, he was more apt to hesitate—and such an opportunity must not be wasted.

The other side agreed that Rosebud and Greasy Grass were indeed messages that the Long Knives would take to heart. However, they were in favor of waiting for them to send their peace talkers, as they certainly would. It was obvious, they said, that from now on the Lakota would speak from a position of strength because of their victories and that no more Lakota blood had to be spilled to win back the Black Hills. The Long Knives had learned a bitter lesson and would be cautious hereafter. This was nothing more than a false sense of security as far as Crazy Horse was concerned—something to be expected from the agency Lakota, who were in favor of friendly relations with the whites.

The idea of sending a large force to attack all the soldier outposts had been circulating among the warriors since the departure from the Greasy Grass. Crazy Horse and He Dog took the idea one step further. If different groups attacked Fort Caspar, Fort Fetterman, and Fort Laramie on the same day, the effect could be devastating. It was bold thinking, yet the reaction to it was largely silence until someone fretted about who would stay behind to protect the women and children.

What was left of the largest gathering ever of Lakota had separated into several encampments along the eastern foothills of
the Shining Mountains. Soon after the departure from the
Greasy Grass, small groups began breaking away to head for the
agencies. Sitting Bull, like Crazy Horse, was deeply disappointed
because they were losing the strength of numbers. Staying together as long as possible would have been safer. But the
Hunkpapa saw that it was the underlying fear of retaliation from
the Long Knives that drove the agency Lakota back. They apparently felt it was the safest place to be. Before a month had
passed, most of the agency Lakota were gone.

Crazy Horse understood that an unbreakable commitment
was necessary to defend the Lakota way of life. For him, the symbol of such commitment was Gall, the Hunkpapa, who was one
of Sitting Bull's most loyal followers. Gall was a tall, imposing
figure and an experienced leader. Both of his wives and a daughter were killed in the first attack on the Greasy Grass. He had
found them when he'd hurried to his lodge to gather his
weapons. Rifle fire from the initial soldier charge had carried
into the Hunkpapa lodges at the southern end of the large encampment. In spite of his grievous loss, he led men in a counterattack, leading the charge that broke the soldier lines and began
the rout that eventually ended with the soldiers retreating across
the river, where they threw up barricades on a hill. Gall was also
chiefly responsible for the defeat of Long Hair's group of soldiers. He had led the pursuit that turned the attempted incursion
across Medicine Tail crossing into another rout. Understandably,
the man had kept to himself after the battle, staying close to his
surviving children.

Gall would have dishonored the memory of his wives and his
daughter if he had chosen to seek safety at the agencies. No one
would have thought less of him if he had, yet he spoke for a
united stand against the Long Knives. They are only men, was
his assertion, and can be defeated.

Despite the best efforts of Sitting Bull, the people scattered. Some made excuses, saying it was time to hunt and make meat for the coming winter, which was more difficult now because of the scarcity of buffalo. Others unabashedly headed for the agencies. Sitting Bull finally headed north to more familiar territory.

Crazy Horse took his people east toward the Black Hills, finding a sheltered valley northwest of the mountains to hide the camps. From there, he led raids into the Black Hills. They operated separately, with He Dog, Big Road, Little Big Man, and Crazy Horse each leading a group of up to a dozen men. This tactic was effective overall, forcing the miners to think that hundreds of Lakota were raiding. A few Sahiyela had stayed with the Crazy Horse camp and their young men joined him in the raids. He was glad to have them along: they were fierce and aggressive and counted their share of kills.

On one of the raids, they found a large tent settlement. Crazy Horse was incensed. Not only were the miners coming in larger and larger numbers, but they were bringing their women and children. They were expecting to stay, to build their square houses, and to plant crops. The Lakota victories at the Rosebud and Greasy Grass meant nothing to these people. Or, perhaps, they hadn't heard. More frightening, however, was the thought that they had heard but didn't care. They cared more about gold.

Impatient and angry, Crazy Horse began to raid by himself and stayed in the mountains for days. Picking isolated camps, he positioned himself and would attack at dawn when the miners were groggy with sleep and their judgment was impaired, or just as they were bedding down for the night, exhausted from their day's labors. In either case there was little opportunity for effective reaction. His expertise at close combat made up for his low supply of bullets, though he preferred the bow and his stone-headed war club. He worked silently and grimly, and without remorse. This was Lakota land. These miners were invaders. Their kind brought nothing but trouble. So, wraithlike, out of the morning mist or moving with the shadows of dusk, he carried on his war—alone, silent, and deadly. If Lakota fighting men couldn't take to the field en masse against soldiers, there were other ways to fight.

At night, he slept in fireless camps always high on a slope where he could hide his horse. He used the terrain to his advantage. He was, after all, a man of the Earth. Black Shawl's dried meat and berry mixture sustained him, and gave him strength. He didn't count the number of miners he had killed, but he wasn't doing it for the numbers. He was removing blight from the heart of all there was.

One day, He Dog found him. His best friend was glad to see that he was alive and unharmed, and then scolded him.

"Recklessness belongs to the young," he chided. "You are a man past thirty and responsible for more than yourself. Never forget again that you belong to the people."

At home, old Worm also rebuked him. Crazy Horse listened to both men without protest because they were right.

Crazy Horse was moving his people closer toward Bear Butte when news came of an attack against the camp of Iron Plume, further to the north near Slim Buttes. Iron Plume was friendly to the whites, but that didn't save him or stop the soldiers from killing women and children. And that was not the end to the bad news. A thousand or more soldiers from Fort Fetterman were in the area. Crazy Horse, with less than two hundred warriors, could do little more than harass them because they were all critically low on ammunition. But he did manage to confuse the soldiers with hit and run attacks, allowing them little rest, taking full advantage of the Lakota horses' superior stamina and speed. When ammunition ran out, he withdrew. Word came later that the soldiers had released the women and children captured from the unprovoked attack on Iron Plume as a result of the continuous harassment.

Three Stars was the one said to have led the soldiers, although no one had actually seen him during the attack on Iron Plume. But as everyone knew, Three Stars was the overall commander stationed at Fort Fetterman. The man would undoubtedly be anxious to make amends for the Rosebud fight, and word came that the Long Knives were very anxious to avenge the defeat of Long Hair at the Greasy Grass. The agency Lakota were wrong.

The Long Knives had learned a bitter lesson, and they were aggressive, not hesitant. He Dog and Crazy Horse were angry that their idea to attack all the forts had not been taken seriously. For that matter, they could have taken the initiative and carried out their plan on their own. Men would have followed them. How many would have been the only unknown factor, and any amount of speculation about the outcome now would be useless—just as much as blaming anyone.

Crazy Horse decided to relocate to the upper Tongue River area where elk were reported to be plentiful. He laughed wryly at a bit of news that drifted up from Red Cloud. The agent there had taken away guns and horses from the agency Lakota, following the orders of Three Stars. What did the Red Cloud people do, he wondered. Did they stand aside quietly like obedient children while the agent confiscated guns and drove off the horses?

"What would you do?" asked He Dog.

"Fight to stay free," replied Crazy Horse, "and die a free Lakota if it comes to that. I will never live on an agency, so I will never give up my horse or my gun."

Sometime in the Moon When Leaves Fall came more news. Scouts who had been along the old Holy Road had seen soldiers leaving Fort Fetterman with buffalo-hide coats and heavy fur caps, a sure, unsettling sign of a winter campaign. A man sent by Sitting Bull arrived with equally disturbing news. A new fort had been built to the north at the confluence of the Tongue and the Elk rivers. The Long Knife in charge there was one called Bear Coat, with the white name of Colonel Nelson Miles. Sitting

Bull's men attacked their supply train and drew first blood. Bear Coat then asked to talk with Sitting Bull. While they were talking, his soldiers attacked the Hunkpapa encampment, destroying winter meat stores and driving off some horses.

Uneasiness came to live in the Crazy Horse encampment. All the news was of the Long Knives escalating their war against the Lakota—a thousand soldiers to the north, a thousand in the south at Fetterman. Furthermore, every soldier was armed with a rifle and a pistol, and spare ammunition was transported on pack mules or in supply wagons. But if the soldiers had an endless supply of ammunition, there seemed to be an endless supply of whites overall. There was only a limited supply of Lakota.

Crazy Horse sent several small raiding parties out essentially to scrounge for rifles and ammunition. Procuring ammunition had always been a significant problem because of the wide variety of rifles. A few Lakota carried lever-action repeating rifles similar to the one given to Crazy Horse. Others had breechloaders, many captured at the Rosebud and Greasy Grass, and there were still a number of single-shot muzzle-loaders that fired round lead balls. But percussion caps to ignite the powder were harder and harder to find. Crazy Horse had carried a back-loading rifle during the Battle of the Hundred in the Hand, with only four round balls.

The threat posed by the Long Knives was the most persistent problem Crazy Horse had to face as a leader, requiring most of his attention. But, in addition, life had to go on and winter was coming. Hunters were busy, but hunting weakened the camp's defenses because the hunter was also the warrior. So Crazy Horse advised the men to coordinate their hunting so that at least half of the able-bodied fighting men were always in camp. Every man hunted as though for two families, bringing in more meat than usual.

The encampment was in a constant state of alert, more so than usual. Early in the Winter Moon the scouts spotted a group of people approaching through the first heavy snowstorm, a heartrending sight. They were Dull Knife's Sahiyela and most of them had no winter robes, many of them suffering from frostbite. As they were brought into camp, they began to tell their story. Soldiers had attacked them ten days earlier. Their winter encampment along a fork of the Powder River had been burned, including all their winter food stores, and their horses scattered. The men did what they could to fight back, but many had been killed and were left behind where they had fallen. Some of the badly wounded had died during the long trek northward. What little food anyone had managed to grab as they fled their homes had been rationed carefully, but it had been so little.

The Crazy Horse people opened their homes to feed and clothe the Sahiyela, and went to work healing wounds and treating the frostbite. The damage to their spirits would be much more difficult to heal. The Sahiyela children often had difficulty sleeping, and many of the adults seemed unusually withdrawn.

Crazy Horse allowed the Sahiyela to rest as long as they needed before the encampment moved further up the Tongue to a more defensible location. Hunters were sent out to replenish meat supplies. Dull Knife informed Crazy Horse that he was forced to consider giving in to life on an agency if it meant his people would be safe from facing continual conflict with the Long Knives. The Sahiyela, he reasoned, were not as numerous as the Lakota; the number of fighting men was far fewer. The fact of the matter was, Dull Knife thought, the Long Knives far outnumbered the Sahiyela and Lakota combined. He was afraid they would not stop until every Lakota and Sahiyela was on an agency, or dead.

The insight of a man like Dull Knife was difficult to ignore. He was a man who always considered the overall welfare of the people above all else. But the implication that the Sahiyela and Lakota should consider that a viable alternative was survival under the control of the Long Knives was a bitter thought. Given the fact that the soldiers were conducting a winter campaign contrary to their usual habits was, in and of itself, cause for concern. But the fact that it was occurring after their losses at the Rosebud and the Greasy Grass was an unmistakable indication of their intent. Moreover, Three Stars' decision to disarm the agency Lakota was the most telling fact. He couldn't risk being flanked if the "wild" Lakota resisted successfully and the young hotheads at the agencies decided to join the fight.

They talked—the old men and the younger leaders of the fighting men—about this alternative, but it was like bile in the mouth. They all agreed that a leader had to consider all the alternatives, to find the path of least resistance, if necessary, in order that the people could survive. And it was coming to that. For most of the "wild" Lakota to be on an agency under the control of the Long Knives was to merely exist—it was simply being alive, not living. That it had to be an alternative was like a black cloud across the face of the bright full moon. But it hadn't happened yet, the younger men pointed out, and it wouldn't happen as long as Lakota fighting men had the will to resist. Nonetheless, the old men countered, wouldn't it be wise to determine if the Long Knives might be willing to avoid continuous armed conflict? If so, then perhaps the "wild" Lakota could use that willingness to their benefit and pick the location of their agencies in return for "surrendering."

The idea was debated long and frequently. Strangely, an opportunity presented itself when messengers arrived bringing word from Three Stars, who had given his assurance that the "wild" Lakota would be allowed to select the location for their own agencies if they signed a peace agreement. The only drawback was that it included agreement to the sale of the Black Hills. In spite of deep-seated suspicions, Crazy Horse agreed that this important issue should be discussed face-to-face with the Long Knives.

He Dog and Big Road suggested that Bear Coat (Colonel Nelson Miles) would likely be the man in charge of agencies in the north, just as Three Stars was in charge of the Red Cloud and Spotted Tail agencies in the south. And it would be preferable to live in the north in the Powder River area. Consequently, early in the Moon of Popping Trees, a delegation of eight good men were selected to meet with Bear Coat.

Crazy Horse and a large detachment of Oglala and Mniconju warriors escorted the delegation north to the fort on the Elk River. From a low bluff, the eight rode in unarmed and under a white flag of truce while the escorts waited. In the space of a few heartbeats, however, any opportunity to honorably discuss the possibility of northern agencies for the "wild" Lakota died unexpectedly.

A group of Crow scouts met the emissaries just outside the walls of the fort, making friendly gestures to indicate their peacefulness. As the eight Lakota rode past them toward the gate, weapons were drawn suddenly and the Crow opened fire at point-blank range on the unarmed Lakota and then fled on horseback. Crazy Horse charged down from the bluff but stopped when mounted soldiers emerged from the fort. Instinctively, the Lakota emissaries turned their horses and galloped for the safety of the bluffs and the protection of the escort warriors. Only three rejoined the warriors. Five lay dead on the ground near the gates of the fort.

Crazy Horse pulled his men back further up the bluffs, wary that the soldiers might open fire with their cannons. But there was no firing of any kind. Instead a group of soldiers went in pursuit of the fleeing Crow scouts while one soldier approached the bluffs, obviously trying to assure the waiting warriors that the soldiers had nothing to do with the ambush. The man's courage was admirable, but the damage had been done. The treachery of the Crow may have surprised the soldiers as well, but there was no way to know.

The ambush at the fort on the Elk River seemed to signal that nothing but difficulty lay ahead. Even the weather seemed to turn against them. Blizzards whipped the land, filling every gully with snow. Crazy Horse moved his camp further up the Tongue on a plateau below a line of sheltering bluffs. Throughout the Powder River region, the encampments of the "wild" Lakota dug in to wait out the winter, hoping that the Long Knives were doing the same.

The harsh winter should have been a deterrent, at least providing a brief respite from worrying about the Long Knives. But it was not to be. Two agency Lakota carrying a bold message from Bear Coat found the Crazy Horse camp. If the "wild" Lakota moved in to the agencies they would be given food but would have to give up weapons and horses. The message immediately revealed heretofore unspoken fears and opinions. To the surprise of those opposed to moving into the agencies, many more were in favor. The debates were long and heated in nearly every lodge, but, in the end, the council of old men turned down the offer and the messengers were sent back with their reply. Under cover of night, however, several families struck their lodges to follow them. Shortly after sunrise, Crazy Horse and several warriors caught up with the runaways.

The people knew Crazy Horse was a man formidable in battle, his often heart-stopping exploits told by men who saw him in action. Most of the people, however, saw him every day as a quiet man, one who worked hard to look after the welfare of all, a generous and gentle man. No one had ever seen him as an angry man, so it was a shock when he ordered the runaways' weapons confiscated and their horses shot. But a greater shock was that the loss of weapons and horses, or Crazy Horse's anger, didn't deter those who seemed driven to take their chances at the agencies. When a few families left, this time in broad daylight, he didn't attempt to stop them. Instead, he rode off into the hills alone to seek out the one friend that would never betray him—solitude.

Winter remained relentless, as did the Long Knives. Late in the Moon of Popping Trees, soldiers entered the valley of the Tongue. They knew that many of the "wild" Lakota winter camps were situated there—the Itazipacola, the Mniconju, as well as the Oglala—because it was common knowledge among the agency Lakota, and among their Crow scouts as well. The soldiers, led by hundreds of Crow and Snake scouts and a few Lakota, struck the lower camps first, with two cannons. The best that the Lakota defenders could do, with their pitiful supply of bullets, was to fight a delaying action while the women and children fled upriver. The soldiers kept coming.

Messengers reached the Crazy Horse camp further up river. The only tactical option was to form a defensive line against the soldiers while the women quickly struck their lodges for a prolonged flight to get as far away from the soldiers as possible. The soldiers came out of the morning fog, and then paused as two cannons were brought up on the line and opened fire. Some of the Lakota moved downslope to within bow range and began to harass the soldiers with showers of arrows lifted high to rain down among them. Infantry soldiers attacked, crossing over the ice at a bend in the river, pouring heavy fire into the advancing Lakota. Cannon fire boomed in the frigid morning air. The Lakota, maintaining cover as they moved, launched a mounted and foot assault and were quickly in the midst of the surprised soldiers. In close combat their heavy buffalo-hide coats were a detriment. The Lakota inflicted heavy casualties before they withdrew, suffering three killed. They had accomplished their objective, to disorganize the Long Knives and stop their advance so that the women and children could get as far away as possible.

Crazy Horse's people kept moving in spite of the freezing cold as Crazy Horse and several men fought a rearguard action, but the soldiers didn't pursue. Eventually the Lakota turned northwest for the region of the Big Horn River. Though they had successfully fought off the Long Knives, their sense of security was gone. The soldiers had attacked Crazy Horse's camp—a lance thrust at the heart if there ever was one. Another thrust came only days later, but not from the Long Knives.

The people had fled the Tongue River camp carrying only what was absolutely necessary, mainly lodge poles, lodge coverings, and little else. Most of the food supplies were left behind. While many of the men were out hunting, help arrived from a most unexpected source—Lakota from the agency. Thirty people, including women, led by Sword came with food and blankets, but also with a message.

Sword, gracious as ever, assured Crazy Horse's people that it was his idea to intervene because he didn't want his friends and relatives dying when peace and a good life could be had so easily. If Crazy Horse would come in—meaning surrender—his people would be given food, clothing, and blankets, and then he would be allowed to return to the Powder River area to claim it as his agency. This was the offer from a soldier named Clark, called White Hat by Sword, who spoke for Three Stars.

One of the thirty agency people was Woman's Dress, garbed in fine clothes as usual. He had given in to the agency long ago, which was not surprising. No doubt he had ingratiated himself to Three Stars or whoever else had power to give Woman's Dress the status he could never earn among his own people. Anyone who considered Woman's Dress anything more than a fop was not to be trusted.

Crazy Horse thanked Sword for the gift of food, but said he could give no answer to White Hat's offer until he had spoken to He Dog and Big Road.

The future had revealed itself again. Young Man Afraid had finally given in. Only he and Sitting Bull were stubborn, or perhaps foolish. How could anyone continue resisting when even a brief battle used up the bullets that took several days of scrounging? Half the people who followed him wanted to go into the agency; they were tired of running from the soldiers, tired of being hungry, tired of seeing relatives die. They stayed because they believed he had an answer of some kind, something that would solve the problem of the soldiers.

Sitting Bull had an answer. He was going up to Grandmother's Land—Canada. The Long Knives couldn't pursue him over the border, and there were still buffalo to hunt. It was an answer, and perhaps the right one for the Hunkpapa. But it also brought a sense of foreboding.

Crazy Horse met quietly with Sword before he departed to return to the agency and asked him to take a message back. If no more soldiers were sent against him he would consider the offer of White Hat and Three Stars.

No more soldiers came. Winter slid into the Moon of the Hard Times and it was a struggle just to find fresh meat. Hunters stalked rabbits as diligently as they did the elk. There was a feeling in the encampment, an unspoken one, weighed down with sadness and even more uncertainty. The old ones would walk to the crest of a hill on a windless day and stand, simply staring out over the land. Black Shawl was alone much of the time. She would find a hindquarter of elk or deer at the door of her lodge some mornings, or sometimes rabbits. She knew her husband was not far away, simply far enough so he could search for answers amid the solitude he so cherished.

Crazy Horse knew what would happen, what had to happen. There was no solution that could rid the Lakota of the Long Knives. Dull Knife was right; the Long Knives would not stop. Their objective was to place each and every Lakota on the agencies—or as one old man said, whoever was left alive. And that was the issue that was the basis for agonizing inner turmoil. For him to die fighting to the last was perhaps his fate; his vision told him that. But what of those left behind? Facing an enemy on the field of battle was one of the most daunting tasks any human being was required to do. But what about facing the Long Knives day in and day out in the confines of an agency at the mercy of their will? The only reassurance was that they would be alive to face it. Perhaps that was the best they could hope for. What of those who had died defending the Lakota way of life?

The breaks along the Big Horn River offered good shelter, usually a cut bank or a low bluff facing away from the wind. In such places, a man could sit and think. He could dig a deep pit to hold glowing embers after the flames of the fire burned down, and with a heat reflector opposite him a man could sit under a thick robe through the long nights, adding wood to replenish the coals. In such places a man could imagine that ghosts would come and sit as though warming themselves.

The living did find him. He Dog and Little Big Man came carrying the worry of his father and his wife. They saw that he was well, perhaps a little thin, but that his spirit was troubled. They joined him at the fire and talked of victories past, of good hunts, of good men, of the good life of the free, buffalo-hunting Lakota. In a voice barely louder than the crackling fire, Crazy Horse told them that, for the sake of the helpless ones, they must seriously consider going into the agency.

Crazy Horse returned to the encampment to learn that his life had taken a strange twist. Thinking to help settle his restlessness, his Sahiyela friends had arranged for him to take a second and younger wife. Unselfishly, Black Shawl agreed, but the young woman, whose family initially also agreed to the marriage, fled at the sight of Crazy Horse. He didn't pursue her or take insult but thought it best to give her back to her family. He and Black Shawl did eventually take in a widow, a Sahiyela. She helped keep the lodge in order and performed the chores Black Shawl could not. She, in effect, become a sister to them both.

The Red Cloud and Spotted Tail agencies were near the source of the White Earth River, fifteen to twenty days of travel from the Tongue River and Big Horn River region. Such a trip was not easy in warm weather, but certainly more bearable than traveling that distance in cold weather. And this winter was par-

ticularly harsh. Even so, another group arrived from the Spotted
Tail agency—Crazy Horse's uncle Spotted Tail himself, and a
hundred people. They had come to convince Crazy Horse to
come in to the agency.

There was fresh meat taken along the way by Spotted Tail
himself, along with many gifts, and visiting with relatives not
seen for several years. Not unexpectedly, the travelers from the
agency spoke highly of it, carrying the promise from Three Stars
brought earlier by the young White Hat Clark. If Crazy Horse
came in, his people would be given food, clothing, and blankets,
and they would be allowed to return to the Powder River country, which would be the Crazy Horse agency.

The visitors were invited into the lodges of their relatives, so
over the days of visiting the same message was repeated: food,
clothing, blankets, and their own agency. The buffalo were gone,
the Black Hills were lost, and so was the old life. Crazy Horse listened to his uncle speak eloquently for the good sense to yield to
the inevitable. Three Stars had sent a man he thought would
have the greatest influence on him. Or perhaps Spotted Tail had
taken it upon himself to talk to him. Either way, Crazy Horse
knew he was probably seeing the last peaceful overture. If he refused, he was afraid the soldiers would come again and keep
coming until they killed him or enough of his fighting men to
make further armed resistance impossible.

But it was the unspoken thoughts that weighed on him the
most, the thoughts not given the substance of words in his presence because his people knew he would be angry and hurt.
Many, perhaps most, of them were thinking that the wise course
would be to go into the agency. They were tired of being chased,
tired of seeing their relatives die, and tired of always sleeping un-
easily. Though those thoughts were not directly spoken, no caring person could ignore the pain of uncertainty in the eyes of the
women who had lost a son or a husband or a grandson. Who
could forget how many of Dull Knife's people would sit staring

vacantly into a fire? Spotted Tail spoke quietly of these realities in the lodge of Black Shawl and Crazy Horse—the same kind of realities that he had to face and base his decisions on.

Spotted Tail was still an imposing figure in spite of the burdens of leadership for over twenty years. Crazy Horse couldn't help but recall the troubles after the Grattan incident, when Woman Killer Harney had come with his Long Knives and carried out a sneak attack on Little Thunder's camp on the Blue Water, and Spotted Tail had led the counterattack against the soldiers, killing several in one memorable hand-to-hand fight before he was seriously wounded. Then he had offered himself to be punished in the place of several men who had been unjustly accused by the Long Knives, and was sent to the Leavenworth prison. Something had changed him. Something that now compelled him to speak for the very people he had wanted to wipe off the face of the earth. Perhaps whatever it was would change them all.

Crazy Horse spoke quietly, feeling his own burdens. "When the snow breaks I will give you my answer."

For the last time in his life he sought the comfort of solitude. But he found no peace, no answers for the turmoil that drove him to seek the shadowy places and the lonely, windswept ridges. Even the nearly endless view of mountains blending with the plains under a bright winter sun couldn't hold back the darkness he knew lay ahead. One day flowed into the next like early morning mist on the water. His ignored his own hunger even as he took his mare to a bare hillside to let her graze.

The land seemed unchanged, but it had been. There were new trails or old ones with new tracks—tracks not made by moccasins, drag poles, or unshod horses. There were new tracks made by wagon wheels, the iron horse shoes, and the stiff boots of the soldiers. And there were the forts, little islands of fear and arrogance, like pimples on a clean face. What the land itself might think of such changes, he didn't know.

Out of the swirl of windblown snow came an old man to sit at his fire. He was a holy man and a grandfather. He had come with a bag of pounded meat and questions in his eyes. Over the fire they sat through the night absorbing every bit of heat they could, surrounded by the melodious baying of wolves and the strident barking of coyotes. They talked of the past because they knew it and it validated who and what they were. They said little of the future because it was a visitor without a face. Sometime after sunrise the old man fell asleep. When he awoke he gathered his buffalo robe around his shoulders and rode away.

Crazy Horse watched the old man go. The holy man embodied all that the Lakota were, and he was riding away growing smaller and smaller in the distance.

In essence, the rattlesnake had come into the lodge and they couldn't crush it. Now they must live with it.

Twenty

✤ *A lake was the first thing he saw, a small still lake. Bursting upward from the blue calmness a horse and its rider shattered the surface and rode out across the land.*

✤

Dust from hundreds of unshod hooves floated up in small swirls to form a choking brown cloud, partially obscuring the riders in the middle and rear of the disorderly mob of sixty or more. Lakota horsemen were nothing new among the rolling hills near the headwaters of the White Earth River. They rode into the hot, late summer afternoon, a procession of horses and stern-faced riders pushed along by circumstances beyond their control and hiding a dark purpose inside the dust.

Nearly a day's ride to the south was the Running Water. Four or five days' ride to the east stood the sharply rolling sand hills. This awareness of such familiar landmarks in Lakota territory was of no concern, however, to the mob. If the man at the center of the lead riders had any thoughts not connected to the heaviness of the moment, he gave no indication. His face, burned brown by the sun, appeared more relaxed than those around him, his light-brown hair unbound. His dark eyes were alert and intense, however. Most of the brown-faced, braided men riding near him wore the dark blue uniform coat of the Long Knives, and were armed with rifles and pistols.

Men and horses on either side hemmed in Crazy Horse solidly. On the opposite side rode Touch the Clouds. Directly ahead was Fast Thunder, who had pleaded with him to go back to Camp Robinson and speak to Randall, the man in charge who would listen and speak for Three Stars. Riding in a wagon were Swift Bear, Black Crow, and High Bear. They didn't have the same feelings about Randall or Three Stars, but couldn't talk Crazy Horse into staying away. There was nothing else that could be done. After he left Spotted Tail's agency, the blue-coated riders had met him on the trail and he immediately knew they had been sent to bring him back to Camp Robinson. No one but Three Stars could have given that order.

The mob all around him was expecting trouble from him. The one man to depend on if any trouble started was Touch the Clouds. Swift Bear, Black Crow, and High Bear had sometimes sided with Spotted Tail against him. It was useless to think of fighting because even if they were all on his side they numbered less than the fingers of a hand. What could a handful do against sixty or more? They would be no more than leaves in a flash flood. Nearby was a man who wanted to be his friend, Lieutenant Lee. Next to him was the speaks-white, Louie Bordeaux, the son of old Jim, but perhaps not so trustworthy as his father had been.

To the west far beyond the sandstone bluffs on the edge of the pine-choked ridges waited the Powder River country and the Shining Mountains. Nearly four months had passed since the Crazy Horse people had arrived at Camp Robinson, 900 people in all, with over 1,500 horses. The soldiers had taken their horses first, and then their guns, and then their hope. In four months, the promise of an agency of their own in the north had turned into an impossible dream. He blamed himself partly because he could do nothing. Perhaps if he had learned to be an agency Lakota and put on the defeated smile in the presence of Three Stars and the other soldier leaders, none of this would be happening.

But the soldiers were not the only ones to cause the turmoil of the past four months. The finger of blame could be pointed at many Lakota as well. In fact, they were mostly to blame. The white agents and the army officers fanned the flames of jealousy and let little minds that could not think beyond the moment, and little men, who yearned for recognition and power, do the rest. There was no other way to look at it. In the end, the Lakota defeated themselves. They had the whites outnumbered and outmanned and did nothing. The entire garrison could have been overrun by enough determined Lakota fighting men with a good plan, if they truly wanted to return to living the old way in control of their lands and their lives. Instead, men stepped over each other to betray their own relatives in order to obtain the power handed out by the whites, a power they couldn't get on their own.

So the disorderly mob of horsemen rode on, and soon the outer buildings of Camp Robinson could be seen. A large group of riders approached, one galloping ahead of the others over a low, grassy rise. It was He Dog. Ignoring dozens of threatening glances, he pushed his way through the front line of riders and took up a position beside Crazy Horse.

Black Shawl was with his father and mother in the Spotted Tail camp, and she would be safe there from whatever trouble might happen at Robinson. Crazy Horse had taken her there the day before. The coughing sickness had weakened her, but the medicine from the post infirmary seemed to be helping. She let herself be taken into the lodge of Worm, who had chosen to be with his wife's Sicangu relatives.

Black Shawl was one reason Crazy Horse had gone to the Spotted Tail camp, but he had also hoped his uncle could help put an end to this foolishness of lies that turned friends against one another. For a time, He Dog had turned away from him and Young Man Afraid was still angry. Crazy Horse had no intention of accepting the power held out to him by the whites, because he didn't want Spotted Tail pushed aside as headman of his own agency. But he did want his uncle to speak for him, to use his influence with the whites, especially Three Stars, to convince them that he only wanted to live in peace. But the lies had gotten to Spotted Tail as well, it would seem. Instead of reassurances he threw down scolding words.

✛

The slender rider wore his hair long and loose, and a stone tied behind his left ear, a lightning mark across his face, and on his chest were painted hailstones.

✛

A buffalo hunt had been promised. But there had been no hunt and Crazy Horse understood why. First, someone with more power than Three Stars had to say that the Lakota could go chasing buffalo. If given the opportunity, Three Stars reasoned, the hunters would keep going, perhaps all the way to Grandmother's Land to join Sitting Bull. Added to that, some among the Lakota complained to Three Stars that if Crazy Horse and his young men were allowed to hunt buffalo, then everyone must be allowed. And it was a Lakota who warned that it was dangerous to put guns in the hands of Crazy Horse.

✛

The unorganized procession came to the edge of Camp Robinson. Hundreds of Lakota were waiting, watching the riders approach. He Dog glanced nervously at Crazy Horse. The sun was near the western horizon and sending the shadows long and deep across the town.

Crazy Horse knew that the trouble started long before he had selected a place along Cottonwood Creek for his camp, a short ride from Camp Robinson. It started when someone, perhaps Three Stars, told both Spotted Tail and Red Cloud that bringing in the last band of "wild" Indians would go far to strengthen their own status with the "great father." Spotted Tail had been the first to make the long trip from the White Earth River, and he had smiled when he said the Lakota at his agency wanted for nothing. Red Cloud had met them along the way on the Powder River. Like Spotted Tail, he had brought gifts. "All is well," he had said. "Come on in."

So two men who had made strong reputations in the free-roaming days and had once looked down on agents and soldier leaders with the utmost disdain, were now forced to do their bidding or face losing the power given to them like one gives a toy to a child. After many of the soldier leaders at Camp Robinson came to Crazy Horse with questions about the Greasy Grass fight and the defeat of Long Hair, the two agency "chiefs" sent messages complaining to Three Stars. Perhaps there was no place for another agency "chief." Crazy Horse thought to reassure his uncle and Red Cloud that he had no wish to be made a "chief" of any kind, but he knew anything he had to say to them would not be regarded as the truth.

But eventually the rumors did fly. It was said Three Stars would make Crazy Horse "chief" over everyone, including Spotted Tail and Red Cloud. To make matters worse, many of the lesser soldier leaders were themselves saying that Crazy Horse could influence the younger men better than the two older leaders could. Through it all, he had tried to talk to Three Stars about the promise of the northern agency, day after day traveling to Robinson from Cottonwood Creek. He grew more and more frustrated each time the general had other responsibilities to attend to first. White Hat Clark sent a message as if to an impatient child. Three Stars was very busy working hard to care for fifteen thousand Lakota, not to mention some Sahiyela and Blue Clouds, and it was the "great father" who had the power to decide about agencies.

If you want your agency, some of Crazy Horse's friends said carefully in low voices—for it was hard to know who might be listening—you will have to travel to their place of power where the "great father" lives and speak to him face to face. Of course, they warned, if Three Stars sends you ahead of Red Cloud or Spotted Tail, they will find a way to make it difficult for us while you are gone. They will find a way to take you down when you return.

He had no wish to travel to the "great father" and curry favor from a man he didn't know. He would be out of place and only something for show, someone to perform for the powerful. Crazy Horse did not wish to be a thing of curiosity. Whites in the east country would see him as the killer of Long Hair and nothing else. And as the old men warned, power does not listen with honest ears to the whispers of the powerless. Furthermore, if there had been truthfulness in the promise of the northern agency, they would be there now. No use to go see the "great father," they said. Stay and protect us against our own kind.

The mob of riders pushed the crowd aside at the edge of the town. Fast Thunder turned and spoke words Crazy Horse couldn't hear. Never had so many people gathered in one place since he had come to Camp Robinson. He grabbed the folded blanket from the withers of his yellow pinto and draped it over his arm. There had not been half this many fighting men at the Greasy Grass fight. There was a strange heaviness in the air like a gathering storm. He glanced toward He Dog, who was suddenly pressed in from both sides and forced to slow his horse. Touch the Clouds, too, was straining to stay close.

Behind them as they galloped was a rising cloud and the deep rumble of thunder and flashes of lightning.

The young men had a plan. They would slip away one and two at a time and scatter their leaving over so many days so the soldiers wouldn't notice their absence. There were nearly ten thousand men between the two agencies, some had heard. Who would miss a few? When enough had gone or all that wanted to had left, then Crazy Horse could slip away in the night and join them at a certain place to be agreed upon, on a certain day. They would have to think of ways to acquire guns and bullets, of course, but that could be done. With enough guns and good horses they could wage war against the whites. They could attack stagecoaches, small settlements, and freight wagons and get the soldiers to chase them out in the open where the big Long Knife horses were at a disadvantage. As a mounted force, the Lakota were much better fighters than the soldiers. Living off the land and without the burden of women and children to protect, they could show the whites that the Lakota understood that killing was the way to win.

Crazy Horse had two concerns about the plan: the whites would retaliate by sending families to the south country, to that place called The Nations where people sicken and die, or, if that didn't stop the raiders, they would start killing their families.

The young men said nothing more about the plan. But some did slip away, it was said, although no one spoke of them or could remember exactly who they were. At times, it could not be remembered if any young men actually did slip away, especially when the whites were asking.

Fast Thunder turned and pointed toward the soldier commander's house. The crowd of Lakota with a few soldiers among them flowed around the mounted mob, forcing them to stop. Crazy Horse recognized a few young men far back in the crowd from his camp and many of the angry faces all around him he recognized as well. Someone shouted, "Clear the way!" and the crowd moved back, but not far. Fast Thunder motioned for Crazy Horse to dismount and follow. Crazy Horse wrapped the folded blanket over his arm and dismounted. He Dog and Touch the Clouds had also dismounted and were pushing to get to him, but blue-coated Lakota scouts working for the soldiers moved in to block them.

People still complained and worried when he went off alone to think. The agents and the soldiers always wanted to know where he was every day. Perhaps it was his place to harangue the whites on behalf of the people, but he had never been one to speak long or loudly. Not long ago, that was a good thing for a man of the people, but now it was a weakness in the face of the whites who seemed to think only in large numbers and loud noises.

Showing weakness in front of his friends and relatives was not the thing to do, so he sought the solitude of Beaver Mountain and Crow Butte. Nothing seemed to exist beyond what he could see in any direction. His lands had grown small, it seemed.

The Sun Dance on top of Beaver Mountain had also been a celebration of the victory on the Greasy Grass. Five of his cousins had pierced and tied themselves to the sacred center tree in his honor. It had been a time of hope and remembering. For a few days, they had all felt strong again and some of the old pride returned to the eyes of some of the old ones. For a few days, they put aside the troubles and told stories, and remembered when they were powerful and flourished over the land.

But the worst trouble came when the Nez Perce—who were a mountain people from the northwest and had their own troubles with soldiers—were trying to escape to Grandmother's Land and were soundly outfighting all the soldiers sent to stop them in the north country. Three Stars had asked for scouts from Crazy Horse's men, hoping that it would take the edge off their restlessness, especially if Crazy Horse himself would join. They would be paid, Three Stars had said, and given a blue coat to wear and a rifle to carry. Three Stars was so certain Crazy Horse would become a scout that he had a blue coat sent to him with the messengers, a blue coat with the three stripes of a sergeant on the sleeves. And a paper had been signed to give him the pay money.

At the same time, White Hat Clark had taken the coats and rifles from two hundred fifty men from Spotted Tail and Red Cloud, saying he no longer needed them as scouts. Red Cloud was quick to complain, especially since he had not been made a sergeant of scouts. But Grabber—the black man from a land no one knew, and a speaks-white who was the go-between for the soldiers—had something to do with the troubles that followed. In reply to Three Stars' offer Crazy Horse had replied, "If we take this trail, we will fight until no Nez Perce is left alive." After the soldier leaders heard Grabber translate his words, they became nervous, and some became angry.

Three Stars also became very angry when Grabber told him Crazy Horse's answer, and the offer of guns and blue coats and the chance to ride after the Nez Perce was taken back. The old men were glad because the Nez Perce were doing something the Lakota should be doing, they said—fighting for their freedom. Crazy Horse agreed. If he could help the Nez Perce, he would, he said to the old men.

White Hat Clark came one day to scold him for the words he had sent to Three Stars. The words Grabber had turned from

Lakota to the white man's language had only convinced Three Stars that Red Cloud had been right, that Crazy Horse could not be trusted.

It was his new wife, Nellie, herself a speaks-white, who helped him to understand Three Stars' anger. Grabber, it seemed, had twisted his words, saying: "We will fight until no white man is left alive," as Crazy Horse's words.

Crazy Horse was aware that some in his camp were angry with him for taking the offer of a new wife, arranged by White Hat Clark, to help take the edge off his anger over the broken promise of the northern agency. She was the daughter of the trader Joe Larrabee and his Lakota wife. And perhaps she had taken some of the words spoken in his lodge with the old ones and warrior leaders to White Hat, but she had not lied about Grabber.

Clearly, the black man Grabber was working for Red Cloud.

The crowd moved like the swirling waters of a sudden bend in a stream and Crazy Horse lost sight of Fast Thunder as well as He Dog and Touch the Clouds. Lieutenant Lee was suddenly in front and pointing off to the left. A strong hand grabbed his arm just above the elbow. "Go that way," a voice behind him said. It might have been Little Big Man in his blue soldier coat.

The horse changed colors as bullets and arrows filled the air, all passing harmlessly. Close above flew a red-tailed hawk.

They stopped north of Camp Robinson and camped for three days, where they feasted and danced and knew the last taste of life without the whim of the white man hanging over them. It was a strange time, as if they were moving from the sunlight into shadow. At the place where sunlight and shadow meet, it is often difficult to see clearly either way. The sunlight seems too bright and the shadow too deep.

In no hurry to put their feet on the new road that awaited them, they broke camp leisurely and finally started toward Camp Robinson when the sun was well past its high point in the sky. Above the soldier town, they were met by White Hat Clark leading a small column of horse soldiers and Red Cloud with a few of his headmen. Clark and Red Cloud led them down into the valley.

His uncle Little Hawk, Big Road, He Dog, and Little Big Man—all dressed in their finest—rode with him, Little Big Man most defiant of all. Behind them came the fighting men, perhaps 150, then the long line of people, some walking, most riding, women holding the lead ropes to the travois horses, dogs and older children still playful even on this day.

This land was not unknown to the Crazy Horse people. Many had traveled this way before, often camping in this very valley with their Sicangu relatives. Off to the east a few days' ride was the sandstone bluff where he had spent the night and dreamed his vision.

The soldier town was not as big as other white-man settlements. As they reached the outer edges, the blue-coat soldiers could be seen, numbering just a few, among the hundreds of Lakota waiting to see them. Then his warriors began to sing a greeting song and the people behind them joined until it seemed everyone was singing. A song of greeting and peace, a hope lifted to the Grandfather that this new road would not be too difficult.

They followed White Hat past the fort, past all the watchers—both Lakota and white—to an open flat beyond the fort. Crazy Horse saw No Water and Woman's Dress among the men riding with Red Cloud. When they stopped, White Hat told them they must give up their horses. There was surprise and grumbling among the warriors, but when Crazy Horse turned over his yellow pinto to the soldier in front of him, all was quiet, and a little at a time the horses were taken. The women worked fast to un-hitch the drag poles from the travois horses.

The warriors talked low among themselves as they watched the horses being led away by soldiers and Lakota men wearing blue coats. Other Lakota, including Red Cloud, waited on their horses and watched. This was a new feeling for the Crazy Horse people. A Lakota warrior without his horse was like sunrise without sunset.

Next, the lodges were pitched, and as the women worked, several white men walked among the people counting and mark-ing on the papers they carried. White Hat Clark went to Crazy Horse and spoke through two men, Grabber and one called Garnier, both speaks-whites. The weapons were to be taken next, White Hat said. There was a silence as before when the horses were taken. And, as before, Crazy Horse was the first to give his rifle to White Hat. One long, silent, angry moment later, the warriors began to lay down their weapons.

It was a time, that first afternoon at Camp Robinson, many people remembered and talked about often. But, of course, it was not a good remembering. Almost in the same breath they wondered how it was up north and if the elk in the Shining Mountains would be fat this year.

The soldier commander's house was off to the right, in the di-rection Fast Thunder had disappeared. Suddenly Crazy Horse was being taken to another place. Perhaps Three Stars and Ran-dall were waiting elsewhere. The surge of the men all around them wouldn't let him turn.

He was astonished, though not surprised. Many Sahiyela fight-ing men had been sent away to places where the whites imprisoned their enemies. Spotted Tail had been held in a place called Leavenworth. From there, he had returned with a new fear of the whites. Perhaps they wanted to send him away so that he would change his way of thinking as well, suggested his young wife. First, they wanted to send him to dance for the "great father." Now they wanted to send him away to a place at the end of their world—all because they thought he wanted to kill Three Stars. Perhaps it was Grabber's words put in his mouth by Red Cloud.

There would be trouble. Soldiers were coming for him, it was reported, with wagon guns. If trouble started in the Cottonwood camp, too many people could get hurt. He had seen what those wagon guns were able to do. His new wife had a place in her father's lodge, but Black Shawl would have no one if they came for him. So he decided to take her to the Spotted Tail camp. There, he could ask his uncle for help as well.

So they rode away at a high lope. The watchers from Red Cloud rode away with news of their leaving, and down the trail, a group of riders led by No Water took after them. Crazy Horse took the lead rope of Black Shawl's horse. With his uncle Little Hawk's method he had used many times before, he let the horses walk up the hills and then ran them down slope. They outdistanced No Water and his men who pushed their horses without stopping until they killed two or three, it was said.

At Spotted Tail, Crazy Horse hurried to the camp of Touch the Clouds where all was in uncertain turmoil. The women were striking their lodges and preparing to find safe places to hide, and the men were making ready for a fight. Word of trouble and fighting to come—Lakota against Lakota—had traveled quickly from Camp Robinson. When No Water appeared, a few of the younger Mniconju charged out to stop him and turned him away. He and his exhausted horses could do no more than head for the lodge of Spotted Tail himself.

Lieutenant Lee, the soldier leader in charge at Spotted Tail's agency, sent word that Crazy Horse must come to the soldier house. Crazy Horse rode out with Touch the Clouds and White Thunder, followed by Mniconju and Oglala. Spotted Tail and over a hundred of his young men met them on the trail. Lee arrived with Black Crow and Louie Bordeaux and was frightened seeing that he was between the Mniconju and Oglala on one side and Spotted Tail's Sicangu on the other. There were shouts and threats hurled back and forth and weapons were brandished, until Crazy Horse raised a hand and a silence slowly fell over the gathering. Lee, now very frightened, told Crazy Horse that he must return to Robinson and make it good with the soldier leaders there.

Spotted Tail waited and then spoke. It was far past the time to learn to live with the whites, he admonished. But there was no room for troublemakers at his agency. The sharp, scolding words were much like those the agents and soldier leaders often threw at the Lakota. Crazy Horse said nothing, then told Lieutenant Lee he would be ready to leave in the morning because he had to see to his sick wife first.

He and Black Shawl spent the night in the lodge of Touch the Clouds. She sat up at every noise to his quiet assurances that young men were positioned all around outside to prevent trouble. Through the night, he sat against a willow chair, listening. There was movement all around, and voices, too. Young men came to the door—earnest, stalwart young men who were the next generation of warriors.

"Lead us north, Uncle," they said. "Take your family and we will travel with you. There is nothing but trouble here, bad trouble."

"There are good men here," he replied, "but not enough to take care of the helpless ones."

The young men nodded sadly, and went away.

So the night passed and the morning came. When the sun arose, he hurried to the soldier house to speak to Lieutenant

Lee, to assure him that he had not changed his mind and was ready to speak with Randall to make things good. So, with Touch the Clouds, Swift Bear, and Black Crow along, they started out for Camp Robinson.

The first group of blue-coated Lakota met them along the trail. They said nothing and formed a wide half-circle around Crazy Horse and the others. Further on, more blue-coated Lakota arrived and now they became a mob of more than sixty. It was then that Crazy Horse knew there was trouble.

On the shore of the lake the people rose up and grabbed the rider, pulling him down from behind.

Fast Thunder was lost in the crowd. So, too, were He Dog and Touch the Clouds. All around was the noise of running and scuffling as if men were pushing each other. Crazy Horse was pushed toward a square house made of logs, a strange place for Randall to be. Before he could help himself, he was through the open doorway. There was a bad smell. A man with dark hair and braids rose from a corner. Then he saw the iron bars.

He spun on a heel and saw a man—Little Big Man—blocking the opening. Crazy Horse shoved the shorter man aside and tried to push past but almost immediately felt Little Big Man grab both his arms from behind. With a great effort, he pulled himself free and reached into the opening of his blanket for the knife. Outside, there were shouts of both soldiers and the Lakota.

"Let me go!" he said to Little Big Man. "Let me go!"

The man, the Oglala warrior who had ridden into battle with him, stood fast. Perhaps it was the blue coat of the soldier that had turned his heart. With a sudden swipe, Crazy Horse slashed the arm of the coat and immediately blood flowed, and Little Big

Man jumped back. With a step, Crazy Horse was outside and there was movement everywhere. More hands grabbed at him from either side, brown hands holding him fast. The strident voice of a soldier yelled.

From the middle of the confusion came a soldier, thrusting with the knife at the end of his rifle. Those near him heard Crazy Horse gasp and saw his knees begin to wobble. Brown hands were still holding his arms even as the soldier withdrew the long knife.

"Let me go," they heard him say quietly, "you've gotten me hurt."

Then he fell.

❖

He was covered with a red blanket on the floor of the post surgeon's office. Opening his eyes, he tried to focus on the form above him, his father, Worm. Touch the Clouds sat cross-legged on the other side, head down. The room was dim, lit by a single lamp.

Crazy Horse had protested when the men who carried him in tried to lay him on a cot, and so they lowered him to the floor. The surgeon gave him medicine to sleep and take away the pain. Touch the Clouds had been alone with him for much of the evening until Worm had arrived. Together, they had watched the slight rise and fall of the wounded man's chest and listened to his shallow breathing. So they had waited, the powerful warrior and the skilled healer, and neither could do anything to fight against death, or to fight for the life of the man on the floor.

With great effort, the man under the red blanket lifted a hand, motioning his father to lean close. His voice was hoarse, barely above a whisper.

"Tell the people they should not depend on me any longer."

The hand fell, the slight rising and falling of the chest stopped.

Touch the Clouds reached over and laid a palm against the scars on the left side of his face, then withdrew his hand to wipe the tears sliding down his own face.

Worm reached slowly down and laid his hands on the top of his son's head. Since childhood, his son's hair had always been soft and fine. Moving a hand down, he gently closed the eyes, and wept.

So ended the journey.

Twenty-one

The old man and his wife drove their wagon through the darkness until they reached the edge of the soldier town and saw the team of horses and another wagon appear as dark shapes. The old woman began to sob softly again when she saw the soldier wagon in the darkness.

The men waiting with the wagon were afraid; someone had pointed a gun at them, they said. Nervously, they helped to lift the body down and place it on the drag poles behind the travois horse Worm had brought along. One of the men said Lieutenant Lee ordered them to turn over the wagon and team, but Worm refused. His son had lived as a Lakota and his final journey across this Earth would be as a Lakota, across the drag poles pulled by a good horse, not in the bed of a white man's wagon. The men unhitched the team and led them away, leaving the wagon.

The old woman pulled aside the blanket covering his face and stroked his hair, then threw herself across his chest and loosed her pain and grief from the very depths of her soul, giving voice to the darkness all around.

"My son! My son! What have you done? Why have you left us?"

Worm waited, wiping his own tears. Anger and confusion were waiting in the night. The young men who wanted to follow his son back to the old life, who hoped he would lead them out, were honing their shock and disbelief into the sharp edge of revenge. In the lodges along Cottonwood Creek, the harangues for war mingled with the tears. Inside Camp Robinson, the soldiers and all the whites waited, wondering when anger would swoop in from the darkness. At the Red Cloud and Spotted Tail agencies, they waited, too, wondering how many would carry out the attack.

The old woman gathered herself together and gently caressed the pale face and lifted the blankets over his head. Worm helped the old woman onto the seat of the wagon and handed her the reins; then he mounted the travois horse. She shook the reins of the two sturdy horses and the wagon creaked. They moved off into the night to begin the saddest journey they would ever make.

Worm wanted to move quickly. He knew that someone was out there. Whether white or Lakota, it didn't matter. They were after the reward for the head of their son. Two hundred dollars.

The sun was rising when they reached Beaver Valley. Already people in the camp were awake. Many didn't know what was happening, but when they saw Worm and his wife with the blanket-covered body, they knew.

The daughter of Bad Heart Bull and two others had been waiting and helped the two old people. They took the travois horse and untied the poles. Worm warned two men who approached that they had been followed through the night and whoever it was may still be looking to cause trouble. The men went back for their weapons.

The young women wept as they uncovered the body. They removed the shirt and washed away the dust and blood from his face, arms, and the wounds with fresh water from two buckets. They cut away the leggings and slipped off his moccasins and finished washing him. Then they prepared him for burial.

Down the sides of his arms, they anointed him with red and wept again as they remembered his words, spoken not two months before: If anything should happen to me, paint my body red and put me in water and my life will return. If you do not, my bones will turn to stone and my joints to flint, but my spirit will rise.

They brushed his hair and painted him as if for war, the yellow lightning mark over the left side of his face and the still visible scar from the pistol wound, then blue hailstones on his chest. To his left ear they tied a reddish brown stone.

Worm next braided a narrow strip down the back of his head, and then cut it close to the scalp. The lock of hair would go into his spirit bundle. Finally, the dried body of a red-tailed hawk was tied to the top of his head.

His mother helped wrap him in new deer hides, tenderly touching his cheek before his face was covered for the last time. Over the deer hides was sewn a buffalo hide with the hair side out. After they finished, Worm smudged them all with sage and sweet grass and sang an honoring song. Then the body was reloaded onto the drag poles.

They led the horse to a meadow above Beaver Creek on the west side. A tree had been chosen by some of the men, a sturdy ash whose main branches were like the fingers of a hand. Across one of its forks, a scaffold had been built and onto it the men placed the body.

That day and into the night, Worm and his wife sat beneath the tree, their clothes cut like ribbons to show they were mourning. Warriors came, among them the five who had pierced themselves in his honor at the Sun Dance. People brought food and ate together to show they shared the grief. Old men stood in front of the gathering and wept as they told stories of he who had left them—of his deeds, of his strengths and weaknesses, of his good quiet ways. What is to happen to us now? they asked.

After sunset the following day, the scaffold was taken down and the body loaded once more onto the drag poles by warriors old and young, by those who had followed him and those who wished they could have. And the people watched as Worm and his wife led the travois horse holding the body of their son off into the darkness. It was their wish to do this final task alone.

The old man and the old woman walked without fear across

the land, for they knew it well. Neither did they fear death, for they knew it well, too. The other mother of their young man had left them before he did.

Across meadows and dry creek beds they moved steadily, now and then stopping to rest briefly, and then finally to the base of a long slope. There, they rested once more, and then found a narrow trail that took them to their final destination.

Sunrise found them back among the people at Beaver Creek. Worm paused to look across the land and went into the lodge that had been pitched for them. The old woman walked to a far hillside and found a rock to sit on. There, she sat looking across the valley until the sun went down.

No one asked the old man or the old woman where they had taken him because they knew that knowledge would go with them to their graves. But many could see that Worm carried the spirit bundle, and when he spoke of his son, there was one thing he would always say:

Life is a circle. The end of one journey is the beginning of the next.

Reflections:
So That the People May Live

I go forward under the banner of the people.
I do this so that the people may live.

—Lakota warrior philosophy

Historians, anthropologists, and other outside observers of indigenous cultures on Turtle Island are still quick to conclude that the native tribes of the northern Plains were "warlike." Catchy phrases may be exciting titles for papers or dissertations or effective leverage to gain funding for a sociological study, but they obscure reality. For example, one anthropologist stated that the Oglala Lakota would start a fight just to see if their bowstrings were taut enough. Such sensationalist pronouncements are nothing more than attempted validation for ethnocentric bias rather than an honest, objective conclusion as a consequence of unbiased study. And, unfortunately, one of the realities obscured is the Lakota warrior's strong belief in serving one's community and nation.

The Lakota fighting man of old has long suffered from an image of flamboyance, aggressiveness, and mean-spiritedness. Those observers who didn't or wouldn't look beyond the feathers and war paint are responsible for foisting that image upon us. Behind the warrior's accoutrements and habiliments was a man, a thinking, feeling, mortal man with strengths, weaknesses, hopes, dreams, and a family and a strong sense of commitment to cause and country. During the recent initial fighting in Afghanistan, American combat casualties were publicized by the press, giving television viewers a personal insight. Consequently the serviceman became more than one of many wearing the same uniform because we heard his name, saw photos of his childhood, the names of his wife and children and parents, the length of his military service, and his particular job in the Army, Air Force, or Marine Corps. We found much in common. We connected him to ourselves, or a father, brother, or close friend who served and perhaps died in combat. But if we chose, for some reason, not to look beyond the camouflage uniform, he would be just another "serviceman," an expendable commodity, a faceless extension of us, one of many sent to a strange land. But we didn't. We did extend our thoughts and prayers to his loved ones because he died in the service of his country; he died for us.

If we as a nation have learned anything from the tragic events of September 11, 2001, and of the issues and challenges that have unfolded since, one of the lessons surely is that we are not immune to attack no matter how strong or invincible we think we are. Within the shadows of that lesson is one as equally important: we must be prepared to defend ourselves. The survival of any group, society, or nation is directly connected to its willingness to defend itself, and the willingness and ability to defend itself is dependent on the depth of the devotion of its people. That kind of devotion is not the exclusive domain of any one culture or race of people. It is a basic human characteristic augmented by cultural beliefs and traditions. Such devotion is part of the history of the Lakota people.

The summer of 1876 was truly exciting and significant for the Lakota and the nation overall. It was a culmination and a turning point. First there was a strong response to Sitting Bull's message to gather. Few, if any, leaders on this continent then and since have had the level of credibility and influence that would galvanize *one fourth* of the population to travel hundreds of miles to meet and discuss issues of national importance. Crazy Horse's considerable reputation and quiet charisma matched Sitting Bull's skill as a politician and orator. Although there were many other well-known and respected political and military leaders present, none had achieved the status of either Sitting Bull or Crazy Horse in the hearts and minds of the people. Together they provided visionary leadership and a sense of cohesiveness and a feeling of strength.

In the summer of 1876 Sitting Bull was undeniably the most powerful political leader among all the Lakota bands. He was still capable as a fighting man but his real strength was in his ability to communicate. He was feverishly attempting to convince enough Lakota to serve the good of all by uniting against a formidable common enemy, one that threatened to destroy their way of life. No enemy had ever faced them with that possible consequence. He knew that his purpose was to bring everyone together under a common cause; after that he was counting on the military leaders, Crazy Horse first and foremost, to step up and lead the Lakota militarily. Both men, each in his way, were calling their constituents to serve, to put their time, talents, and experience to work to solve a very large problem. Therefore, as Sitting Bull watched Crazy Horse invoke the ancient ritual of *Wica Mnaiciyapi,* he probably felt an overwhelming sense of satisfaction that his message was getting through.

As Sitting Bull watched the throng of fighting men answer the call, he certainly realized what they would encounter in combat, but he may not have fully considered what lay ahead for those several hundred warriors as they left the encampment. History has not focused as much on the battle toward which Crazy Horse was leading his men. It is known as the Battle of the Rosebud because it occurred in the valley of Rosebud Creek, one of the tributaries that flowed north into the Yellowstone River. It occurred on June 17. There is obviously more attention to the battle of eight days later, the Battle of the Little Bighorn. But to understand fully the reason for the outcome of both battles, we should examine the significance of the night of June 16, 1876, and what it reveals about service to one's cause and nation.

The Lakota encampment on June 16 was near Ash Creek, a few miles from its confluence with the Greasy Grass (Little Bighorn) River. The scouts had reported the soldiers to be in the area where Goose Creek flowed into Rosebud Creek, a distance of about fifty miles from Ash Creek in a southeasterly direction. Crazy Horse and his men departed from the Ash Creek encampment at dusk. The summer solstice was days away, so daylight lingered further into the evening. From today's perspective that meant the warriors left the encampment around 10 P.M. on June 16 and the first shots were fired seven hours later at dawn, or about 5 A.M. on June 17.

Moving troops at night is a sound tactical maneuver but can often prove to be a logistical problem. In this instance at least three factors contributed to the success of this action. One, the Lakota, especially men from Crazy Horse's band, knew this particular area well. Two, at least one scout who had ridden north with the news of the soldier column was leading the way back, over the trail he had traveled only hours before. And three, riding great distances at night was nothing new to the Lakota and the Sahiyela. Nevertheless, anyone who knows the West or is an experienced rider understands that the seemingly simple act of riding a horse for fifty miles is not, even in the daylight. The fact remains, however, that several hundred riders, many leading a second horse, traveled through the night over the rough, uneven terrain of the Wolf Mountains.

Fifty miles and some seven hours afford ample time to think. No one knew specifically what would happen when they reached their objective or where exactly the enemy would be. The one unavoidable fact facing them all was that there would be a battle. Many of the men riding through the night were combat veterans and many had fought against white soldiers. They knew what to expect. But this particular situation had an added dimension. The older veterans understood the circumstances and concerns that had brought them all together at Ash Creek. They knew that riding through the night to face a persistent enemy was part of the process of alleviating the threat to the very existence of the Lakota. This was not a war party to demonstrate how much braver the Lakota were in battle. This was a mission wherein the enemy had to be thoroughly defeated, where body count was just as important as tromping the enemy's spirit. It was the message Crazy Horse had been preaching: Kill the white enemy because that's how he counted his victories and assessed his defeats.

Most, if not all, had answered the call in this particular instance because of the man issuing the call: Crazy Horse. Riding into battle with such a man was something to tell the children and grandchildren. But once the initial fervor had dissipated somewhat, reality set in. Thoughts of family rode with them and certainly thoughts of the enemy they would face. Many prayed for courage, strength, and victory. And those with little or no combat experience were likely plagued with uncertainty about themselves, hoping and praying they wouldn't break and run when the shooting started.

So they rode through the night—eager, apprehensive, circumspect, perhaps talkative, but most of all silently introspective—picking their way up the western slopes through the sagebrush and prickly pear cactus, and over the divide and down the eastern side. At dawn they reached their objective and immediately engaged the enemy. In spite of the fifty-mile trek, they and their horses, without any significant rest, had enough stamina to engage in combat for ten to twelve hours. Half of that time was under a fierce sun.

The enemy was cavalry and mounted infantry of the United

States Army, a 1,000-man force augmented by 300 Shoshoni and Crow Indians, under the overall command of Brigadier General George Crook, known as "Three Stars" to the Lakota. They were encamped along Rosebud Creek in a valley a few miles northeast of the present town of Sheridan, Wyoming.

The scrutiny of hindsight suggests that the battle was a draw. Crazy Horse and his men withdrew from the field in the late afternoon, and Crook's soldiers could do little more than watch them leave, although there was one aborted attempt at pursuit. Perhaps it was a draw because of the weariness of Crazy Horse's warriors and their horses after an all-night ride. If Crazy Horse could have engaged his enemy with fresh men and horses the outcome would have been a decisive victory. But that they could fight a numerically superior and better-armed force to a standstill *after* a seven-hour ride is testament to commitment. Although the Lakota and Sahiyela suffered many wounded, incredibly only eight were killed in action.

Crazy Horse's warriors displayed a devotion to duty because the course of human events too frequently causes men and women to take up arms in defense of life, community, nation, or ideals. Their efforts were nothing new, unfortunately, in the annals of human history. And there have been many similar examples since throughout the world. But during the summer of 1876 the foundation for Lakota victories in two significant battles eight days apart were established during that long night ride over the Wolf Mountains. That long and arduous journey to battle taught them much about themselves individually and collectively. It taught them, or reminded them in many cases, that engaging in combat is only part of the commitment to serve, that sometimes commitment and devotion to duty is a long, quiet ride.

Honoring songs are common at Lakota pow-wows, sung in recognition of a notable accomplishment, a noteworthy deed. The gathering, hence the community, pauses to give recognition.

Many honoring songs are sung for Lakota military veterans, sometimes as a general commemoration and sometimes specifically to honor those present at the gathering. One of the lines of the honoring song is:

> *Oyate kin ninpi kta ca lecamu yelo,* or, "I do this so that the people may live."

In Lakota society of the past, woman was the source of life and man was the protector of life. So what is the "this" that "I do" for the people? Women gave birth, taught the children for the important first formative years of life, and nurtured the family. Men had to provide the material for the family and community to survive, grow, and prosper, and to ensure that there was the freedom to do so.

In the Sun Dance, the most solemn of Lakota religious ceremonies, males are the primary participants, some as helpers and observers, and some make the focal sacrifice and are pierced. Those who are pierced practically and symbolically offer and give the one thing that is truly theirs: themselves. The giving of self is the core philosophy of the fighting man, the warrior. The male as the warrior is prepared physically, emotionally, and spiritually to give all that he is on behalf of the people. It is a process that begins at the age of five or six and continues throughout a lifetime. If a man does not die on the field of battle and reaches that part of his life where his physical skills are not as sharp, he enters that phase where his experience and wisdom are just as important as his physical skills and his deeds once were.

Crazy Horse did reach that point in his life—a culmination of the forces and influences of destiny and the circumstances of the times he lived in, rather than the infirmities of old age.

After the Battle of the Little Bighorn, the United States government stepped up its military campaign against the Lakota. Sitting Bull was forced to flee into Canada in 1877 and the U.S.

Army attacked Crazy Horse's own encampment during the winter. Other influential leaders such as Spotted Tail of the Sicangu Lakota and Red Cloud of the Oglala were already settled at their own agencies. Indeed, most of the Lakota bands were on agencies or reservations by early 1877, already living under the control of the United States government. It was inevitable, they said, and they sent messages to Crazy Horse's band that it was time to consider that living on reservations was preferable to being hunted down and killed by the whites.

With Sitting Bull in Canada, Crazy Horse was the most influential leader among those Lakota who refused to surrender. In fact, the Crazy Horse band of nearly a thousand people were for all intents and purposes the final holdouts. When Sitting Bull finally returned south of the Forty-eighth Parallel in 1881, it was in capitulation rather than to continue the fight.

Crazy Horse and his advisors realized that it was a numbers issue. He had less than two hundred able-bodied fighting men. The whites could send ten times that many men against him at any time. Furthermore, the whites had more guns and more bullets. The deciding factor, however, was the lack of resources to sustain his people in the field. The buffalo were gone, but there was probably enough elk and deer to provide them with the fresh meat they needed. However, when men had to devote most of their time to fighting to defend their families, there wasn't much time left to hunt.

A number of the younger men proposed hiding their noncombatants in some secret location and taking to the field as a highly mobile force against the whites. The idea had strong appeal, especially with those who thoroughly detested the thought of life on a reservation and those who knew that man for man the Lakota could outfight the whites. The idea was appealing to Crazy Horse the warrior, but to Crazy Horse the family man, to the leader responsible for the welfare of all the people, he knew that leaving the women and children unprotected would not be wise. Sooner or later the whites would find them, and he didn't want a ghastly reoccurrence of the Little Thunder or Sand Creek massacres. Therefore, the cold hard reality was simply and inescapably picking the lesser of two evils. Continue to resist until the soldiers killed them all, or surrender.

Almost a year earlier Crazy Horse had mounted his horse and ridden around the encampment on Ash Creek, and with each circuit more and more warriors fell in behind him. In May 1877, the circumstances were nearly the opposite. If he had decided to fight, every able-bodied male, from the very young to the very old, would have followed him anywhere. Most certainly more than a few women would have taken up arms also. But now he had to put the warrior aside—push him into the shadows, so to speak. It would have been completely understandable for the warriors to fight and die, because the very survival of a nation and a way of life was certainly worth dying for, but that would mean leaving the helpless ones to face the whites alone. So the choice was made to surrender.

Crazy Horse realized that a new kind of war was being fought to save the very essence of being Lakota. To fight in this war meant that the right kind of leadership was even more critical because the enemy was not only the whites but those Lakota who had essentially "gone over" to the other side. Crazy Horse knew that surrendering militarily didn't mean surrendering identity, and he detested anyone who pandered to the whites. To survive physically was necessary to prevent further bloodshed, but it was just as critical to survive culturally. That would mean hanging on tenaciously to language, values, and beliefs no matter what the whites might do. To fight that fight he knew that, as he had done on the battlefield, he had to take the lead and set the right example. The prospect of living in close proximity with white people *and* under their control was distasteful and detestable. Nevertheless it was a call to duty and service to the people he couldn't ignore. He had to do it so that the people could live. If he suspected that it would cost him his life, he spoke of it to no one, but he must have wondered about that part of his vision in which his own people pulled the rider down from his horse.

Afterword:
Honoring Song for a Thunder Dreamer

✜   Crazy Horse still lives in the shadows of my mind, as he always will. The boy in me sees him as a glorious warrior. The man I've become sees him as someone who reluctantly answered the call to serve and who became a leader in the most trying of times.

There were struggles within me from time to time, between the temptation to make Crazy Horse into a shimmering legend and the need to see him as a real person. He is certainly both, but it is immeasurably reassuring and inspiring to know him as a real man. Legends *are* like fog. Sooner or later the heat of the sun does burn them off. The scrutiny of unvarnished truth is like the sun. Bit by bit it dissipates the misty aura of legend. We do need our legends, it would seem. We hold them up as sort of a standard that we can try to attain, knowing we never can. But if we dare to look at them as people, it is frequently possible to understand them, their motives, their attitudes, and how and why they did what they did, or didn't do. If we accept them as people, we can find a connection to them, a connection woven by reality and humanity—for, after all, they fulfilled their journey just as we are fulfilling ours, on the same Earth.

Crazy Horse should be a hero, but not one of conjecture. Many have misjudged him or made him into something he is not, and as a result, Crazy Horse pretenders cross our path with annoying consistency. They seem to be everywhere. Some are living grand adventures in the wide-eyed imaginations of "Indian lore" enthusiasts, or are stubbornly fighting a losing war in the pages of pulp western history magazines as another dark icon opposing the inevitability of manifest destiny. These Crazy Horses are almost never without a weapon in hand, frequently wearing a feather "war" bonnet and riding at the head of a mass charge. They are from the "an Indian is an Indian is an Indian" view of indigenous cultures, which will swear that Crazy Horse and Geronimo spoke the same language and that "war" bonnets are standard issue for all Indian males over the age of twelve. This type of Crazy Horse is the darling of those who find lost causes somehow appealing. They know nothing of the reasons Indians fought so hard to protect their lands and their lives, but only that they were "noble savages" because they fought knowing they would lose.

Then there is the "conqueror of Custer" version, the purveyor of violence ready to fight at the drop of a "war" bonnet, his hate for white people dripping like venom—meaning, of course, that Crazy Horse has no validity without Custer. Kill a famous white man and insure your place in history. That's almost as popular as the glory-seeking egotist suffering from violent mood swings—a quiet camp dweller one day and a screaming savage on the warpath the next. Close behind is the overrated leader who owes his place in history to the fascination of white people, a first cousin to the one who owes his celebrity to offing Custer. Popping up in the crowd is "Chief" Crazy Horse because there are those among us who seem to think that we can't make history unless we have a title in front of our names; like general, duke, emperor, governor, mayor, judge, president, or chief. And then we have the Crazy Horse that could be one of the richest men in the world if he were paid endorsement fees for the use of his name on anything from tobacco products to malt liquor, designer clothes, salons, saloons, jewelry stores, and Paris burlesque houses.

The Hollywood Crazy Horses are an eclectic bunch. In a 1955 feature film his vociferousness was as out of place as his "war" bonnet. In a 1990 made-for-television miniseries (about Custer), he was a moody, reticent pedestrian (literally). A feature film the same year in which he shared equal billing with Custer attempted the "untold story" approach, but it went awry soon after the opening credits. Between 1955 and 1996 he has appeared as a background or minor character in several westerns, and once as an insect-eating captive in a western television series about Custer that lasted only slightly longer than the Battle of the Little Bighorn. A 1996 television movie came the closest. But overall, screenwriters should know that it takes more than an occasional smile on an Indian face and lovemaking on the prairie to portray the human side of Indians and give us a realistic insight into Indian culture. It is progress, I suppose, for non-Indian writers to realize that we smile and make love. Fortunately there hasn't been a preponderance of movies because they probably would have done nothing more than burden us with Crazy Horses of conjecture.

Photographs of Crazy Horse also pop up now and again. I'm inclined to react to those who purport to have or know of an "authentic" photograph of him much the same way I would to anyone who wants to sell me the Brooklyn Bridge, or argues that Custer really won the Battle of the Little Bighorn. There is, of course, no way to state unequivocally that no photographs of Crazy Horse exist. But we should consider two factors when discussing this topic: first, he was very suspicious of white people in general and, second, he probably would not have sat or stood still (literally) for the minimum five or ten minutes required to pose for a photograph. A few people have suggested that a photograph could have been taken of him without his knowledge, but, again, given the photographic technology of the time it would have been impossible to take a "snapshot" of him. Furthermore, until he took his people to Camp Robinson, he was rarely in the presence of whites and only once anywhere in the vicinity of a photographer. From that encounter came the anecdote of his refusal to pose and the words, "Why would you want to take from me my shadow?"

Western writer Louis L'Amour gave him gray eyes and someone else suggested he was part white because of his brown, slightly wavy hair. (I think it was the same writer who postulated that the Lakota won the Battle of the Little Bighorn because Sitting Bull was secretly trained by Jesuits at a military school in Europe.) The "part white" theory explains, to some folks, why Crazy Horse was such an outstanding warrior and tactician. The white blood made all the difference.

Historian Stephen Ambrose called him a man of violence, and the subtitle of his book *Crazy Horse and Custer* labels him an "American warrior." If Crazy Horse is an American, then Joe McCarthy is a friend to Communism, Ralph Nader loves Chevrolet Corvairs, and Kenneth Lay is the champion of the working class.

Larry McMurtry seemed mostly mystified with his slant on Crazy Horse and almost hesitant to write about him, but he did venture a point that I do agree with. Neither historians nor writers have an accurate insight into the deeds of Crazy Horse, much less his soul.

There will always be pretenders because Crazy Horse is many things to many people. Even among us Lakota there are tendencies to deify him. It's difficult to say if the real Crazy Horse will ever outmaneuver the ethnocentric opinions, the paternalistic pronouncements of those who think they have the final word on history, or the plain, unmitigated hero worship. But strangely enough, each time a pretender steps into the limelight of someone's ignorance, it is an opportunity to unveil the real Crazy Horse. For it was as a real person he left tracks both on the Earth and in the hearts of men and women who truly know him.

I have walked the ridge north of Buffalo, Wyoming, where he led several hundred Lakota and Sahiyela fighting men to victory over the infantry soldiers from Fort Phil Kearny in the Battle of the Hundred in the Hand, or *Opawinge Napogna Wicayuhapi*—also known as the Fetterman Battle or Fetterman Massacre. I went there alone on a cold December day and transported myself back to a like day in the Winter Moon of 1866. The wind stung my face and numbed my fingers as I walked the snow-covered ridge along the old Bozeman Trail. I could hear the deep boom of fifty-caliber rifles, the sizzling hiss of flying arrows, and the voices of men exhorting one another in Lakota, Sahiyela, and English as they fought or screamed in pain as they were mortally wounded. In the eerie aftermath of combat I could see Crazy Horse riding the slippery eastern slope of the ridge to discover his boyhood friend Lone Bear disabled by a grievous wound and face down in the snow. I could see Crazy Horse turn his friend over gently and brush snow and ice from his face and hair, and then his own features distort with anguish and grief as the young man died in his arms.

On more than one hot summer day I have stood and looked over the ridges and rolling hills along the Little Bighorn River north of where Ash (Reno) Creek flows into it and where, 128 years ago, another battle was fought.

Like Crazy Horse himself, the Battle of the Little Bighorn is still often misunderstood. It was, of course, reported as a massacre of the cavalry troops led by George Custer. In fact it was three hard-fought distinct and separate engagements over two days. More than half of the six hundred or more troops survived the battle, although Custer himself and the five companies he commanded (over two hundred men) were completely wiped out in the second engagement.

Crazy Horse was one of several combat leaders who had a definite impact on the outcome of that battle. The others were Gall, Crow King, and Black Moon of the Hunkpapa Lakota, Big Road of the Oglala Lakota, Red on Top of the Isanti Dakota, He Dog of the Sicangu Lakota, Touch the Clouds (about seven feet tall, it was said) of the Itazipacola Lakota, and Two Moons and Wooden Leg of the Sahiyela.

If we look at that battle as only a military action—or, as many white historians like to say, "an episode in a clash of cultures"—we limit our awareness. Any battle or conflict is, at the very least, an interaction between two (or more) distinct groups of people. An interaction between people is a human endeavor driven or caused by human characteristics such as obedience, loyalty, greed, anger, curiosity, fear, patriotism, and so on. If we consider these as factors then we cannot help but put a human face on such an interaction or endeavor. Having gone that far, we need then to look into the soul represented by that human face. When we've been touched by the souls of those who have gone before us we will gain a new perspective on history and we will likely realize that the phrase "clash of cultures" does not begin to describe it.

Walking the hills above the Little Bighorn River on a hot June day can provide an insight into the souls, the humanity, of both sides of that conflict. To feel the hot breeze and the burning sun on your face, to feel the same dusty soil beneath your feet, to gaze on the same landmarks such as Medicine Tail Coulee and Last Stand Hill and Sharpshooter Ridge, and to watch the sunlight flashing off the slow-moving river puts you in touch with a particular event in our collective past—an event that will never change no matter how long or how vociferously we debate the details of that conflict, and it will remain a part of each of us who goes there. At some point most of us will dare to wonder how it felt to be there. How did it feel to hear the continuous gunfire? How did it feel to run through the dust on that hot day? How does one react to the sound of bullets hitting into the flesh of one's comrades? What did the mothers, wives, and grandmothers in the great encampment, or as they fled from it, think, knowing that their husbands, sons, brothers, and grandsons were facing an enemy who always had more guns and more bullets? Surely some of them paused to look toward the gunfire across the river, trying to see something through the cloud of dust. Surely some of them paused to pray, clutching their children and grandchildren to them, wondering if their loved ones lost in the dust were alive. And surely even as the soldiers were dying, many of their final, conscious thoughts were also of loved ones far away from the dusty hills and ridges that would become a final resting place.

The Little Bighorn Battlefield National Monument contains and preserves some of the actual 1876 battle site, but there is much more than the tangible physicality of the place, more than geography and landmarks. Marble headstones to mark where soldiers fell and the mass grave atop Last Stand Hill are powerful reminders, but there are some things from the past that are not as tangible. Stories are there, riding on the breezes, sometimes flashing in the sunlight, but always reaching across the gulf of time. To learn these stories one must know as much as possible of the moment in time they originated. One must also be willing to shed skepticism, put aside the arrogance of the present, and forget the ethnocentric bias that too many times obscures the truth. And then the truth will come, likely in bits and pieces, but it will come.

Crazy Horse was not perfect or so overwhelmed with righteousness that he was incapable of dark thoughts or doubts. Nor was he impervious to all the foibles of being human. He was very human. He learned his lessons, he laughed, he loved, he was driven by loyalty, anger, patriotism, and he did his best not certain it would be good enough. He knew cold and hunger and fear and self-doubt. Seeing men die in combat and losing a daughter made him much too familiar with grief. As a very young man he lost—twice—the woman who was likely the love of his life, so he knew the bitterness of heartache. He knew the responsibility of leadership on and off the battlefield, and the satisfaction of a job well done. Walking among the shadowy pines of the Shining Mountains he enjoyed the fresh, exhilarating scent of pine mingling with fresh air. From below the sky-lines of many hills he watched the setting sun bathe low autumn clouds with an impossible hue of lavender and felt the presence of Wakantanka. In the Moon of Falling Leaves he reveled in the high, lonesome call of the snow geese heading south for the winter, and probably wondered what it felt like to fly and see the land from their perspective. In short, he was a man like many others, and in many ways he was a man like no other. He will always live in my mind and my heart as a quiet man, a humble soul, a good husband, a loyal son, a doting father, an unrelenting warrior.

There will always be some kind of debate about Crazy Horse. What exactly did he do at the Battle of the Little Bighorn? Did he have special powers through his vision? Why was he such a private person? Even his contemporaries were divided over their opinions of him. Then and now, however, there is probably one factor that most of us can agree on. He was a leader. Whether he came into it by accident or by design, whether he was good at it or not, he was a leader. And he led by example. Lakota culture wouldn't allow him to do it any other way and neither would his own character and personality, because he was not an authoritarian. If there is one thing and one thing only that we can learn from him, it would be leadership by example. He didn't invent it but he used it and it worked for him.

The time of Crazy Horse is past, but his leadership style is not passé. Those of us who study him without the obtuse filter of cultural bias see him not as legend but as an example. An example of making the best of the talents and abilities one has, at the very least.

The current moment is fleeting, the past grows with each passing moment, and tomorrow is shaped by what we do today and what we are willing to learn from yesterday. The basic difference between us and our ancestors is technology. The fact that we can perform a task more quickly because we've improved on a tool only proves that we, at least in one instance, have become more efficient, but it doesn't necessarily mean that we've grown wiser. And if there is one aspect of our modern society in which we cannot afford arrogance, it is in the development of our leaders.

Crazy Horse didn't rise to the pinnacles of leadership because he came from an influential family, or because he recited his record of heroic deeds publicly, or because there were no leaders among the Lakota. He rose to leadership because he actually led. He didn't direct or point to where others should go while he waited. He led.

He has been called a mystic, that he had powers because of his vision. Perhaps he was a mystic and perhaps he was given power through his vision. One thing is certain: he believed what he saw in his dream and his power came from that belief. And it wasn't necessarily otherworldly power. Crazy Horse used a power that was available to most warriors and warrior leaders of his day; the power of example. He went first, he took the lead, he was the first to face and meet the challenge. When he had to be daring he was, sometimes to the point of recklessness as it certainly appeared to most of his fellow warriors. It is what set him apart from other leaders. But the other factor that enabled his rise to leadership was his humility.

Crazy Horse was truly humble about his achievements. Both those traits endeared him to many and evoked jealousy in some. He understood that what is accomplished in the name of and for the people belongs to the people. He set aside his reputation.

Why, I've often wondered, did he do that? Was it because he was so shy and humble that he shunned the public limelight? That is certainly part of it in my opinion, but I think there was another reason.

I can still recall the quiet, utterly respectful statement made by one of those old men, that day in my boyhood by the Little White River, as they sat and talked of the old, old days and of *Tasunke Witko. Wankinyan ihanbla ske,* one of them said. They say he was a Thunder Dreamer. I had felt a shiver go through my body. Even at the age of six I knew that a Thunder Dreamer had powers because the *Wakinyan,* the Thunder Beings came to him or her in a dream or during a vision quest. Such a person literally had a vision that was a connection to the most powerful natural element on the Plains and spiritually becomes a *heyoka,* a wise fool, or a sacred clown, if you will.

A *heyoka* is a walking contradiction. His or her behavior at times may seem crazy or against his or her own character, but in behaving contrary to good sense or one's basic character or habits, the *heyoka* is actually performing a spiritual ceremony. A *heyoka* sacrifices his or her ego and reputation for the sake of the people. I believe that Crazy Horse was a Thunder Dreamer. That was his journey because the *Wakinyan* came to him in a vision, and that vision showed the *way* he was expected to live his life. The vision likely didn't provide specifics, only that he was to walk the path of *giving* as opposed to *gaining.* That would seem to explain why Crazy Horse always wore plain clothing and never donned a feather bonnet, which he was certainly entitled to as an accomplished warrior. That would seem to explain why he didn't participate in the *waktoglakapi,* the *telling of one's victories.* He did, in fact, sacrifice his own ego and reputation for the sake of his people. And in doing so he was honoring his journey.

Crazy Horse, the Thunder Dreamer, will always live in the shadows of my mind, sometimes waiting in the margin of my awareness and sometimes stepping into the focus of my awareness. I will always see him as a man, but sometimes there is that mist that flows around him. Perhaps his bones have turned to stone, as he said they would. But his spirit has risen because he does live in the minds of many Lakota, and also because he has found his place in our hearts. And that, I believe, is the best place for him to be because the human heart is stronger than stone.

Tasunke Witko!

Lakota wica!

Hokahe!

A Story:
The Lightning Bow

A thin covering of snow had fallen over the land in the first days of the Winter Moon. The Bow Maker wandered, searching the never-ending prairies for just the right young ash tree. It could be no wider than his forearm and straight and at least as high as he was tall. He could no longer walk as fast as he did in his youth. There were many strands of gray in his nearly waist-length hair. But he still had endurance and could maintain a steady pace, thus he went from one valley to the next. Though they were now leafless he could still easily spot stands of ash trees in the bottomlands along creeks and rivers, for that's where they grew in abundance. Years and years of experience told him in a heartbeat if a tree was straight enough and had the spirit to make a powerful bow. So he kept searching.

The right tree was waiting somewhere, he knew. It was only a matter of time. But as he traveled he wondered if he would live long enough to see that it would be cured properly. Every ash tree that was split into staves then had to be air-dried for five years. Then, and only then, would the stave be ready to be made into a good bow. Whatever is to happen will happen, he told himself as he journeyed on.

The Bow Maker no longer had the strength of his youth, but he had the strength of wisdom that comes from the journey of a long life. The old ones know that wisdom and experience are the greatest strengths of all. So he traveled on, watchful for enemies but unafraid, secure in the knowledge that he had lived a good, long life and that he was ready for the next.

In a wide valley where he remembered playing as a boy and hunting as a young man the Bow Maker found an expected gift. A once sturdy ash tree, many times as tall as a man, had been split in two. One half lay on the ground. The Bow Maker cried out in joy for he had found what he thought he would never see in his lifetime, an ash tree split by lightning. Such a tree had been dried and cured in one heartbeat by the awesome power of the lightning sent down by the Thunders. A bow made from such a tree would have power like none other.

The Bow Maker found a secluded spot and made his camp. He made offerings to the Thunders and smoked his pipe, and then he set about splitting the lightning tree into staves for bows. He worked for several days and made several staves, each of the proper length and width. One of them felt different in his hands when he held it. It was no longer or wider than the others yet there was something about it that made him want to touch it. The Bow Maker could feel a certain force, perhaps the spirit of the Thunders themselves.

Though the days and nights were growing colder the Bow Maker decided to stay in his camp and build a bow out of the stave he liked. He worked and worked, slowly and patiently. With his tools of stone, bone, and antler he shaved and then shaped the stave until it became a bow. He sang songs as he worked calling on the skills taught to him by his father and grandfathers, and he sang songs of honor to the Thunders and their power. In his weathered and rough hands, hands that had turned many staves to bows, this bow of the lightning tree took shape. It was thickest around the middle, where it was two fingers wide. From the middle it gradually tapered to each end where it was the size of the tip of his little finger. Each limb or wing was as equally long as the other, and as graceful.

The Bow Maker worked using all the skills and the knowledge he had gathered in his lifetime. As he watched the bow take shape he marveled at its feel and balance. Never in his lifetime had he made a bow as fine. When he tied on the sinew string and drew it back for the first time, he knew it was the most powerful as well. Pulled back and drawn to an arc, it resembled the thinnest new crescent of the new moon. It was appropriate, for as all bow makers know, the moon is the mother of the bow.

Arrow after arrow he sent from his new bow, farther and faster than any bow he had made or shot. Truly, this bow had a power and a spirit he had never seen, or felt, in any other. The Bow Maker returned home to his village with six staves from the lightning tree and his new bow. All the hunters and warriors were curious as he took his new bow to the river to shoot arrows into a sandbank. To a man they marveled at the speed and power of the bow. Each arrow flew almost faster than thought and drove itself deep into the bank.

Men of the village came with offers to trade for the powerful new bow made from the lightning tree. Word went out to other villages and although it was winter many came. The Bow Maker allowed each man to shoot the bow. Not one of them had ever seen such a bow and all praised its strength.

Offers were made for the bow; each man who touched it and used it wanted it and promised anything the old Bow Maker would want in trade. The Bow Maker patiently listened to all the offers but said nothing. Days passed and the men in the village were growing impatient, some returned and increased their offer of payment. The Bow Maker didn't want to trade. He had enough to make his life comfortable for he required little in the way of material things. He had it in mind to give the bow to the man he thought was most deserving. So he patiently waited.

More days passed and the village was growing restless, anxious for the Bow Maker to make a trade, but nothing happened. The men began to talk among themselves, asking what they must do for one of them to have the bow. Some suggested there be a contest of some kind, a foot race or a test of strength, and the winner would receive all the possessions of each man who lost and then he could trade for the bow. But others had different ideas and arguments grew, some men became angry and accused the Bow Maker of some kind of trickery. Fights broke out among some and families joined in until there was a deep unrest in the village. The Bow Maker watched and was sad. He hoped that one man would show himself worthy of owning the bow from the lightning tree, a bow with the power of the Thunders. But a bow such as that could not be given to anyone who was willing to stoop to anger or deceit to own it. The old Bow Maker was heart broken. He had not meant to cause such trouble. Even the best of gifts can bring out the worst in some, he had learned. He was just as sad that not a single man could prove himself worthy of the bow from the lightning tree. There was only one way to fix the difficulty he had caused.

The Bow Maker sent a Crier through the village to announce that on the sundown of the fourth day hence, he would have an answer. The people grumbled that it was about time. During the night the Bow Maker slipped away unseen from the village with a sad heart and a long bundle under one arm. The people noticed that his lodge door was tied shut and grumbled all the more. On the sundown of the fourth day the Bow Maker returned, empty-handed.

"The power of the bow made from the lightning tree is a special gift," he told the people when they gathered to listen to him. "It is more than a thing to be owned. I did not want to trade. Though I made it, it did not really belong to me. I would have given it to the man with the humility to own it. All I saw was arrogance and anger and how you made yourselves more important than the gift. Therefore I have given it back to the Thunders. I still have six more staves from the lightning tree, someday before I die, perhaps I will make another bow. Perhaps . . ."

The people were ashamed of what they had done, of the manner in which they had behaved, and expressed their regret to the Bow Maker. And all hoped that someday he would make another bow from the lightning tree, before it was too late. The Bow Maker didn't have to remind them that until then they would all need to live in a good way, so they could be worthy of such a bow if one were to be made again.

Sources

Storytellers from the Rosebud Reservation—Sicangu Lakota

Horse Creek Community
This district or community was named for the creek that drains into the
Little White, or Smoking Earth, River.

Albert Two Hawk	Annie Good Voice Eagle Two Hawk
Isaac Bear	Nellie Bear Doctor
Moses Rattling Leaf	Lucy Rattling Leaf
Maggie Little Dog	Paul Little Dog
Hazel Two Hawk Marshall	Joseph Marshall II

My maternal grandparents were Albert and Annie. Lucy and Maggie
were my grandfather's sisters. Lucy married Moses Rattling Leaf. In the
1950s when many Lakota were still using horses and wagons (and buggies),
Grandpa Moses had a very good-looking pair of matched draft horses for
his wagon. Maggie married Paul Little Dog, who was also known as No
Two Horns.

My parents are Joseph and Hazel. My mother has patiently answered
questions in the past three years, especially concerning the names in this
Sources section. I was not surprised to hear various bits of family, cultural,
and historical information from my father in the years before he died;
which I always suspected he knew, and am exceedingly glad he finally saw
fit to divulge.

Sam Brings (aka Brings Three White Horses)	George Brave

Sam told me of a place along Horse Creek where he had found arrowheads and flint chips when he was a young man or boy. My grandfather and

I later found stone flakes there, too, but no arrowheads. The site was bull-dozed when Highway 83 was widened in the 1960s. George was an avid hunter and later in his life drove a bus route for the local school district that hauled only Indian students.

Harris Lodge Skin Menard   Millie Menard

Harris and Millie lived west of us on his land that bordered the Little White River, adjacent to my grandmother Annie's land. We walked to their log house often, especially in the summers. I remember trying desperately to stay awake as he and my grandfather would talk far into the night about the old days.

Swift Bear Community
The Swift Bear district or community is located on the northern edge of the Rosebud Reservation. Its northern border is the Big White or White Earth River. It is named for one of the Sicangu Lakota headmen, Swift Bear, also known as Quick Bear. All of the following were in some way related to my maternal grandfather, Albert.

Isaac Knife   Richard Mouse
Eunice Black Wolf Running   James Yellow Cloud
  Horse

Ring Thunder and Soldier Creek Communities

Katie Roubideaux Blue Thunder   Blanche Roubideaux Marshall
James Provincial   Ollie Lodgeskin Provincial
Sam Provincial   Mercy Provincial
Lulu Lodgeskin   Laban White Sr.
Narcisse Brave

Katie (Katherine) Roubideaux Blue Thunder and M. Blanche Roubideaux Marshall were sisters. Blanche was my father's mother. Their mother (one of my great-grandmothers) was Adelia Blunt Arrow, a Sicangu Lakota, and their father was Louis Roubideaux, a mixed-blood of French descent and a district agent and interpreter for the Indian Bureau at the Rosebud Agency. My grandmother Katie lived to be nearly 101 years old.
Sam and James Provincial were brothers. Sam was a very distinguished-

looking man with a strong baritone voice. By contrast, James was very soft-spoken. Sam's wife was Mercy and Jim's wife was Ollie Lodgeskin Provincial. My maternal grandmother Annie and Ollie were first cousins, and had known each other since childhood. Ollie's mother, Lulu Lodgeskin, was a small woman who also lived to be a hundred years old. I never heard her speak English.

My father's older brother was Narcisse Brave. Both of them were involved in tribal politics with the Rosebud Sioux Tribe at one time or another. My father was a council representative from the Horse Creek Community and Uncle Narcisse was tribal vice president.

Laban was my uncle by marriage. He was married to my father's sister Adelia. He, like my grandfather, the Reverend Charles Marshall, was an avid fisherman. Uncle Laban liked to tell stories as he fished.

Storytellers from the Pine Ridge Reservation—Oglala Lakota

Wilson Janis   Alice Janis
Rev. Charles J. Marshall   Adolph Bull Bear

Wilson and Alice lived along a creek bottom not far from my grandparents, Charles and Blanche Marshall, near the town of Kyle on the Pine Ridge, in the Potato Creek District. They walked a lot because Wilson was blind and Alice, as I recall, didn't drive. Alice had extensive knowledge of midwives in the old days, and Wilson just knew a lot. Adolph was my uncle by marriage, married to one of my father's sisters. He was not an old man when I first met him, when I was eight, but I suspect that much or all of what he knew historically and culturally he learned from his father, Guy Bull Bear, who lived through some interesting times. Bull Bear, is, of course, an old and distinguished name among the Oglala Lakota.

My grandfather Charles was tall and very distinguished. He and my maternal grandfather, Albert, had a deep mutual respect. Grandpa Charles, in his life, was a rancher, a gold miner (having worked in the Homestake Gold Mine in the Black Hills), and an ordained Episcopalian deacon. I remember watching him play baseball when he was fifty-five years old. He was the son of a Frenchman, Joseph Marshall (probably originally Marichale). (Joseph and his brother, Francis [François] had an interesting journey that eventually led them to the Pine Ridge Reservation, via Fort Yankton and Fort Laramie, among other places. They both married Lakota women and raised large families.)

Many of these people from Rosebud and Pine Ridge were related to me, or took me as a relative. Each of them gave me a piece of themselves because of a story or stories they told me, or because they taught me something. My grandfather Albert taught me to make bows and arrows, for example. Grandpa Isaac Knife taught his son, Israel (my cousin), and me to weave fish traps out of sandbar willows. I can't remember who it was that taught me how to play the Snow Snake game first, sliding willow rods on the river ice. All my grandmothers showed me about beading and quilling, and hide tanning. The list goes on and on. Most of all they all taught me to be aware of who and what I am, and always to be proud of it.

Suggested Reading

Andrist, Ralph K., *The Long Death*. Macmillan, 1964.

Brown, Dee A., *Bury My Heart at Wounded Knee*. Bantam, 1970.

Buecher, Thomas R., ed., *The Crazy Horse Surrender Ledger*. Nebraska Historical Society, 1994.

Hardoff, Richard G., *The Oglala Lakota Crazy Horse: A Preliminary Genealogical Study and an Annotated Listing of Primary Sources*. J.M. Carroll and Company, 1985.

Kadlecek, Edward, and Mabel Kadlecek, *To Kill an Eagle: Indian Views on the Last Days of Crazy Horse*. Johnson Books, 1995.

Sandoz, Mari, *Crazy Horse: The Strange Man of the Oglalas*. University of Nebraska Press, 1942.

Scott, Douglas D., Richard A. Fox, Jr., Melissa A. Conner, and Dick Harmon, *Archaeological Perspectives on the Battle of the Little Bighorn*. University of Oklahoma, 2000.

Index